COLORED, NEGRO, BLACK:
CHASING THE AMERICAN DREAM

by

Bernard C. Watson, Ph.D.

JDC Books
Philadelphia, Pennsylvania

COLORED, NEGRO, BLACK: CHASING THE AMERICAN DREAM

Published by
JDC Books
Philadelphia, PA

Library of Congress Catalog Card No.: (pending)

ISBN: (pending)

10 9 8 7 6 5 4 3 2 1

First Printing, January 1997

Printed in the United States of America

TABLE OF CONTENTS

ACKNOWLEDGEMENTS

Dorothy Innes Blanchard has been my research assistant for almost ten of the past thirty years. A graduate of Bryn Mawr and Temple University, she is a fine writer, an even better editor. To paraphrase a well-known TV commercial: she doesn't make the product, she makes it better. Working with me on this memoir was very difficult: we learned some things about each other and ourselves. Without her questioning, criticism, arguments, and encouragement, this project might have been delayed or, perhaps, abandoned.

I want to express my thanks to the former colleagues and friends who refreshed my memory of past events. Among them are Graham Finney, David Horowitz, Robert Poindexter, and Tom Rosica. The staff of the Urban Archives at Temple University were also very helpful in locating newspaper clippings and other documents to substantiate my recollections.

The people who read and commented on all or part of my manuscript—including Ramona Edelin, Ella Evans, Dick Gilmore, Wilson Goode, Fasaha Traylor, and Paul Vance—deserve a special tribute for devoting themselves to what must have been a tedious task. I take full responsibility for any errors which escaped their careful reading and recommendations.

Clarence Currie not only read the final draft, but agreed to write an introduction. For this task, I wanted someone who knew me well but who would be honest. As he says, our friendship began in childhood and has remained firm for many years. Some of his comments are far too flattering, but I appreciate them anyway, as well as the time and effort he put into his brief recollection.

Words fail when it comes to conveying my gratitude to my family. My wife and children inspired this project; they made helpful suggestions along the way; and, most important, they put up with me throughout the time it took to complete this memoir.

Bernard C. Watson, Ph.D.
Philadelphia, Pennsylvania

INTRODUCTION

Bernard Watson is my great and good friend. During our teen years, Bernard was my best friend. We were in daily contact with each other. After school, we checked out the joints together, dodged bullets together, and, in that pre-television era, engaged in nightly wrap-ups and pontifications about the state of the world, the future, and our role in effecting change. Bernard is a great talker. I am a great listener. Bernard is extroverted, competitive and a doer. I am more reticent, more dreamer than doer.

Bernard says I have a great brain. In all modesty, it must be at least partially true, because Bernard does not "suffer fools gladly." He is polite to everyone and has an uncanny ability to espy talent in unlikely places and to make everyone around him feel good. Still, he surrounds himself with bright, good-looking, successful people who are focused, and on their way to doing something meaningful and important.

When I say that Bernard is thus or so, I mean he has always been that way. He is the same today as he was when he was six years old—exuberant, loud, optimistic, and reaching out to people. I have never known him to be down or depressed or pessimistic—except once, when he got a "B" in college sociology. You and I know the grade should have been an "A," and he was actually more angry than depressed.

Bernard is fearless. One night, as we made our rounds, we chanced upon a major altercation at 20th and Broadway in our steel city. All of the dudes who usually stood on the corner engaged in verbal repartee were ducking behind cars and trams, trying to avoid bullets which were pinging off everything in sight. Watson walked right up to Tommy Anthony, one of the baddest dudes in town, who had just grabbed a gun from his antagonist and was about to blow him away. Watson calmly convinced Anthony to put the gun down and let the man go. Of course, I was a hero for about two weeks, simply because I was close to Watson and had seen it all happen.

Watson has led a charmed life with incredible achievements. For many years, I have been convinced that he operated from a secret folio, known only to him and God, which allowed him to turn the pages confidently and find out what he was to do each day. How else does one explain his unerring sense of timing. He has always known exactly when to stop any given activity and move on to the next stage. While others routinely wrestled and agonized over assorted options, Bernard invariably understood what to do and when to do it.

Not only could he do this for himself, he could do it for others. Sometimes I felt that my life must be in the book also. In the tenth grade, I was content to take classes and watch the passing parade. One day, Bernard said, "Currie, it is time for you to become an officer in the Hi-Y Club." Just like that. Not next week or tomorrow, but today, right now. That advice changed my life. With that beginning, I later became president of the student body and president of the senior class. I enjoyed every minute of it. Bernard had seen something I had no inkling was there. He did the same with other friends—prodding, encouraging, challenging—whatever it took to pull amazing talent out of reluctant hosts (all the while, no doubt, turning the pages in his secret book of the future).

I was able to pay my way through college because of Bernard. We joined the Air Force together in August 1951. The Korean War was still going on. Watson convinced me that the GI Bill was more important to us than the mere lives we were placing in harm's way on behalf of an improving, yet bigoted and uncaring country. (Years before Martin Luther King, Watson and I had already engaged in restaurant sit-ins in Bloomington, home of Indiana University.) Once again, however, right in the middle of basic training, Watson turns the page in his secret life book and finds that it is time when he must become an officer. He announces the fact forthwith, puts in an application, and is one out of about 300 to be selected. Unbelievable.

After the service, he returned to Gary, working in the school system at his beloved Roosevelt High School. Soon he had married a beautiful wife and had built his own ranch- style home. Any ordinary human would have been supremely happy. Before I could blink an eye, Watson says, "Currie, I'm getting a Ph.D." (I knew he had been looking in the book again.) Naturally the book told him to pick the toughest school he could find within striking distance—the University of Chicago. He worked himself to a frazzle. I was afraid for him, that his dogged determination would do him in. He looked gaunt, nothing but big nose and big eyes. He got his degree.

The rest, as they say, is history. He moved onward and upward, reaching unprecedented heights of accomplishment, nurturing hundreds of millions in investments, consultant to U.S. presidents, role model to young black kids in Gary and around the country. There is much more I could tell you. About his love for "Bird," "Prez," Sarah, Miles, and the great Art Hoyle; about our work in the steel mills, learning Spanish from the Mexicans; double dating at the prom. His telling is much more interesting. What is astonishing to me, even more than my being allowed to say a few words here, is the fact that Bernard is opening his private book to the world. We are better for it, but I am convinced that he has known what you are about to read for at least 50 years.

Bernard is one in a million. Or, since there are about 33 million blacks in the U.S. population, maybe I should say he is one in 33 million. Few individuals have accomplished what Bernard has in such a short time, against all odds, with such impact and from such modest beginnings. Modest is perhaps a misnomer. The Watsons had modest finances. They were rich in love, intelligence, persistence, compassion and loyalty to their fellow human beings. I had the privilege to grow up beside Bernard, and I am better for it.

Dr. Clarence R. Currie
Gary, Indiana

PREFACE

When I was younger, black Americans were almost invisible. Because of conditions beyond our control, we lived and worked in almost total isolation from our white countrymen, confined to the poorest part of town and limited to jobs that were the most dangerous, demeaning, and exhausting; jobs with the lowest pay; jobs that nobody else wanted to do. Positive stories about black Americans generally appeared only in the black press: the *Pittsburgh Courier*, the *Philadelphia Tribune*, the *Chicago Defender*, the *Baltimore Afro American*, *Jet*, *Sepia*, and *Ebony*.

Today, black Americans seem to be everywhere: television, newspapers, magazines, and movies. Most of them, however, seem to fall into one of two groups. The first includes celebrities, entertainers, actors, gangsta rappers, and sports superstars (the crazier or more bizarre the better, it seems, from the standpoint of the media). The second group is made up of drug dealers, teenage muggers, murderers, car thieves, and jailbirds (also the crazier the better). For many Americans—including, I regret to say, many black young people—there appear to be two choices: a black person is either notable or notorious. You applaud one, you're afraid of the other.

That's a distorted and nonsensical picture, of course. There are about 33 million black people in this country, and the vast majority of us are not household names for any reason, good or bad. Like our fellow citizens of other groups, we differ from one another on every conceivable measure: appearance, education, lifestyle, attitudes, and beliefs. The one thing we all have in common is race. Race has defined many, if not all, aspects of our lives, and continues to do so, even if in more subtle ways than in the past. I believe it is important for people to know about black Americans who are neither celebrities nor criminals. I am one of those "others" and this is the story of my life and times. It is a story which could be told by many others, especially those of my generation.

I have been extraordinarily lucky—lucky in the parents I chose, the city in which I was born, the public school ("Dear Ole Roosevelt") I attended, the friends I made at an early age, the woman I married, the children we raised, the opportunities which came my way. I am lucky because I am one of the few African Americans of my generation who has lived the American dream. In spite of all the difficulties, the barriers, the mean-spirited people who placed obstacles in my path; in spite of the words and acts designed to break a person's spirit and force me to say "I quit, I give up," I never did.

Too stubborn, I guess. Too determined to prove that America belongs to all of us, despite the racism of individuals and institutions. I did exactly what the books and movies and magazines and radio programs and movies taught us to do: "Believe in America." Perhaps that message was not meant for African Americans, but I embraced it anyway, and so did a lot of others. We acted on it, we pursued our goals and tried to fulfill our aspirations, whether we were meant to or not. Some succeeded beyond anyone's wildest dreams, in spite of the system.

It wasn't easy. A lot of us failed or quit, out of exhaustion or fear or pain or frustration or weariness, perhaps because of other responsibilities. Some of us got killed. Or wounded. Or locked up. Or institutionalized. Some of us put our skills and abilities, our education, our inventiveness, our inspirational ideas, in cold storage. Instead, we worked to sustain ourselves and our families in jobs and careers that had little or nothing to do with our potential, our willingness to work hard, and our desire to contribute. We did what we had to do. We kept our humanity and we still loved this country, our country, even when it didn't love us back.

We too felt our hearts swell with pride as we heard the stirring notes of "The Star Spangled Banner" or, more to our liking, "America the Beautiful." And before or after these patriotic songs, we sang our own: "Lift Every Voice and Sing," the Negro National Anthem, which expressed our pain, our disillusionment, our sadness, but also our faith in the ultimate triumph of justice: "...sheltered beneath thy hand, may we forever stand, true to our God, true to our native land."

How did I decide to write this account of my own experiences? It began when I was half way around the world. In the summer of 1988, I spent two weeks in the People's Republic of China as a guest of the Chinese government. The visit had been arranged by Dr. John Chen, a mathematician and my colleague at Temple University. During that time, I discussed issues in higher education with the Secretary of Education and the presidents of a number of colleges and universities, including Huanghe University, then the only English-language university in the country and where Dr. Chen had been chairman of the board. My son, Bernard, Jr. (whom we call Chuck), had just finished his junior year of high school, and he accompanied me on that trip. For fifteen days we were together around the clock, as he was permitted to sit in on every meeting, dinner, lecture, and discussion.

Among the gifts I had taken to present to Huanghe University and to government officials were materials on the African American experience: *Autobiography of Malcolm X, The Invisible Man, Why We Can't Wait,* and *Eye on the Prize.* During the course of our visit, my son read the *Autobiography of Malcolm X*—and that led him to ask a series of questions about my own early life and what the conditions were when I was his age. He knew that I had met many famous people, such as Thurgood Marshall, A. Philip Randolph, Coretta Scott King, Roy Wilkins, the Rev. Leon Sullivan, and the Rev. Jesse Jackson, and he wondered how our paths had crossed. He wanted to hear about his grandfather (my father) who had died before Chuck was born. I was surprised but gratified that he was interested in these things, and I was delighted to answer his questions.

After several days of these discussions, he asked if I planned to put any of this in writing. Such a thought had never entered my mind! His next comment surprised me: "As close as we are, dad, I didn't know any of this. I am sure Barbra [his sister] doesn't, either. You need to put some of this down so people my age will be able to understand what life was like in the 'olden days.'" Eight years later, here is my attempt to describe for my children at least a part of what my life was like in the time before they were born and how things changed as they grew into adulthood.

This memoir was written for you, Barbra and Chuck.

CHAPTER I
MY FAMILY AND EARLY EDUCATION

Negro Life at the Turn of the Century

The context and culture into which we are born inevitably shape our attitudes, our actions, and ultimately our destinies. As I look back at my earliest years, therefore, I think of my parents not simply as individuals whom I loved and admired, whose behavior so strongly influenced my own, but as members of a race which was then, as now, struggling to attain the opportunities and privileges which were its moral and legal right. My mother and father were born in Alabama in the last decade of the 19th century. To understand my parents, and therefore myself, I must recall the world in which they began their lives.

It was a world of incredible horror and amazing courage, of vast injustice and boundless determination, of daily humiliation and unflagging creativity. The Civil War had ended some thirty years before their time; its devastating aftermath, the period of Reconstruction, was over; and the old Confederacy had been left to its own devices in regard to the political, social, and economic arrangements for the millions of Negroes who lived within its boundaries. Like the Third Reich, the Confederacy was based on racism—the belief that certain peoples were innately inferior and were destined for subjugation at best or even elimination. But the Allied response to Naziism was very different: war criminals were brought to trial, reparations were paid to the survivors of the concentration camps, and every attempt was made to stamp out the hateful doctrines of racial superiority. In the south, in the late nineteenth century, racism was codified in both law and custom.

The withdrawal of federal troops from Louisiana in 1877 marked the end of northern protection of or even interest in the fate of the former slaves (except as a source of cheap labor). Meantime, poor white farmers in the south found them a convenient scapegoat for their own economic problems and a handy target on which they could focus in order to bolster their tenuous self-esteem. Although the Ku Klux Klan had been formally disbanded in 1869, it continued to terrify Negroes and anyone who sympathized with their cause. During the 1890s, there were 1,107 lynchings of Negroes (including women), many for trivial "causes."

Those who gained control of the state governments quickly moved to disenfranchise Negroes through such measures as a grandfather clause, a poll tax, or educational requirements. Jim Crow laws were passed, enforcing segregation of the races in education, public transportation, housing, restaurants, and other public facilities. Lamentably, the United States Supreme Court approved these measures, most notably in Plessy v. Ferguson (1896), which established the doctrine of "separate but equal" accommodations for Negroes—a decision which remained in force until 1954.

Yet it was also during the 1890s, in spite of discrimination and fraud and murder and other forms of violence, that the indomitable black spirit began to emerge and flourish. Certainly there were arguments among Negroes—particularly between Booker T. Washington and W.E.B. Du Bois—about the best methods to promote their welfare, but their goals were the same: progress through racial pride, solidarity, self-help. If Negroes could not achieve their objectives with the aid of whites, they would manage to do so on their own.

There was new interest in Negro history, and especially in the African origins, typified by the establishment of the Society for the Collection of Negro Folk Lore (1890) and the Negro Historical Society of Philadelphia (1897), as well as by Arthur A. Schomburg's declaration: "The American Negro must remake his past in order to make his future... For him a group tradition must supply compensation for persecution, and pride of race the antidote for prejudice." Libraries and literary clubs, magazines, musical and arts groups flourished, and the American Negro Academy, to foster cultural activities, was founded in 1897.

With little or no access to financial and business support from the majority group in either south or north, Negroes banded together to protect and expand their own interests. Professional organizations were formed for black teachers, doctors, and lawyers. Black hospitals for both care and training purposes were begun: Provident in Chicago, by Dr. Daniel Hale Williams, a pioneer heart surgeon, and Frederick Douglass (now Mercy-Douglass) in Philadelphia. Banks, like the Alabama Penny

Savings and Loan Company and the Nickel Savings Bank in Richmond, Virginia, were established, along with insurance companies such as National Benefit and North Carolina Mutual. Hampton and Tuskegee sponsored conferences on topics of interest to farmers, as well as on economics and social welfare. The National Association of Colored Women— which was started in 1896 by educator Mary McLeod Bethune and predated the NAACP by sixteen years—represented the wide proliferation of women's charitable and cultural organizations.

When Du Bois became the first Negro to earn a Ph.D. from Harvard University in 1895, he is said to have replied to someone who was congratulating him on his success, "The honor, sir, is Harvard's." I like that wry comment. Somehow, it sums up the dignity and fortitude and audacity with which nearly nine million individuals, many of them former slaves, confronted and conquered a world they had not made. They were people with attitude.

***

My father, Homer Bismarck Watson, was born in Alabama on March 24, 1898, the son of Antiney Watson and Nancy Gamble Watson. Both of Homer's parents died early: his mother when he was ten and his father seven years later. After his mother died, my father was essentially reared by his older sister, Essie Draper. Like so many children (especially Negroes) in the rural south in the early twentieth century, he attended school only sporadically and, as far as I can determine, he never went beyond the second or third grade. Education was secondary to work.

I never knew much about my father's family. I did meet his sister and I knew a number of his cousins, the Gambles. Like thousands of other southern Negroes, they had moved north in search of better jobs and a less oppressive racial climate. Nathan and Wiley Gamble wound up in Gary and lived on the east side, near my family, but they were the only relatives on my father's side we knew.

When he was still quite young, my father became an apprentice to a white man who owned a horse and wagon with which he delivered ice to businesses and private homes. My father became quite skilled at cutting the ice to precise poundage, delivering it, and collecting the money. When his employer died, leaving no relatives, my father continued to serve the customers, buying the ice, cutting it to specifications, and paying the bills. I don't know how this could have happened in the south—maybe another white man took over the route. He probably worked in the

Alabama mines as well. At any rate, he supported himself until he entered the U.S. Army on October 28, 1917. He was nineteen years of age.

My mother, Fannie Mae Browne, came from a large family of seven girls and two boys. Her father (my grandfather) was employed by the Birmingham and Southern Railroad as a fireman. In those days, fireman meant fireman: he shoveled the coal into the belching furnaces which provided the steam for the engines. It was dirty, hard work, but it was one of the better jobs available to Negroes of that time. When the railroad decided to build a new roundhouse in Talladega, my grandfather was assigned to work with the engineers from Chicago who were supervising the construction and installation of the equipment. By the time the roundhouse was completed and the engineers were ready to return to their offices in Chicago, my grandfather knew as much about the roundhouse as anyone. As a result, he never returned to his old position as a fireman; he spent the rest of his days in the roundhouse, teaching white males how to operate and repair the equipment and serving as a troubleshooter.

He was still considered a fireman, of course. He was never given the title or the wages that should have gone with his actual responsibilities. Many other African Americans and other minorities had the same experience—long after my grandfather's time with the railroad: they had valuable skills, but they could not get the pay or recognition which their contribution merited. In fact, when we were teenagers, my friend Hosea Hopkins and I were considered "laborers" at the U.S. Steel Gary Works because that was the highest category open to blacks. Our job? We read the flues in the open hearth, computed the results, and turned them in to the white males who were getting paid to do the work.

My grandmother was a housewife; she kept house and saw to it that her children were educated and raised to be respectable. The family lived in a large house with a garden in the rear and a large front yard. My mother and her sisters attended the laboratory school at Talladega College, which was down the hill about a block or so from where my grandparents lived. When she finished the lab school, she went on to the college and was graduated *magna cum laude* in 1915 at the age of seventeen. Several years ago I found her diploma, which I had restored and framed; it hangs in my study. My mother apparently returned to Talladega for additional study because she was honored in 1991 as a member of the class of 1917. That same year, the state of Alabama issued her an elementary teaching certificate, but she became a teacher at Decatur High School in Decatur, Alabama. All the Browne girls, except for the eldest, Gertrude, eventually settled in the north: New York, Michigan, Indiana, Illinois, and Wisconsin.

I think it's very likely that my grandparents encouraged their girls to leave the south, especially Alabama. In those days, black women were considered fair game by white men; if they were attacked or raped, little would be done about it by the authorities. I remember my mother and her sisters talking about how their father had insisted that they all learn to shoot with skill and safety. My mother was proud of the fact that she could handle a double-barreled shotgun, a rifle, and a pistol. It's easy to understand this preoccupation with safety and survival when you consider what life was like for Negroes in the south 80 or 100 years ago.

My grandmother was born before the Civil War, and she died in 1945 at the age of 96. I remember that day very clearly. My mother left Gary, Indiana, on Christmas Eve to go to Talladega and prepare for the funeral with her sisters.

Negro Service in the Military

In 1917, the United States entered World War I. Negroes had served in the military since the American Revolution, as soldiers and sailors in the Continental army and navy. In fact, Crispus Attucks, an escaped slave, was one of the first people to die facing British troops in what became known as the Boston Massacre. Negroes also participated in the War of 1812. And they had strange and interesting roles on both sides of the War Between the States.

Freedmen in the north were at first banned from enlisting in the Union Army, but after the Emancipation Proclamation in 1862, Negro units were organized—although the colored private's pay was only half that of the white's. Meantime, riots broke out and lynchings of Negroes took place in New York City, because Irish immigrants, resenting conscription and unable to pay for a substitute, blamed their dilemma on the Negroes. The Confederate Army utilized Negroes in supporting roles—for instance, as army cooks or laborers in the war industries—but in the last desperate days of the war, Jefferson Davis called on the Confederacy to provide more troops regardless of color.

Several Negro units participated in the Spanish-American War, and by the war's end the number of Negro officers had risen from one to over 100. When the United States declared war on Germany in 1917, more than 700,000 Negroes registered under the terms of the Selective Service Act, and by the end of the war 367,000 had been drafted. But it was not until 1948 that segregation in the military was finally outlawed by executive order of President Truman.

For men like my father, with little education and few decent job prospects, army service may well have seemed a reasonable alternative. After entering the U.S. Army in 1917, he was sent to Camp Dodge, near Des Moines, Iowa, for basic training and was assigned to Company I, 366th Infantry Regiment, 92nd Division. Shipped overseas to France, he served in the American Expeditionary Force (AEF) from June 15, 1918, until February 28, 1919. He was honorably discharged at Fort Oglethorpe, Georgia, on March 26, 1919, with a record of participation in the following battles, engagements, skirmishes, and expeditions: St. Vosges, Meuse-Argonne Offensive, and Marbache Sectors (August 23, 1918, to November 11, 1918).

My dad's regiment, the 366th, consisted primarily of men from the mining districts of Alabama. They were mostly uneducated and were described as "... the worst looking lot that ever reported to any of the camps." During their training, from the autumn of 1917 until early in the spring of 1918, the regiment spent so much time at non-combat work that they were derisively called "the fatigue" regiment by neighboring white divisions. Actually, this practice was routine for black troops: they were restricted to low-grade service jobs until or unless they were absolutely needed in combat. When the war was nearly over (and commanders were trying to save white lives), they fought in the final battles.

The 92nd and 93rd Divisions were the first consisting entirely of colored troops to be assembled to prepare for combat. They had colored officers and non-commissioned officers, but all field and staff officers (as well as one-third of the others) were white. Great care was taken to assure that no white officer in any individual unit was outranked by any black officer. The 92nd Division was the successor to the "Buffalo Soldiers," legendary black soldiers who helped to settle the west. Both divisions were sent to France, but the 92nd (which was largely comprised of draftees) remained part of the American Expeditionary Force under U.S. command, while the 93rd was placed under French command, over General Pershing's protests.

The 92nd fought in the war's final battle—the assault on the Hindenburg Line—and its 367th regiment was awarded the Croix de Guerre. About three-quarters of the members of the 93rd Division were National Guardsmen. Three of its regiments—the 369th, 370th, and 371st—also received the Croix de Guerre. The 369th fought for 191 consecutive days and was the first unit to reach the Rhine. It received more citations than any other unit in the American Expeditionary Force and was welcomed home with a triumphant victory parade up Fifth Avenue to Harlem.

The experiences of black soldiers in World War I illustrates the tangled history of black Americans in all their country's wars. They were demeaned, their valor was under-reported or overlooked. When they were recommended for citations and medals by field commanders who were in the trenches with them, higher-ranking officers, acting out of prejudice or ignorance, routinely denied or "lost" or downgraded the recommendations. Nevertheless, black soldiers—and sailors and airmen, for that matter—continued to love their country, to volunteer for military service, and to respond when drafted. It is a history which is galling, even though today the first black chairman of the joint chiefs of staff (now retired) is among the most popular and respected men in the country.

My father earned his decorations and got out alive, although he was never able to focus his rifle or shotgun with his right eye after the war. He always aimed with his left eye, although he was right-handed. It didn't make any difference: he could still use a rifle and a shotgun better than either of his sons or his hunting buddies.

My father never spoke to us about the war. When my older brother, Homer, Jr., volunteered for the U.S. Navy in World War II, and again when I enlisted in the Air Force during Korea, my father's only comment was that we didn't have to go. But he never said why he was not thrilled with the prospect of his sons entering the armed forces. My father, like many of his friends who were veterans of World War I, belonged to American Legion Post 99, a segregated post in Gary, Indiana. His fellow veterans, most of whom had been in the AEF and had seen combat, were equally unwilling to discuss the war. Even when my father was dying of cancer in a hospital in Waukesha, Wisconsin, where I visited him every weekend and spent literally hours with him alone as he wasted away to nothing, he would never talk about his war. By this time I was a veteran, but it made no difference.

Some years later, I became friendly with a number of Vietnam veterans through a program I helped organize at Temple University. In a conversation with one of them, a very highly decorated veteran, he mentioned that one of his uncles had served in France in World War I. As we talked, I discovered that his uncle had responded the same way: he would never discuss his experience in World War I.

My interest was piqued. I began to read about the experiences of colored troops in World War I. I knew there was absolute racial segregation and blatant discrimination, but I was not prepared for the details of that experience. Then I called my good friend Charles Blockson, curator of the Blockson African American Collection at Temple University, who gave me citations and references not only about the general experience of colored troops, but also references for the specific division, battalion, regiment, brigade and company in which my father had served overseas. This information led me to review my father's service record and discharge more carefully.

I could not understand how my father could have been in the battles and engagements listed on his discharge, as well as obtaining the performance and character ratings which were stated, without receiving even a good conduct medal. As a result, I wrote to the Defense Department. To make a long story short, exactly seventy years after the Armistice was signed in 1918, I received the three decorations my father had earned in World War I. Had I not inquired, I would not now have them in my safe deposit box for his grandchildren and future generations. Unfortunately, my mother, my two brothers and two sisters did not live long enough to share this information.

It was not until 1993, however, that I finally understood my father's reluctance to talk about World War I. On October 10, 1993, the *New York Times* carried a column by Richard Wald, senior vice president of ABC News, describing his father's aversion to discussing the war. As I read the column, "My Father's War," a light went on. Wald, on Armistice Day, sees his father with tears in his eyes. In response to his "What's the matter?", Wald's father reveals to him the bitterness he feels about the timing of the World War I Armistice: the 11th hour on the 11th day of the 11th month. "They had to wait, to make a symbol. They let it go on so they could look wonderful later. I had friends who were killed while we waited. The bastards."

Then, I understood the last piece of the puzzle. From Wald's description, his father had many of the same characteristics as mine: quiet, stolid, a rock in the storm, rarely showing emotion. But there were differences. My father was a black man. Colored troops in his division, particularly in his brigade and regiment were assigned accelerated front line combat and activity in the final days of the war, immediately before the Armistice. I understand more now. But I still wonder what hurts that man carried with him to the grave; what disappointments he tried to forget; what dreams he once harbored; what emotions he never felt free to express openly, even to his children who loved him dearly.

In Search of Work

As demobilization quickly followed in the wake of the Armistice, millions of American men found themselves looking for jobs. A brief period of post-war prosperity was soon succeeded by a depression, beginning with disastrous drops in Midwestern grain prices. As in all periods of economic uncertainty, racial and ethnic animosities flourished. Peddlers of hate called for "100 percent Americanism" and whipped up fear that communists, Jews, Catholics, and Negroes were "taking over." For many people, including recent immigrants, the message was clear: your jobs are in danger. From 1917 to 1920, hundreds of people died and thousands were wounded in riots which erupted across the country—in Washington, Chicago, Philadelphia, Omaha, East St. Louis (Illinois), Longview (Texas), and Chester (Pennsylvania). In some places, federal troops had to be called out to help the local police quell the riots.

For black Americans, the post-war outlook was particularly dismal: after helping to liberate Europe from the Kaiser, they returned to find that nothing had changed at home. The few professionals—chiefly ministers and teachers, but also doctors, dentists, and lawyers—could continue to practice within their segregated communities. For the greater number without much or any education, the choice was largely limited to providing smalltime services, like my father's ice business, or working in the mines or in the fields under conditions which were not very different from the days of slavery. Years before the mechanization of the cotton fields drove five million Negroes to northern cities, many Negro veterans decided to leave the south and seek employment in the great manufacturing enterprises which had grown up in or near Chicago.

Situated midway between the iron deposits of Lake Superior and the Appalachian coal mines, easily accessible by both water and rail, the Chicago area—stretching from lower Wisconsin to northern Indiana—had become a center for trade and industry well before the end of the nineteenth century. In 1905, the U.S. Steel Corporation decided to build a mammoth steel mill complex on the southern shore of Lake Michigan, just over the Illinois state line. For about $800 per acre the corporation purchased a tract of 9,000 acres. Mostly swamp and sand dunes, and very lightly populated, it was an ideal site. Construction of the giant works started in 1906 and within three years, production began. The corporation also laid out streets and provided utilities, creating areas where its executives and laborers could live. A real "company town," it was named for Judge Elbert H. Gary, chairman of the board of U.S. Steel.

Like other industrial towns and cities, particularly those dependent on a single company, Gary suffered from a series of economic booms and busts. Growth of the steel works was rapid in the first few years, then there was a recession which, in turn, was followed by an expansion during World War I. A post-war depression led to massive layoffs and the famous strike of 1919, organized by labor unions seeking better working conditions and increased wages. Gary's mayor, William Hodges, crushed the strike by bringing in the army and declaring martial law. The strike leaders were jailed, sympathizers were called "Reds" (the overthrow of the Russian czar and the establishment of a communist government had occurred just two years earlier), and aliens were threatened with deportation if they did not return to work. People who were willing to work, black and white, were recruited to work in the mills. My father was one of them.

❧

To this day, I do not know how or when my mother and father met, whether it was before the war or after he returned home from France. I do know that they married in 1920, after his discharge, and were married to each other all of their adult lives. Once they were married, an agreement was reached, whereby my father would work and take care of the family and my mother would run the house, raise the children, and be a wife and mother. She would never teach or hold a full-time job again.

My mother and father left Talladega, Alabama, shortly after their wedding. Negroes were leaving the south in droves, heading north to "the promised land" and a degree of freedom undreamed of in Alabama, Arkansas, Mississippi, and Georgia (the home states of most of the Negroes who migrated to Gary after World War I). Like many of his peers, my father had little education. For poor people, education in the south was awful. For Negroes, it was even worse—when it was available at all. White people didn't care whether Negroes were educated or not. They were expected to work, obey orders, remain deferential to white people, and keep their mouths shut. Anyway, most people thought Negroes were too dumb to learn.

After growing up in this environment, and then being exposed to a wider world in the army in Iowa and in France, it is not surprising that my father and others Negroes of his generation decided to leave at the first opportunity. My parents first went to West Virginia, where my father worked at the coal mines. When the foreman told him he had to give up his topside job and go into the mines, my father decided it was time to move on. He told my mother that God didn't intend for a man to work in a hole in the ground. The next stop was Akron, Ohio, because of its rubber industry. By this time, their first child, Helen, had been born—the only one of the five of us who was not a native of Gary. My father stayed in Akron until word came that the steel mills were hiring in Indiana. He and my mother left Akron and moved to Gary, where he found a job in the Gary works of U.S. Steel, the largest integrated steel works in the world.

My father went to work in the coke plant and spent the rest of his working life there. He was never laid off, although he sometimes worked only one day a week or a few hours a week. He did not leave the coke plant until he came out, on medical disability, to die of cancer which had ravaged his body after years of exposure to carcinogens from the coke ovens. He died approximately five months after I returned from "my" war, Korea. I think about him sometimes when I look at my own children and wonder if they realize how different life is and has been for them.

My father always worked hard—hard, physical labor in unpleasant, hazardous conditions. I know the kind of work he did because he taught me his job one summer when I was in high school. My father was a pusher operator in the coke plant. A pusher was a very large machine which combined some of the elements of a crane and a bulldozer. It was two stories high and ran sideways on steel tracks, like railroad tracks. The operator, sitting in a small cab, lifted the doors from a bank of coke ovens with one part of the pusher. Then, using another part which resembled a battering ram, he pushed the coke from the oven into a "hot car," which was driven along a track behind the coke ovens. Once the coke was removed, the door was replaced and the process repeated on the other ovens in the bank.

Through it all, the air was filled with coke dust, sparks, smoke and whatever other pollutants came from converting the coal and ore to coke. It was a dangerous and dirty job. You had to wear goggles, a respirator, gloves, a hat, and long-sleeved shirts. At the end of an eight-hour shift, your clothes were filthy, you were filthy, and everybody looked alike, whether you were white or black. You were constantly ingesting carcinogens. Most of the people who worked there all of their lives died of cancer, as my dad did. But the job was the highest and best-paying one available to Negroes. My dad was good at it, so good that he was never unemployed, even during the Depression. And he was respected; he was a no-nonsense person.

The foremen did not yell at him or curse him, a common practice in the mills. And they didn't "goose" him either. White workers and foremen would sneak up behind the older Negro men in the mills and stick their fingers between their legs, causing the Negro men to jump and make funny noises—to great guffaws from the whites. It was all play-acting, but it wasn't funny. It really pissed off the younger Negroes. Nobody ever goosed them. Nor did anyone touch my father; the white employees spoke to him, were civil, and left him alone. He didn't talk much; he did his work and went home to his family.

I could tell he was proud that I learned the job so quickly and that I paid attention. He was gratified when the foreman and others would tell him what a good worker I was and how smart I was, adding that I would not spend my life out there doing what they did for a living. Toward the end of the summer, I actually got to operate a pusher when someone was late or until a man could be convinced to work another shift. When the summer was over, my father told me he didn't want me in the coke plant again, that there were better places in the mills to work. There was never a question about whether I would take a full time job after graduation from high school. My father had not raised his children to become laborers in the steel industry.

I watched my father work himself to death, although I didn't know it at the time. He was like all of the other men who were trying to support their families: doing jobs that paid well enough to buy a home or purchase a new car periodically or take summer vacations; encouraging their children to carve out a better life. He achieved his goals, but I have rarely seen anyone exert himself as hard as my father did, without complaint. He worked the swing shifts, like most of the workers: 8 a.m. to 4 p.m.; 4 to midnight; or midnight to 8.

During World War II, the shifts were frequently ten or twelve hours, six or seven days a week, with time-and-a-half pay for overtime and double pay for certain days and hours. My dad took advantage of most of those extra hours and shifts; so did I, after I became sixteen and after high school graduation. These earnings not only enabled my father to buy a house and other luxuries, they also helped me to attend and graduate from college. I worked in the blast furnaces, the coke plants, the sheet and tin mills, and the open hearths. Those experiences were an important part of my development and maturation, experiences I value to this day.

Life in Gary

America was changing. The waves of immigration which peaked in 1907 had brought increasing numbers of people, not only from northern European countries, but from Russia, Italy, Austria-Hungary, and the Balkans. The Chicago area was particularly attractive because of the job opportunities in that industrial capital, and as early as 1890 immigrants and their children comprised 78 percent of its population. By 1920, immigration had increased Gary's population to over 55,000, and in the following decade, it doubled to over 100,000. In 1910, there were only 383 Negroes in a population of 16,802, but that number grew quickly following the influx of Negroes from the south after World War I and the steel strike of 1919, when many were recruited as strike breakers. Racial antagonism increased as well.

There was a good deal of Klan activity during the 1920s. Ku Klux Klan rallies were held in Hammond, Valparaiso, and in Ridgelawn Memorial Park on West Ridge Road in Gary itself. Klan activity in Indiana continued with some force and visibility until D. C. Stephenson, Grand Dragon of the Indiana Ku Klux Klan, was convicted of violating federal white slavery statutes. (As late as the 1940s, however, hand-printed crude signs announcing Ku Klux Klan meetings were tacked on trees on the Bloomington campus of Indiana University. They were just as regularly removed by Negro World War II veterans, students, and others as we proceeded to and from classes.)

Meantime, Gary's downtown area flourished with banks and stores and businesses. Civic groups like Rotary, Kiwanis, and Lions were founded. U.S. Steel expanded and instituted an eight-hour day to temper worker discontent. There were 12 theaters, six of which had live entertainment. By the mid-twenties, Gary had become Indiana's leading convention city. But crime, poverty, social fragmentation, and cultural dependency on nearby Chicago existed simultaneously—conditions exacerbated by Gary's domination by absentee corporate leadership. Mayor Roswell O. Johnson's toleration of speakeasies, brothels, and gambling led to his conviction on federal charges of violating the Volstead Act, and he was sent to prison in 1923. His replacement as mayor was Floyd Williams, who was alleged to have ties with the Ku Klux Klan, a major force in Indiana state politics during this period. In 1929, however, Johnson was re-elected mayor of Gary, after having received a full presidential pardon.

The Depression was tough on everyone. Ten of eleven banks closed; Gary defaulted on its debt and paid in scrip. Teachers were forced to *accept a salary cut and a reduction in the school year. Mill production dipped below 20 percent of capacity, and workers considered themselves lucky if they were hired to work one day in five. Black workers had a particularly difficult time of it, but Mexicans—who had been welcomed when workers were needed—were prodded into leaving town on freight cars.*

◄►

Through good times and bad, my parents were devoted to each other and to their children: Helen, Homer, Jr., Ernie (who died in childhood after a sled accident, a tragedy from which my mother and father never fully recovered), Bernard, and Dee. Their life revolved around the family. We always had dinner together (except when my dad was on the 4 p.m.-to-midnight shift) and our conversations—which ranged from what was happening in our community to events in the nation and the world—frequently continued well into the evening. My mother, who was a voracious reader and had her face in a book even while she was cooking, encouraged us to use the library nearby; we also went to the movies on the weekends. All of us were members of the First Baptist Church and attended regularly. In fact, my mother was in the choir for thirty-five years.

My childhood was a happy one. We enjoyed playing with neighborhood and school friends, and like kids everywhere we invented our own games. The summer that I was ten, I started attending overnight camp where we pitched our tents, cooked over fires, and hiked for miles. The camp belonged to Delaney Methodist Church and was run by a local settlement house. Sometimes we all piled into the family car for a trip to Detroit to visit relatives, and once we went all the way to Talladega, where I met my grandmother, aunts and uncles, and saw the family homestead.

I remember clearly our visit to Alabama. It was in 1936 and I was eight years old. I remember young white boys, teenage or younger, calling my father "Homer," just as their parents did. I thought that was strange: only adults called men by their first names in my neighborhood. As I think about it, nobody *ever* called my mother by her first name, unless they were the same age as she was or even older. It didn't matter whether they were white or black.

Music was a central part of our family life. There was always a piano in our home, even when we were renting. My mother would play church songs and popular music while the rest of us sang, and each one would be given the opportunity to sing a solo or take the lead—whether we wanted to or not! My mother gave piano lessons to neighborhood children, and she saw to it that we all learned something about music. Helen played the piano and was a violinist in the school orchestra. Homer studied saxophone and piano, while Dolores—the most talented of the children—not only took piano lessons for ten years, but was the first chair clarinetist in the high school concert band and orchestra. I was the only one who did not learn at least the rudiments of piano (a fact which I regret to this day). I was involved in so many activities at school and the settlement house, in Boy Scouts and the junior choir at church, that I was able to avoid piano lessons. Later, when I started feeling my oats about my musical accomplishments in band and orchestra, Homer quickly demonstrated how little I knew, and when I began playing in lounges and taverns, he reminded me that I was a novice, entering the real world of sometimes dangerous and irresponsible adults.

We were a close-knit family. We were taught that brothers and sisters could disagree and argue, but whatever your differences, you didn't fight one another. The older ones were responsible for protecting and guiding the younger ones. There was a clear pecking order based on age, but we always looked out for one another. Helen got me a job in the short-order kitchen of the States Hotel, the major Negro hotel in Gary. When, at age twelve, I started a shoeshine business with two local white boys as my assistants, my brother and his friends provided protection when we ventured out of the neighborhood.

My father built me a wagon with removable sides (so it would load more easily and carry more), and I delivered groceries from the neighborhood store. My brother taught me how to charge and collect my money in advance. I also made trips to and from the local distribution center of the U.S. Department of Agriculture for people who were eligible for surplus food from the government—juices, fresh fruit like oranges and grapefruit, corn meal, flour, canned goods, and so on. It was a form of relief, before food stamps. The Watson family, cousins and all, never received welfare or surplus food. My father was part of a group of black men (most black men in Gary belonged) whose motto was: "Never been on welfare; never been arrested." This slogan, or boast, says a lot about conditions then, even in the industrial north. Capricious police action and arrests were not common in Gary, although they could occur; they were much more frequent in Chicago or in other Indiana towns, like Hammond, Whiting, and Indiana Harbor.

There were rules in our home. You did not "sass" your parents or disagree with them in an impertinent manner. It was fine to argue and defend your point of view if you did it appropriately—without showing disrespect and raising your voice in anger. We were expected to attend school every day and to be on time. We were expected to do our homework, get good grades, and respect our teachers. We were expected to demonstrate, in our speech and behavior, that we were a part of a God-fearing, law-abiding, respectable, and hardworking family. Woe be unto anyone who violated these rules.

Both parents handled discipline, although all my father had to do was look at us. No words needed to be spoken, no warnings or threats: his authority was unquestioned. He never administered corporal punishment, although my mother dispensed it when she felt it was necessary. My parents did not always agree. We heard them argue, but it was never loud, angry, or personal. Their disagreements could be heated and they sometimes went on for days, but eventually they would be settled and life would go on.

Helen, the eldest child, became a housewife after high school. Hortense, Helen's daughter, was the first black captain of the cheerleaders at Froebel High School. She became the administrative assistant to the dean of Meharry Medical School in Nashville, Tennessee, where she met and married her husband, an air traffic controller. In 1967, tragedy struck: she was the only survivor of an automobile accident which killed her husband and her brother- and sister-in-law. She was a paraplegic from 1967 until her death in 1993.

Homer, Jr., the next in line, became a jazz musician, playing reeds. Despite efforts to get him to go to Purdue with his best friend to study engineering, he went to the Chicago Conservatory of Music. While there, he supported himself by working in the chemical laboratories of U.S. Steel. He and his lifetime friend, John Gates, were the first blacks to work there. Homer was also a composer and arranger, and I still have the copyrights for a number of the songs he wrote. He became the first black employee of Lyon and Healy (music publishers) in their Cleveland store, but he died less than a year later, just before he was to join the Tiny Bradshaw band. If the medical knowledge of the 1990s had been available, he would be alive today.

Dolores, the youngest of the five children in the family, was clearly the most musically talented. Dee, as we called her, was so gifted that her first piano teacher advised my mother that this child should receive the very best instruction. Accordingly, my parents found some way to put aside a weekly fee for piano lessons from a person who was known as a "fine teacher." Dee raced through her lessons and soon was giving recitals while continuing to study. When she went to high school, she enrolled in the band and began to play clarinet. Within one year, she was holding down the solo chair in the school band and the school orchestra.

She should have become a professional, but in those days there were very few opportunities for black musicians, especially classical instrumentalists. Dee studied accounting and became a secretary/bookkeeper after high school. She finally went to Indiana University to study elementary education, but she hated it. (Ironically, Dee's roommate at Indiana University was opera singer, Frankie Weathers.) Dee decided she didn't want to become a teacher, so she never finished her last year, but she continued to love music above all else until the day she died. She returned to Gary, married, and had a son who is now a public accountant in Cincinnati. At the time of her death, she was working as assistant to the former chief financial officer of the city of Gary, Maurice Baptiste.

My father was a quiet man who kept his thoughts to himself. Standing only five feet, eight inches, tall, he was slender, but all muscle and sinew, partly as a result of the kind of work he did. He rarely expressed his personal feelings or shared his emotions. Only twice in my life did I see him overcome. As I mentioned, my older brother died at age 26, just when his career as a musician was beginning to take off. After the funeral, when friends and relatives came to our house to comfort the family, I noticed my father's absence. When I took the trash out, I found him sitting alone in the darkness in a corner of the garage crying softly. I pretended I didn't see him, but that image remains vivid to this day. Both my brothers died at an early age, and I think I understand why people say that the most devastating thing parents can experience is the death of a child.

Dad was passionate about baseball, however, and he and his cronies would argue and joke about the game. He was a lifelong fan of the St. Louis Cardinals—even after Jackie Robinson joined the Brooklyn Dodgers and became the first Negro player in the major leagues. Of course, almost everybody followed the exploits of the teams in the Negro leagues, especially when they played post-season games against the all-white major league teams. Negro teams—including some good amateur and semi-professional ones—were a big deal in the black community. My father took my brother and me to a couple of games in Gary, and it was one of the few times I saw him, his cousins, and his neighborhood or work buddies really excited and enjoying themselves. I had no interest in major league baseball: there were no Negro players when I was growing up, and furthermore, really good baseball was played by American Legion and semi-pro teams. To this day, I have never attended a major league game.

My father loved listening to ball games on the radio, and he loved working on his automobile. He could take a car apart and put it back together. If anything was wrong, he fixed it himself. I can remember when I was a little boy meeting my father after work on the corner of 16th and Virginia Streets, a block from our apartment. He would let me in the car (a 1929 Ford), sit me on his lap, and allow me to "drive" the car home. I thought I was really something special! Most families didn't own cars at that time, so none of the other children in the neighborhood could do that. In 1936, when he received his second World War I veteran's bonus, he purchased a brand-new, black, four-door Ford V-8. He—like the rest of us—was so proud of that automobile. Until he and my mother were able to buy a home a few years later, he kept it in a rented garage. That Ford was the magic carpet which took us some place every summer when my dad was on vacation: Michigan, Illinois, Ohio, and once to Alabama. He took such good care of the car that when he died in 1954, it was still running and in pretty good condition.

My dad could do almost anything with his hands—skills and abilities I never acquired. With our help as we got older, he replaced and extended the front porch on our house, laid new sidewalks on the side and rear of the house, added a patio in the back yard, replaced the garage doors, and repaired the brick foundations. He could and did fix the faucet and sinks, he painted the exterior of the house every two or three years, and he did all the painting and papering inside. Painting was the only skill I learned from him, and I could do this without supervision. I also had full responsibility for taking care of the lawn and shrubs, but otherwise, I was a total disaster, the object of derision from my siblings as they observed my feeble attempts to help with other tasks. Only under my father's supervision was I adequate. (I am still the object of scornful laughter—from my wife, my children, and my good friend, Richard Gilmore—when I attempt to do anything requiring mechanical ability or skill in construction.) But in spite of my limitations, I enjoyed spending the time with my dad: we all did. He would say, "We start at six in the morning." We had no idea *what* we would start, but you can bet we would be up and ready on time. Once we began, there was very little conversation except for instructions, comments, and compliments. To get the job done, we all had to work together—a lesson I have never forgotten.

Something else we did together was going to American Legion Post #99, the only Negro post in Gary, which sponsored a number of youth activities: baseball, marching, softball, talent shows. My father and his friends would sit around and talk about the old days and the war—but we were never allowed to participate in that; it was for adults only. As I said earlier, I never heard my dad or his friends or my cousins discuss their experiences in World War I.

My mother was more outgoing and engaging than my father. She helped neighbors, white and Negro, with paperwork and business matters. Sometimes she did record-keeping and prepared reports for both the Republican and Democratic parties. She gave piano lessons for neighborhood children. When we were young, we thought that she knew everything. There seemed to be nothing we could ask her about that she couldn't help us learn. She had taught reading and music in Alabama, and although she never held a full-time job after she married and moved north, she read constantly—biographies of famous people, current novels, and westerns (she especially loved Zane Grey). All of us were introduced to libraries at an early age. U.S. Steel had placed branches in almost every neighborhood, and there was one near us wherever we lived.

I became an insatiable reader, just like my mother: it didn't seem to matter whether it was fairy tales or facts, I was interested in everything. The library had copies of *Boy's Life, Life, National Geographic,* and the *Saturday Evening Post*, and I read them all. My friends, like Clarence Currie, competed to see who knew the most about a subject or who had seen the latest on the topic, and then we would hang around and talk about interesting people and places, dreaming of our future. We also read black newspapers: *Chicago Defender, Pittsburgh Courier*, plus the local *Gary American*. My mother passed on to me her love for books and their magic, and I will always be grateful. Today my personal library includes almost 2,000 books.

Because I stayed at home until I was almost seven, my mother and I developed a special relationship which lasted until her death in 1978 at eighty years of age. She was a wonderful woman, a great mother. We talked for hours about all kinds of things. She understood my dreams, my ambitions, my anger at the injustices of racism and discrimination, and above all, my drive to confront, to compete, to achieve, to try to do everything in which I had an interest.

Today, I wonder if those long conversations were as much a reflection, a mirror image, of her own dreams and ambitions, as they were of mine. I wonder how she, as a well-educated woman, felt about being a housewife and mother, never using the skills and education she had acquired—at some sacrifice to her parents, I am sure. Perhaps she knowingly and willingly lived her dreams of a better, less pernicious, less restrictive and oppressive world through her children.

I know my dad did. The one thing all of us remember about my father was his saying in twenty different ways that we did not have to have the kind of life he had lived or endure the indignities suffered by his generation. My mother was even more explicit, encouraging each of us to pursue our interests and goals, whatever they might be. Both our parents drilled into us that we were responsible for what happened to us. We could not control the world or all of our surroundings, but we could be prepared for any opportunities should they occur.

I learned so much from both my parents, just by watching them or listening to their informal, offhand conversations. I also became a dreamer. Through what I found in books, magazines, and movies, I could transport myself almost anywhere, and by the time I was in grade school I was spending a lot of time in my own private world of ideas and imagination. I became a very private person, one who guards his real thoughts and feelings zealously—a habit my friends and family tell me I still continue.

*E**ducation in Gary*

The Gary Public School System was planned and directed by Dr. William A. Wirt, a nationally-acclaimed educational innovator and visionary. Dr. Wirt introduced what was known as the "Work-Study-Play" system. The school day began at 8:15 a.m. and ended at 4:15 p.m., with an hour for lunch. On Saturday, there were classes from 8:15 a.m. to 12:15 p.m. for students who could not keep up during the regular week. There was a full summer school for those who needed to repeat courses or make up work they had failed during the regular school year, as well as for people who wanted to accelerate graduation by taking extra courses.

Dr. Wirt's plan was both ingenious and comprehensive. He believed that the school should accommodate all the children from the local community, from kindergarten through high school, providing them with not only classroom instruction by faculty who specialized in one subject, but recreation and participation in school operations, such as plant maintenance and the cafeteria. Each school had a gymnasium, playground, auditorium, and shops, and careful scheduling saw to it that "platoons" of students spent half the day in academic work and half in the extended program, with activities appropriate to each grade level. From kindergarten through the eighth grade, every child took classes in music, drama, and speech every year; these subjects were also required for high school students.

In Dr. Wirt's view, which was commended by John Dewey in Schools of Tomorrow *in 1915, developing discipline, social skills, and a sense of responsibility was as important as learning English or math. (I noted with interest a recent* New York Times *article on education in Japan, a system* much admired because its students rank so high in international achievement tests. There are similarities to the Wirt plan: tight organization, the sense of community, and the requirement that students share janitorial tasks, including cleaning bathrooms.)

The population of Gary included many ethnic groups: Polish, Hungarian, Greek, Lithuanian, Italian, Mexican, Chinese, Russian, German, and others—each trying simultaneously to be American and to maintain its cultural and ethnic identity. On the east side of the city (where I grew up), Poles, Hungarians, Italians, and Negroes lived in relative harmony in houses rented from U.S. Steel or private landlords. The west side also contained a mix of ethnic groups, including a small number of Negroes and most of the Mexicans in town. Most Negroes lived on the south side, along with a few Germans, Poles, and others. Despite this unusual residential mix, children attended schools which were racially segregated in one way or another.

It didn't start out that way. Initially, some of the schools—like Emerson on the east side—served all students in the neighborhood, as Wirt had envisioned. But in 1927, as the Negro migration to Gary continued, the Board of Education transferred Negro students out of the integrated schools and reinforced a policy of blatant racial segregation. Even here, however, there were exceptions. It was truly a weird system as far as race was concerned.

On the east side where my family lived, there were three schools: Emerson, which was changed from integrated to all-white in 1927; East Pulaski, the school for Negro students, with an all-black staff; and West Pulaski, on the same campus as East Pulaski but with an all-white student body and staff. For children who had lived side by side, sometimes in the same building, segregation began when they reached school age. Those who were white and Roman Catholic and could afford the tuition went to St. Hedwig's; the others went to West Pulaski, then on to Froebel, Emerson, or Lew Wallace. Black children went to East Pulaski, then a few to Froebel and most to Roosevelt.

On the west side, there was Froebel School, which was integrated only because there was not enough room at Roosevelt for all the Negro students. But they could not swim in the pool except on Friday (the water was changed over the weekend), participate in student government, or attend the prom. They had their own association called the Junior-Senior Club and their own separate social activities. For many years, Froebel had no Negro teachers or coaches, despite the fact that many of its star athletes were Negroes. In fact, they were the only Negro athletes in the city who could compete against white schools. *(Teams from Roosevelt, the segregated school I attended, could not compete against other Gary teams until World War II. Before that, Roosevelt travelled all over the country to participate in contests with other Negro schools—in Missouri, Arkansas, Virginia, Texas, North Carolina. There was even a national Negro championship in football, basketball, and track.)* Also on the west side, but downtown, there was Horace Mann, widely viewed as the academic school. One of its best-known graduates was Tom Harmon, the All-American football player who later became an outstanding member of the Los Angeles Rams football team and then a movie star.

On the far south side, in a section called Glen Park, Lew Wallace was the school. It was all-white and served a neighborhood largely populated by white people, former residents of the east side, who had purchased small homes with lawns and backyards. This school also produced some of the finest athletes in the city, including the Karras brothers of National Football League fame.

Far to the east, along the shore of Lake Michigan, sat William Wirt School, named after the first superintendent. This was the closest thing to an elite school to be found in Gary. The well-to-do citizens lived in this area—which was definitely off limits to Negroes. *(The "public" beach here was also off limits, but because the Indiana dunes were part of a state park, some areas were open to all and even had facilities for barbecues and picnics. Dunes State Park later became a part of the national park system, thanks to the leadership of Senator Paul Douglas of Illinois.)*

H. Theodore Tatum, previously principal of East Pulaski School, became principal of Roosevelt in August 1931. He was to become a legend.

⟡

As a child, I was very small for my age. My mother and father decided that I should not begin school until I was older and larger. One of my brothers had been bullied by older, bigger children, a not-uncommon occurrence in that steel town. After enduring a number of fights and other incidents, my parents determined that the same thing would not happen to me at Roosevelt, the K-12 school I was scheduled to attend. So, when all of my friends started school after their fifth birthday, I stayed home. I didn't enter school until the beginning of the second semester in February, a few weeks before my seventh birthday on March 4th.

Helen and Homer, my older sister and brother who were already students at Roosevelt, accompanied me to school on the first day and left me in the office, where I waited until the clerk asked me what I wanted. I gave her my name, told her I wished to enroll in first grade, and presented my birth certificate and the other required papers. Mrs. Griffin, the head clerk, took the materials, conferred with the other secretaries in the office, and asked me to please step behind the counter and into a small office. I did so, answered a number of questions, and was duly enrolled. One of the clerks then took me to Mrs. Lane's classroom where I began my formal education. I didn't go to kindergarten because I was too old; besides, I could already read. My mother had taught me at home while I followed her around the house, watching her cook and clean and pay the bills. I can't remember when or how I learned, but I could read, as my first grade teachers soon discovered

I loved school. It was so exciting and I really enjoyed the work. I also liked being at Roosevelt with the junior and senior high schools on the same campus. We started school at 8:15 and the last class was over at 4:15. In addition to the "three Rs," all students were required to take physical education, auditorium, speech, drama, music, art, and industrial arts (for boys) or home economics (for girls). Everybody took the same courses until high school when students began to follow certain tracks in mathematics and science. Except for art, where I clearly had no talent, I was almost a straight "A" student.

The first week I was in school, I had a big fight. I didn't start it, and in fact I was petrified. It was with a retarded student (the son of a very prominent and well-off family) who was in the special education section except for physical education, art, and some industrial arts classes. Anyway, he started in on me while we were in gym, and when I outplayed him, he decided to "kick my ass." Now, I couldn't take that lying down, especially in front of a gym full of my classmates. Even more important, my father, mindful of what had happened to my brother, had told me not to let anyone run over me. "If you have to fight," he said, "do it. It doesn't matter if you lose; you must serve notice on people that they cannot take advantage of you. Once they know that they have a fight on their hands, even if they win, they will think twice before messing with you. Most of them will leave you alone. Besides, you will also win your share of the fights."

I jumped in his face and chest like a cornered rat or a treed cat. I must have hit him ten times before he got over the surprise, but by the time he did, he was on his back and I was on top of him. All the time, I was scared to death, breathing heavily and wondering how he was going to dismember me. Fortunately, he started crying because all of the kids who were so afraid of him were laughing and cheering me on. They made so much noise that the coach and several teachers came into the gym from the hallway. They broke it up and, in the process, probably saved my life. This dude was big and strong, three or four years older than the rest of us. After that incident, my reputation was made: I was a little runt, but I had heart and would fight. These were important traits of character in a steel town. I never had to fight again, although there were a couple of near misses.

After fourth grade, I skipped fifth and went directly to sixth —a "double promotion," in recognition of outstanding grades and top scores on citywide tests. Of course, I liked that, because it put me in the grade I would have been in had I started school at the appropriate age. However, when another double promotion was recommended at the end of seventh grade, Mr. Tatum, the principal, wisely decided not to give his approval. He thought I was not mature enough to be in high school classes with students who might be considerably older. You see, in those days it was unusual for people to graduate from high school before the age of eighteen, or even nineteen or twenty (the maximum age for participation in sports). I didn't like it at the time, but that was probably the best decision for me. Later, I understood and appreciated Mr. Tatum's wisdom. Oh, I could have done the work without much trouble, but I clearly would have been a misfit socially and would have had no chance to participate in sports and other activities.

High School

I stayed with my class and entered high school, which began with ninth grade in those days. I finished my freshman year with a straight "A" average; I received one "B" in my sophomore year, but I was in the junior and senior honor societies. It's a wonder that I had time to do this well academically, because I participated in so many activities: essay contests, plays, student government, debate, and sports. I was elected president of the freshman class, president of the sophomore class, assistant secretary of the student government (as a freshman), and later vice president. I played quarterback on the freshman city championship football team—and was almost killed in the process, was a member of the junior varsity basketball team, and ran varsity track. I played saxophone in the Knights of Rhythm Jazz Band (the best in the city), and clarinet in the concert and marching bands and the orchestra. Somehow I also managed to be president of the chemistry club and the Spanish club, treasurer of the Senior

Hi-Y, sports editor of the school paper, on the yearbook staff, and in the sophomore and junior plays. I was busy! I loved high school, just as I had loved elementary and junior high school. I loved all of it.

While all of this was going on, I worked at U.S. Steel during weekends, holidays, and summers, thereby making enough money to buy my own clothes and my saxophone, save a little for college, and help out at home—something every boy did in those days. My friends and I could work at the steel plant after we turned sixteen because so many men were away fighting in World War II, a war which started when I was in the sixth grade. If you were eighteen and could handle it, you could even work full-time (on the afternoon or night shift) and go to school in the morning. Principals and teachers ignored it as long as you got to school on time and did not sleep in class.

I remember the first day I entered the Gary U.S. Steel plant at age sixteen. I was assigned to the #3 Open Hearth, and when I walked into that cavernous building, it seemed that all hell had broken loose. Fire, noise, cranes and other equipment operating everywhere at full roar. Scores of men proceeded to do their work with a degree of nonchalance I found wondrous to behold. It was exciting and just a little scary. Those of us who were minors had large red badges pinned to our work clothes, but we were real steel workers, helping in the war effort and making a man's wages: $6.24 a day. I remember resting in the tower of the conveyor house, during a break on the midnight shift, looking out at the city and vowing that when I was an adult I would never hold a job that required me to work shifts and to be dirty all the time. Most important, I promised myself that I would never work in a situation where I had to take orders from someone every day. I was a little guy, weighing only 128 pounds when I graduated from high school, but I had big dreams, and nobody was going to break my spirit.

On weekends and evenings during the summer, I worked jazz gigs in lounges and other assorted joints. Again, we could do this because of the war: every lounge and bar wanted live music, but many of Gary's professional musicians were in the armed forces. Chu Crump, Skeeter Hart, the Ferguson brothers, John Goosby, and Arthur Hoyle—to name a few—worked the top clubs where people demanded the best. The rest of us worked the second- and third-level places. We could work and learn; go to listen to better musicians and steal their stuff; go to jam sessions and get cut up. But you would go back to the woodshed and practice, practice, practice if you wanted to play. The 1940s were cool, because you also got to see the greatest, stars like Sarah Vaughan, Duke Ellington, Count

Basie, Nat King Cole, Lionel Hampton, and Ella Fitzgerald. Wow! What a time. It wasn't so great for the people fighting the war, however.

From the time I went to work in the steel mills at age 16, I took care of all of my personal expenses, bought my own clothes, and purchased my first saxophone (a French Selmer) from a pawn shop. I also contributed to the household, as did most young people who were working but living at home. As a matter of fact, I paid to have a modern bathroom installed on the first floor of our house, and later I purchased a new gas furnace and water heater. Like many other blue-collar families, we used to bathe in a large corrugated tin tub.

By the way, I am proud of the fact that I became a member of two unions while I was still in my teens: the Steelworkers Union, of course, and also the American Federation of Musicians. In those days, the AFM was segregated, and I had to join the black local, Number 622—an experience that, many years later, gave me special empathy with Philadelphia's Clef Club, the jazz organization whose founders had also been in a black AFM local. Later, when I taught in Gary, I served as vice president of the American Federation of Teachers—a position I had to give up five years later, when I was promoted to vice principal and thus became a member of the administration. I was active in the principals' organization and have thus had seats on both sides of the bargaining table.

My parents wanted to do something special to celebrate my high school graduation, so they bought my class ring. Earlier, my mother had given me gold cuff links and studs for my junior prom, and my dad gave me a set in ivory for my senior prom. These and other mementos were among the things stolen when thieves and vandals broke into our house in Chestnut Hill in July 1976. There is no way to express what a loss like that means.

Race relations were horrible, even during the war. I remember a very tense time during my high school years. Across town, at Froebel High School, there was a white student whose parents were immigrants. I am not sure whether he or his parents were citizens—my memory is murky here—but I do know that they were recent arrivals to the city, perhaps to this country. Yet, here he was, in one of the few schools which had both black and white students, preaching race hate and arguing that black people should not attend Froebel, a school they had attended for generations. This student even led a walkout and demonstrations by white students. Unfortunately, he began to attract media attention and support from some white students in other schools. We were close to having open rioting between black students and white students across the city. What made us really furious was the knowledge that black people were fighting and dying in the segregated units of all the services.

Just before the city exploded, a Gary organization, the Anselm Forum, called a city-wide assembly of high school students and arranged for Frank Sinatra to fly into Gary. Alone, on the stage of Memorial Auditorium, Sinatra told the students in no uncertain terms that this country was not going to tolerate divisiveness and racial hate. He didn't plead with the students, he didn't patronize them: he told them. He wasn't smiling, he didn't try to charm them. He sang "That's America To Me" and "The House I Live In"—at that time, the most popular ballads of brotherhood and racial tolerance. Sinatra told the kids to go back to their schools and to act like Americans while our troops were risking their lives to defend freedom and democracy abroad. He was magnificent. The assembled students responded with a stunned silence and quickly left the auditorium. We, the black student leaders, were surprised by the response to the no-nonsense lecture. Like the police and school officials, we had fully expected to have open warfare between the races break out after the assembly. I will never forget that day and the courage Frank Sinatra showed, putting his popularity on the line for what, at that time, was not exactly a popular position. It worked, however, and things cooled out. The troublemaker was quieted and, as I remember, left the school and the city shortly after.

It should be noted that wartime racial animosities were so serious that they exploded into full-scale riots in several places, most notably in Detroit and Mobile, Alabama, when white workers in defense factories objected to working alongside Negroes. The racism that festered throughout the war years continued unabated during the post-war period—just as it had following the end of World War I. In 1946, a Negro veteran was fatally shot in Georgia because he had dared to vote; a fistfight between two white veterans and a Negro in Alabama escalated into a riot involving a mob estimated at 2,000; Columbia, Tennessee, erupted after a Negro veteran defended his mother, who was protesting unfair treatment in a local store; and there was a brief riot in North Philadelphia involving over 100 Negroes and whites. So widespread were such incidents that President Truman created a presidential committee to study the situation. Its report, *To Secure These Rights*, issued in 1947, became the basis for the civil rights proposal he sent to Congress in 1948. Not only was it defeated, but it split the Democratic party and endangered Truman's election.

Meantime, as I said, I loved going to Roosevelt High School. One reason I liked it was because it was the envy of most people in the city. For Negroes, it was the pinnacle. Even the white schools envied Roosevelt, although they would rarely admit it. Our campus was the prettiest and the cleanest, despite the fact that our buildings were overcrowded. Classes averaged 35 or more, and in high school and junior high, it was not unusual to have classes of over 40, even in academic courses. The thing that made the school unique, however, was its faculty and its administrators. Many of these teachers were truly special—and they were all specialists in their subjects.

For instance, I remember Mrs. Graham, my third-grade social studies teacher who taught me how to write. All of her tests included both short-answer and essay questions, but most of the grade was based on the essays. Ann Rogers Childress recommended me for my first double promotion—and was still teaching and inspiring students when I became a junior high school principal in the same school. They were just two of the many outstanding individuals who were devoted to the school and to each of their students. Particularly memorable was Quentin P. Smith—called Q.P. behind his back—who was a tall, muscular, good-looking dude when he taught me in the eighth grade. He had been a pilot with the legendary Tuskegee Airmen and would probably have become a general, like the late General Chappie James, had he not been so outspoken and uncompromising on racial matters. I'll get back to Q.P. when I describe my own military experiences.

Perhaps the most celebrated members of the faculty were the coaches. Lane, Smith, Douglas, and Mallard were the pioneers who trained, led and inspired the next generation: Dowdell, Campbell, Kimbo, Heflin, Stearnes, and Taliaferro. Bo Mallard was unique, the only coach in Gary who had won state championships in cross-country, basketball, and track. The youngest of the original group of coaches, he represented a new style of coaching, more analysis to supplement outstanding athletic ability. All the coaches stressed academic achievement and used sports as a means of getting college scholarships for those who otherwise could not have afforded to attend. All of them had been outstanding athletes, but they knew the importance of getting a good education: athletic fame was fleeting. They also knew how to compete, because they had earned their degrees from predominantly white colleges and universities—although, despite their abilities, they could participate in only football and track, not basketball.

So many memories of Roosevelt rush back as I recall this period of my life. I remember the first time I went to the school and saw all the students on the grounds and in the main building where I enrolled. I was awed, a little nervous, but glad to finally be a part of Roosevelt. The hallways were crowded but orderly, and there was a relaxed atmosphere as each went his or her way. I was a little guy then, but I knew that as the years passed I would become one of the upper classmen. I remember my first public performance in a play; being admitted to the concert band and the marching band; my first saxophone solo with the jazz band; my first May Dance, my last high school prom; representing Roosevelt at Hoosier Boys State.

One memory is bittersweet. I had won first place in a city-wide essay contest, and the award was to be presented by the superintendent in Roosevelt's auditorium. Many dignitaries were to attend the ceremony, and it was a big deal for the school. The problem arose because I was supposed to wear a dark suit for the presentation, and I didn't have one. One of the teachers, the wife of a prominent dentist, even offered to buy me a suit, but I refused. When I told my parents about this, they were not happy. They made it clear that the clothes I wore to church—nice sport coat, dress pants, white shirt, and tie—were quite appropriate for the ceremony. Anyway, the Watson family did not need charity or assistance from anyone. They were not angry at the teacher, but they resented the emphasis she had placed on the suit. I wasn't angry at her either. She was a nice person and an excellent teacher who, I am sure, was simply trying to do the right thing.

There was never any doubt that I would attend college. The problem was that I didn't have the money. I was lucky in one way, however: we had conscientious men and women on the faculty. In those days there were no counselors—for college admission or anything else—and some students simply didn't have access to information about the application process, scholarships, and other important aspects of getting into college. Not long before graduation, Haron Battle stopped me in the hall between classes and asked if I would be interested in attending DePauw University in Greencastle, Indiana, on scholarship. I was stunned: I knew that DePauw did not enroll Negro students and was in a very prejudiced part of Indiana. After a brief discussion, I declined the offer. I would have been the only Negro student on campus—probably the first Negro, a distinction Vernon Jordan endured some years later.

A short time later, Miss Ida B. King, who had always shown an interest in me, came up to me, asked about my college plans, and said she had secured a scholarship for me to go to Howard University. But I had attended a segregated school all my life, and I wanted to go to a large predominantly white university where I could openly compete with white students who, as I knew from my contacts and competitions, were no brighter or more knowledgeable than their Negro peers. So Howard was out, although I knew it was the premier black university. (Several of my classmates attended and graduated from Howard. One became an air force general; another became a lawyer, senior foreign service officer, and regional director of the Peace Corps.) When I told her how I felt, Miss King arranged for me to take an examination for a scholarship to Indiana University in Bloomington. I scored high enough to win a Special Merit Scholarship which would pay half my tuition. (It turned out to be the only aid I received until I entered my junior year.) I wanted to attend Indiana University because it was cheap, large, and attended by a fair number of black students but—as I will describe in Chapter III—finding the money wasn't easy.

Many times after my graduation from Roosevelt, I would remember how much I had learned there. Perhaps one of the most important ideas was this: that you didn't have to be the best at everything; you were probably not even going to be *good* at everything. There was always somebody who was as competent as you were and, in all likelihood, someone even better. As usual, the students knew who the really smart students were, not only in general but in each specific subject. We had a pretty accurate idea who would go to work in the mills and who would go to college, who would get out of the city as soon as possible and who would get married.

We recognized which students were able to get people to follow them; who could fight; who was the most sophisticated; who had real self-confidence; who had responsibilities at home. We knew lots of stuff that the faculty and administration did not know—like who the best teachers were: those who demanded and received respect; those who got real effort from every student; those who didn't talk much, but who knew each student. Graduation was a turning point for everyone. We would scatter. Some would always be friends.

What were the lessons I learned at Roosevelt? There were so many...

- To accept my strengths with grace and my weaknesses with a sense of proportion, confidence and self-esteem intact;
- To see other people as multidimensional, with both acceptable and unacceptable aspects, and to tailor my relationship with them accordingly;
- To refrain from judging people (including myself) too harshly or on only one dimension;
- To avoid making predictions about people's capabilities; to understand that as important as ability may be, other qualities like focus, hard work, persistence, clarity of purpose, and resilience are even more significant;

- To see that practice, honing skills, and knowing the context always improves the probability of success;
- To recognize the importance of dreams, a vision for the future—and the necessity of backing them up with realistic plans, confidence, and the willingness to work hard.

By far the most profound lesson was the insistence on excellence. I learned that there were standards to be grasped and to be observed, standards of conduct and standards of performance. Roosevelt had little time for or patience with the notion that one person's accomplishment was just as good as another's: we were taught that certain criteria existed and that they—not our own feelings—were the basis for judgment. This was a tough lesson, but one I've never regretted. It bothers me to see today's educators worrying about their students' self-esteem and trying to administer it as though it were a new vaccine. They apparently don't understand that self-esteem is the result of meeting one challenge and gaining the confidence to try the next; the result of knowing that you have intrinsic worth as a human being.

This was Roosevelt's legacy to me and to many others: a credo that would help us to find that most things were possible, even for black people in this country. It was part belief, part hope, and part the naivete of youth. But it was also the willingness to confront and contend without flinching.

For me and others of my generation, attending majority institutions of higher education was our way of looking for dragons to slay, of testing the limits imposed upon us as black Americans. We were sure we were up to the challenge and eagerly sought it—just like those who were the first to join the armed forces, take a corporate position, or seek opportunities hitherto unavailable. We were called "Race Men," people prepared to "meet the man" on his own turf and, despite whatever he threw at us, to prevail—without losing our humanity, without succumbing to hate. We must have truly been out of our minds, but most of us actually did it. I wonder how many face today's renewed racism with this degree of confidence, self-esteem, and realism. I wonder how many have been prepared for the reality of the 1990s: racism, however subtle.

CHAPTER II
ROOSEVELT AND MR. T.

Roosevelt was an extraordinary school—and one which means a great deal to me. I was a student there for eleven years and later returned to serve as teacher, counselor, and administrator. For many years, it was led by H. Theodore Tatum, universally known (although no one ever dared address him so informally) as Mr. T. He was such an outstanding principal that he deserves a chapter of his own. In a time when hope and dignity were difficult to come by, Roosevelt was an oasis of promise and pride, the cornerstone of self-respect for many individuals. This was Mr. T.'s goal when he came to Roosevelt in the early 1930s and one which stayed with him throughout the thirty years he was principal.

To really understand what Roosevelt became and what it took to make it happen, one must know what education was like in the 1930s, 1940s, and 1950s. Many white Americans are familiar with the practices in the states of the old Confederacy, but they are not often aware of similar or identical practices in the north—"up south" as most black Americans called it. Schools throughout the United States were basically segregated, separate and unequal in every way. Until several court cases challenged and eventually overthrew separate salary schedules for whites and blacks, black teachers and administrators at all levels made considerably less than their white counterparts. In fact, a white teacher could earn more than a black principal. In the south, where most black Americans lived until World War II, there was a dual system of public education, with separate schools and central offices. Those for blacks mirrored those for whites, but at lower cost and quality.

Almost all black Americans who attended college in those days went to one of the Historically Black Colleges and Universities (HBCUs). They had little choice. Remember, during this period of our history, none of the colleges and universities in the states of the old Confederacy would admit black students, while few outside the south admitted them with any degree of fairness or without quotas. Then too, the predominantly white institutions were far from hospitable to their few Negro students or were even hostile to them. They had to contend with a double standard of grading: blacks had to earn an "A" to receive a "B." Many professors held the prevailing attitudes about the low capabilities of black Americans and treated them accordingly. It was a major accomplishment for a black person to obtain a degree, especially a graduate degree, from a good white college or university. It wasn't fair, it wasn't just, but it was common. Blacks who chose to attend white schools knew the situation and adjusted their behavior and study habits to deal with that reality. They knew they had to be better than their white counterparts to compete on anything like an equal basis. Only after the end of World War II and the creation of the GI Bill did conditions begin to improve, and slowly at that. Significant change for black Americans did not occur until the late 1960s and afterward.

In the HBCUs, it was a different matter. Because most black Americans were poor, they fared better at the HBCUs which were generally more affordable. But the most important difference between the HBCUs and the majority institutions was the former's nurturing, supportive, yet demanding atmosphere for their students. Not only were students prepared in their subject matter areas, they were prepared to cope with the racially oppressive society they would face upon graduation. They were prepared to challenge and change the conditions under which they labored and achieved. Race, pride, and responsibility were taught along with history, algebra, physics, English, and French.

Black Americans who wanted to teach—at any level—were restricted to black schools and colleges. As a result, institutions like Howard, Fisk, Morehouse, Spelman, Hampton, and Tuskegee, to name a few, could attract and retain the outstanding faculties for which they became noted. In this period of our history, the predominantly white colleges and universities were not interested in hiring Negro professors, whatever their qualifications and experience. Few majority institutions had any minority faculty at all; fewer still had Negro faculty.

Once the positions in the HBCUs were filled, even people with doctorates were happy to get jobs in the public schools. In the 1930s and 1940s, it was not unusual for teachers to have two-year diplomas from teachers' colleges, known as normal schools. Roosevelt, however, had faculty members with baccalaureate and master's degrees from such schools as Columbia, Morehouse, Hunter, University of Michigan, Hampton,

Northwestern, University of Illinois, Tuskegee, Indiana State, Howard, Fisk, and North Carolina A & T.

Although Roosevelt's teachers and administrators were the victims of discrimination and segregation, although their options, opportunities, even their dreams, were diminished at best and destroyed at worst, they passed on many of their ambitions to their students. They encouraged them to imagine and to hope. They taught them to fight, to persevere, to face their adversaries without fear, and to run through, around, or over whatever obstacles were thrown in their path.

It was not a very pleasant time for black people in this country. Lynchings were common. Housing was rigidly segregated by law and practice, as were public accommodations—not only in the south but in most of the rest of the country. Even the armed forces were segregated and continued to be so until 1948 when President Truman issued his executive order mandating integration throughout the military (an order which took several years to be fully implemented). Employment discrimination was so pronounced that the National Urban League and the NAACP were fighting to get black Americans jobs as milkmen, truck drivers delivering bread, bank guards and tellers, clerks in department stores, secretaries, government workers, policemen, and firemen.

In Gary, as I explained earlier, almost all black children attended black schools; almost all white children went to white schools. There were a few exceptions, but even in these schools, the separation of the races was underscored rather than reduced. Although the Frederick Froebel School was integrated—at least for classes and some sports—there were black children who lived within a block of the school or even across the street who were assigned to Roosevelt. Conversely, white children who lived near Roosevelt always attended other (white) schools, usually Froebel. All the teachers, coaches, counselors, secretaries, and administrators at Froebel were, until the 1950s, white.

As I mentioned before, there were two unit schools which occupied the same site: East Pulaski for black students and West Pulaski for white students. This was particularly ironic because the students who attended these schools were from the most multi-racial section of Gary, the east side. It was in this section that Poles, Hungarians, Italians, and black Americans lived rather peacefully together, sometimes in the same buildings, always in the same blocks. Mr. T. had been principal of East Pulaski before his appointment to Roosevelt, and for twenty-five years he was the only black high school principal in the city.

Introducing Mr. T.

He was the boss. Make no mistake about that. Always correct: standard white shirt, starched; two-piece dark business suit; subdued tie. He was usually unsmiling and brisk, but always courteous and not unfriendly. Everybody knew he was the boss: students, teachers, parents, the superintendent, the Board of Education. He never said he was their final authority; you didn't have to be reminded of it. But if you ever forgot that he was in fact the final authority, you would never, ever forget it again. There was a pride and dignity about Mr. Tatum. He understood power and he had the inclination and the will to use it when necessary.

Looking back over the years, one could relive a typical assembly program in the school auditorium. The halls are clean, empty and quiet. Approximately sixty percent of the students are in their classrooms and instruction is proceeding as usual, but in the auditorium, second largest in the city and filled with more than eleven hundred students, teachers and parents, all eyes are riveted on the man at the podium, his right fist raised and clenched, the forefinger extended toward the ceiling. His words flow with an eloquence and spellbinding power in a style reminiscent of black Baptist preachers or stars of the lecture circuit. His speech, inspired by an intense pride in the virtues, potential, and power of black people through the ages, is punctuated with illustrations from his vast knowledge of history and the classics. As he finishes, the audience emerges from its rapt attention and subdued excitement and literally explodes in enthusiastic support of the man and his message. Mr. T. is clearly respected and admired .

These are not the 1960s or the 1970s. We are talking about a time long before the days of Black Power, Black is Beautiful, Martin Luther King, Jr., and Malcolm X. This is Gary, Indiana—Steeltown, USA—in the midst of the Great Depression, and the auditorium is in a school described in the official literature of the district—as late as 1954—as having been built for the "little colored children." The man at the podium who accepts the applause with dignity and poise is the principal of the Roosevelt School. To the audience he is more than just a black man filling an administrative position. He is their man; he is the boss. For thirty years, he demonstrated the power of his beliefs and imbued black students with pride by building his school and the surrounding black community into something very special.

As the auditorium empties, teachers and students return to classes through halls lined with pictures of black men and women of achievement: George Washington Carver, Benjamin Banneker, W.E.B. DuBois, Philippa Duke Schuyler, Toussaint l'Ouverture, Marian Anderson, Frederick Douglass. The air still rings with the echo of Mr. T.'s words and the strains of the Negro National Anthem, "Lift Every Voice and Sing," which opens every Roosevelt assembly and which every student is required to learn. The faces in the corridors, however, tell us something about the times. Students are of all ages, some in elementary school, others in high school; some are older than most seniors and approach the ages of the youngest teachers.

Roosevelt, like many other schools in Gary, Indiana, is a unit school, a part of the famed William Wirt plan which was popular in this country during the 1930s. The times were difficult and many children and youth had to end their formal education before reaching high school. The Wirt K-12 unit school gave every age level an opportunity to use all the facilities (rather than delaying such experiences until high school). The unit school also provided an educational continuum and a chance for younger and older students to cooperate and learn from one another. Speech, drama, physical education, music, art, and shop were required along with the three "Rs." It is the irony of the Depression years that some people were forced out of school too early while others had no place to go and no opportunities except school.

Mr. T. did not come to Roosevelt as an answer to the school's quest for a man who could revolutionize the institution, transform it body and soul—although it was clear that Roosevelt needed such a person. Instead, he was selected by the all-white Gary school board to serve as a buffer between board members and "the coloreds." It was a common practice for teachers in Gary to complain to the superintendent's office when they were unhappy with their principal. Black teachers were no exception. There was one essential difference, however: the superintendent did not want black teachers visiting his office with complaints that should have been handled within the school. The Gary school board and the superintendent wanted a man who could eliminate this problem.

When Roosevelt's first principal departed in the early thirties, the school board found the logical successor in Mr. Tatum. He was, after all, the best educated black man in the Gary public school system. In fact, Mr. Tatum's education and training, like everything else about the man, was rather special for the times. During the Depression, most teachers, both black and white, were graduates of two-year normal schools and most principals, if they had earned degrees at all, had completed only baccalaureate degrees. Mr. T., however, had an impressive and varied background.

It began with graduation from high school in his early teens, followed by a degree (with highest honors in mathematics and science) from Wiley, a small black college in his home state of Texas. After earning another bachelor's degree (in education), he became a teacher and principal in a high school in Louisiana. Following this experience, he earned a master's degree in administration from Teachers College, Columbia University, and pursued additional graduate work leading toward the doctorate. While attending Columbia, Mr. T. supported himself by working at a variety of jobs, including waiting on tables and operating an elevator. In Gary, because of his education, personality, and social contacts, he quickly became the most prominent black man who was not a dentist, physician or lawyer. In every respect, he was a dominant figure in the life of Gary's black community.

And so, Mr. T. was appointed as Roosevelt's principal. He knew when he took the position what the school board and superintendent expected of him. He had been told, subtly but pointedly, that his job was to maintain order among the students and keep the faculty under control. For a man of his convictions, Mr. T.'s acceptance of this role represented a compromise, no question about it. But he understood that by working within the conditions and very real limitations that confronted him, he could reach for his ideal: making Roosevelt the best public school in the country for poor black children.

With the confidence of a strong man and the patience of a long distance runner, Mr. T. turned the school board's racist mandate into the foundation of his power and the beginning of Roosevelt's transformation. He began by insisting that the school board make him principal in fact as well as in name. The school board responded quickly and willingly, for their buffer, to be effective, had to have real power. This gave Mr. T. the opportunity to begin to assemble a faculty on which he could depend to be the backbone of the school's development and the creator of Roosevelt's new spirit.

Mr T.'s Philosophy

Mr. T. believed that pride and discipline were especially important. Teaching was the central, the defining activity, but you couldn't teach unless there was discipline. A teacher, no matter how intelligent and well prepared, could teach little if students were raising hell. A teacher whose class was out of control had to answer personally to Mr. T., who knew (as most competent educators know) that discipline was not so much a question of control as it was a product of respect, cooperation, and a sense of doing something worthwhile. To establish discipline, Roosevelt had to do its job as a school—and that meant striving for excellence in academics and in the arts, as well as providing an aura of school pride, building an esprit de corps to which athletics was obviously the key. Mr. T. wanted academic excellence, excellence in the arts, *and* athletic excellence—a tall order. How do you achieve it? Move forward on all fronts simultaneously.

When a student didn't toe the line, he had the awful experience, the unforgettable experience, of a personal confrontation with Mr. T., who could handle the biggest and toughest of his students. Yet he rarely used corporal punishment. Mr. T.'s very being conveyed authority, and his verbal encounters with a student, faculty member, or parent, were both direct and disarming. His discipline was never capricious, emotional, or irrational. When Mr. T. called you on the carpet, you were told exactly what actions had brought you there, which principles you had violated, and what consequences you would have to face. Many a six-foot-plus, 200-pound young man, tough as nails, would swagger into Mr. T.'s office for one of these sessions— and emerge fifteen or twenty minutes later changed in important ways. Some walked out with the memory of their own tears slowly rolling down their cheeks; most with the realization that they had some shaping up to do and knowing exactly where and why.

Faculty Recruitment

Before Mr. T. became principal of Roosevelt, all faculty assignments in the schools of Gary were made by the central office. After Mr. T., the procedure remained the same in a technical sense, but in fact nobody was arbitrarily assigned to teach at Roosevelt. Mr. T. always had the final word. In all cases, all the time. This power was not his by delegation of the superintendent or central administration. It was a practice acquiesced in by the central office because of Mr. T.'s forceful and persuasive arguments on behalf of quality education for Roosevelt students—and his rigorous, dedicated, and untiring search for faculty members who could provide that quality. Mr. Tatum built and strengthened his control by effectively assuming a responsibility that others in the Gary schools administration were willing to abdicate to him. Mostly, they just wanted peace. It was a propitious beginning for Mr. T.'s administration.

The entire country was Mr. T.'s territory in his search for faculty. Friends, acquaintances, colleagues, and neighbors were contacted for nominations of promising black teachers. The black half of the dual public schools systems in the southern and border states was raided. Mr. T. searched, cajoled, bargained, and persuaded to get the kind of teachers he wanted. Each record, each transcript, each recommendation was checked and double-checked. Hobbies and interests were reviewed, educational beliefs assessed. Mr. T. interviewed every candidate and approved every assignment. Most of those who finally received appointments had been recruited personally by him. The Roosevelt faculty began to grow in breadth, depth, and commitment.

His requirements were simple and straightforward: academic achievement, dedication, and absolute loyalty to the school, the student, and the principal's goals. People on Mr. T.'s staff had, above all, to believe in the potential of the black students who attended Roosevelt. If teachers demonstrated competence in teaching and spent their classroom hours teaching, they had little to fear from the principal. Even if Mr. T. did not personally like an individual teacher, it made little difference; teaching performance was the crucial determinant of the principal-teacher relationship. If children were learning, the teacher could do just about anything within reason: adapt or revise the curriculum, introduce other materials and books, use whatever techniques and methods seemed appropriate.

Having decided that the quality of the faculty was the single most important factor in his educational plans, he was fearless and totally dedicated to attracting the very best. His assistant principal, an English scholar, had a graduate degree from the University of Michigan. His teachers had earned degrees from some of the best colleges and universities in the country. The list included HBCUs, like Howard, Hampton, Lincoln (Missouri), and Fisk; public institutions such as Hunter, Illinois, Indiana, and Indiana State, Michigan, NYU, and Ohio State; and private universities like Chicago, Columbia, Northwestern, and St. Louis.

To assemble such a faculty during this period was infinitely difficult. People were not always willing to move to a blue-collar, industrial town, or they were married and their spouses had jobs which could not be easily duplicated in Gary. Some preferred to work in federal government jobs which offered good benefits, like the post office or bureaus located in Washington, where there were some of the social amenities, even if segregated ones. Perhaps more important, many of the best candidates elected to stay in the segregated schools in the south, because that was where they felt most at home and where there was a well-developed social and cultural life. In any case, the number of college graduates was limited, and there were even fewer of the kind Mr. T. tried to recruit—superb, committed people. Nevertheless, Mr. T. sought and found outstanding teachers.

Mr. T. was not above creating controversy in his recruitment of outstanding faculty. T. Roger Thompson and Ethel Pannel were teachers in the state of Virginia. Thompson taught algebra, geometry, and trigonometry; Pannel taught English. Both epitomized the individualism, professional expertise, and dedication to students that Mr. T. sought in his faculty. Both happened to be available because they had been fired by their school systems—not because they were incompetent, but because they were "troublemakers."

Virginia was like most other southern states. Schools and faculties were rigidly segregated by race—but to add insult to injury, white teachers were paid more than black teachers, regardless of education or experience. Ethel and T. Roger decided there was something fundamentally wrong with this, so they joined their peers and filed suit, demanding equal salaries. They fought the case through the courts and won. Black and white teachers were placed on the same salary schedule. For their efforts, Ethel and T. Roger were fired, despite outstanding records as teachers and as leaders in their profession. Both came to join the faculty at Roosevelt; Mr. T. sent for them.

A short, stocky woman (she stood all of four feet, eleven inches tall), Ethel Pannel was more than a match for the biggest and strongest student, parent, or teacher that Roosevelt—or any other school for that matter—could boast. Business-like, alert, with eyes that filled with fire when she was challenged, she clearly indicated that she was not someone to be trifled with under any circumstances. She had been a Master Sergeant in the WACs in World War II and she knew how to command. Ethel taught English to juniors and seniors and she became their taskmaster, a teacher whose discipline they accepted because it was meted out with fairness and deep concern for the students' welfare. She knew how to make students work without killing their adolescent spirit, and she was rewarded by the pride they showed and the prizes they won in essay and poetry contests or other literary competitions.

It was something to behold, watching this little woman pinning a six-foot, six-inch basketball or football player against the wall. She would tell him he was going to use his mind, write his papers, and behave like a gentleman—or she would personally beat him down to her size or at least break his arm. And then, this kid with a lopsided adolescent grin would say..."Aw, Miss Pannel, you know I'm gonna do it for you." Varsity athlete or star, it didn't matter: her standards had to be met. But she didn't rely on demands alone. She entered into secret agreements and operated in collusion with coaches, counselors, teachers, and parents to enforce her standards. She was usually successful. This was the kind of teacher Mr. T. looked for, fought for, supported, and took pride in: a teacher who knew how to do her job with her heart as well as with her mind and whose first concern was always the lives of her students.

Not surprisingly, Ethel was involved in many activities outside the classroom. Like Mr. T., she knew that it takes more than just disciplined learning to make a school a place where students could find their identity and develop great loyalty. It takes far more. Inspired by her energy and organizational skills, a booster club for athletic teams was organized at Roosevelt. The club became so large that by the late 1950s and early 1960s, it was not unusual to see thirty busloads of students, all dressed alike, going to out-of-town basketball and football games. Their behavior was impeccable—and their numbers intimidating, a fact not lost on competing coaches and teams. They were the talk of the state of Indiana.

The student government also progressed under Ethel's watchful eyes. So did a literary club. Ethel transformed the senior yearbook from a drab document into a first-rate publication which won awards. She was involved in everything but, for all their diversity, in each activity Ethel's one abiding concern was the students. Nobody was neutral about Ethel. They either liked her or disliked her, but all of them followed and worked with her because she produced results.

Mr. T. understood the value of teachers like Ethel and made good his commitment to that quality by getting the wherewithal to hire them and by expending the energy and time to find them, wherever they might be, and bring them to Roosevelt. They came, in the thirties and forties, the fifties and sixties. At first, they had to be sought out and recruited, but soon they came on their own, searching out Roosevelt and asking to become a part of it. Roosevelt had developed a national reputation, a mystique, like Dunbar in Washington, D.C., Booker T. Washington in Memphis, and Sumner in St. Louis.

The Case of Mr. Johnson

But even a visionary and taskmaster like Mr. T. made mistakes and he had to live with them. Not every teacher he selected and hired lived up to his standards and expectations, but when that occurred, Mr. T. took decisive action. A teacher we shall call Mr. Johnson is a case in point. A well-educated teacher of mathematics, Mr. Johnson was initially assigned to teach several classes of college preparatory mathematics to some of the best students in the school. There were honor students with top grades, well-above-average scores on citywide tests, high ambitions, and good motivation. These students were doing well in all of their other classes under demanding, competent, experienced teachers.

In Mr. Johnson's classes, however, they were receiving below average grades. In one class of thirty-three students, twenty-one received failing grades and five received "D"s. In an Algebra II class, the grades were even more disturbing: fifteen of twenty-one students failed and one student received a "D." Yet in all their other classes—physics, chemistry, English—the lowest grade received by any student was a "C." They were scoring in the top twenty percent on nationally normed, centrally administered achievement tests. The seniors had above-average and superior scores on the SAT and the ACT. Several became National Achievement Scholars. In Mr. Johnson's opinion, the fault lay with the students. They were, he said, "stupid," "ill-prepared," and "lazy"; they were below average and not of the calibre of "good white students" in college preparatory classes in other schools. He actually believed black students could not achieve at high levels.

Parents were angry, students were in tears. Other mathematics teachers who had taught and tutored these students were at a loss to account for Mr. Johnson's behavior. Despite repeated attempts, they were unable to persuade him to change his attitude, which at best was unrealistic and at worst, oppressive. At this point, Mr. T. took over. He consulted with Mr. Johnson several times during the course of the semester, but the teacher refused to change, insisting that his Algebra I and Algebra II students would have to perform at a completely unrealistic level to qualify for grades above "C."

As a former—and demanding—mathematics and science teacher himself, Mr. T. realized that he was dealing with something other than an insistence on high standards of student performance. In fact, he was dealing with a combination of things: Mr. Johnson's glorified sense of his own knowledge, his unrealistic impression of how white students perform (he had never taught white students), and a basic contempt for the abilities of poor black students. More important, however, Mr. T. saw what the ultimate effect of such experiences would be on the students: the crushing of their spirit and determination at a crucial and especially vulnerable period in their lives. This, of course, he could not and would not tolerate.

After department chairmen, assistant principals, and Mr. T. himself had made repeated and unsuccessful attempts to persuade Mr. Johnson to alter his approach, a letter was sent informing him that his algebra classes would be transferred to another teacher. It is not an exaggeration to say that, upon receipt of this letter, Mr. Johnson went into a state of shock from which he did not recover for weeks. None of the students or faculty said a word to him about the reassignment. Nobody gloated. But Mr. Johnson had discovered once and for all what it meant to cross Mr. T., when crossing him meant violating the rights and interests of the students at Roosevelt. Mr. Johnson learned something about himself and something about teaching as well. As time passed and the lesson was absorbed, he became a better teacher and a better person.

Administration

Mr. Tatum knew he needed help from his assistant principals. He also knew that opportunities for advancement were limited for black administrators, especially outside of the dual system in the south. In the north, there were few black principals even at the elementary level and almost none at the junior or senior high school level. First, he organized Roosevelt into two schools. Mr. Anderson became principal of the elementary school and assistant principal of the high school. Later, when Mr. T. had several assistants, he assigned one to head to the elementary school and one the junior high school; both were assistant principals of the high school. In effect, Mr. T. was supervising three schools; the total enrollment at one point exceeded 4,000 students. By organizing his operation in this manner, he gave his assistants experience—unattainable elsewhere—in all aspects of administration and supervision, enabling them to learn and grow. Working as an assistant to Mr. T. was a rare opportunity, and most of his assistants went on to become principals and central office administrators in Gary and other cities.

Each of the departments also had a chairperson, providing additional opportunities for growth and development. Chairs of the mathematics, foreign language, physical education, guidance and counseling, industrial arts, music and speech and drama departments all became principals, central office supervisors, or directors. Roosevelt was a magnificent training ground.

The Physical Plant and Equipment

Although Mr. T. spent much of his time recruiting good faculty, other things had to move forward simultaneously. First, there were the physical aspects of the school itself. A school that generated pride had to be a school that looked as if people cared about it. Mr. T. saw to that. Walls needed cleaning; floors had to be sanded, waxed and buffed; sidewalks needed sweeping or clearing of snow; uniforms had to be laundered; books and supplies had to be stamped and delivered to classrooms; dishes had to be washed; tables had to be set and cleared. Students worked in the offices and alongside the full-time custodians. There was work to be done and so Mr. T. put the students to work—in the process providing much-needed extra income for those who would otherwise have lacked the few cents needed to buy milk in the cafeteria or pay for the hot meal provided through the school lunch program. The pay came from the National Youth Administration (NYA), the Public Works Administration (PWA), and the Works Progress Administration (WPA). Whatever alphabet soup was available, students at Roosevelt got their share.

Roosevelt looked like a very small college campus. It had a large, beautiful front lawn with trees and shrubbery which were maintained by the custodial staff as if they were the gardens surrounding a private mansion. Woe be to anyone, adult or student, who dared set foot on that lawn or disturbed the shrubbery. At the rear of the main three-story brick building, there was a playground with a few pieces of equipment—swings, a cinder track donated by the local U.S. Steel plant, and a field covered with a mixture of grass, clay, and straw, which could only charitably be called a football field. There were two tennis courts that, as far as anyone could remember, had never been finished. The concrete was pitted, with weeds growing through the cracks.

Not everything was the way Mr. T. would have liked it to be, but there were no graffiti to be found anywhere, inside or outside: not in classrooms or hallways, not in washrooms and toilets. The buildings were old, but they were spotless, squeaky clean. However, Roosevelt was a black school and, like other black schools, it received much of its furniture and equipment in hand-me-down fashion from white schools which had been given new items. Many of the books, especially those issued to high school students, had already been used for several years by white students elsewhere before they were shipped to Roosevelt. There was no attempt to remove the name of the sending school from the books. Students at Roosevelt were regularly issued books stamped Horace Mann School, Lew Wallace School, or William Wirt—all of them white high schools. Mr. Tatum and the teachers hated having to use second-hand books and equipment, but although they fought against this practice, at first there was only so much they could do about it. It continued throughout the 1940s.

Parent and Community Support

As Roosevelt began to move forward and make progress on his goals, Mr. T. used his community contacts, and the parents' group which he had formed and still led, to get some of the equipment that the school badly needed. With their support behind him, Mr. T. forced the school board to provide Roosevelt with books, equipment, and other items it should have received routinely, but in fact never got without a struggle. The Parent-Teacher Association (PTA) was a venture that was nourished and enriched through the years. When Mr. Tatum retired from Roosevelt, the paid membership was more than 900.

Slowly, the struggles began to pay off. Mr. T. demanded and received new pianos, new band and orchestra instruments. His kitchen equipment was of the highest quality. In Roosevelt's auditorium—the second largest in the city and the largest in the school system, seating almost twelve hundred—everything was first-rate: draperies, seats, stage equipment, and lighting. The auditorium served as a major center for community events. When school district officials balked at certain requests, the black community took over with increasing enthusiasm and support. Fish fries, chicken dinners, other fund-raising projects, and outright donations helped to get the necessary items. Sometimes they were second-hand, even castoffs, but what they lacked in newness was more than offset by pride and excitement.

Within a few years, Roosevelt had earned the reputation as the cleanest and best-maintained school in the entire city. Mr. T. would often chuckle over the fact that visitors, especially white visitors, were always shocked to see that a school for black students looked so good. Roosevelt soon became the showcase for Gary's black community and the center for what was happening for blacks in Gary. There were a few black lawyers, physicians, dentists, social workers, and ministers. There were a few firemen (all assigned to one station), a few mom-and-pop businesses, and the black underworld. Everyone else worked in the industrial plants in and around Gary—except, of course, the teachers, most of whom worked at Roosevelt under Mr. T. and his administration. Because they were a unified group under a strong executive, the school almost inevitably assumed the role of leadership, although there was no indication that either the school district or even the black community expected Roosevelt to take on this responsibility.

However, the community responded with increasing enthusiasm as Roosevelt began to demonstrate a new direction under Mr. T. When he went after cultural and academic innovations at Roosevelt, he was hardly breaking precedent or making outrageous demands. On behalf of his students, he was simply attempting to keep Roosevelt on a level with the two leading white schools in the city: Horace Mann and William Wirt. He was never able to obtain the materials or space or equipment or support that these two schools received, but he did manage to get enough for his students to have confidence and pride in their school's capabilities—and to move on to colleges and universities.

The bare bones college curriculum had offered only two years of mathematics and two years each of French and Spanish; Latin and chemistry were offered every year, but physics only in alternate years. Over the years of his leadership, Mr. T. developed a broader curriculum, including five years of mathematics; four years of two languages and two years of two other languages; chemistry, physics, and advanced science every year. Every student was scheduled for speech and drama at the elementary and secondary levels, and every student was required to learn the rudiments of parliamentary procedure, using Robert's Rules of Order. There were classes in music theory and composition. Classical music was a required study, but so was music by black composers, Negro spirituals, and jazz. Art was also required, and it was taught by specialists with earned degrees.

As the curriculum expanded, so did the number and variety of student activities: marching, concert, dance, and jazz bands; orchestra; chamber music groups; madrigal singers; boys' and girls' glee clubs; mixed chorus; cheerleaders; Hi-Y; student government; honor society; tutoring club; masque and gavel; ROTC. Clubs seemed to keep pace with the curriculum, and by the 1940s there were groups for almost every subject: chemistry, physics, art, math, Latin, French, Spanish, business, social science, and dance. There were nine varsity sports, each with its own group of student and adult boosters.

In every undertaking, high achievement was the goal, and excellence was the standard. The fact that Roosevelt was treated as a second-class school by the superintendent and board of education was no reason for the faculty, administration, or students to believe or to act as if that were true. Thus, Roosevelt students were expected to and did enter all manner of competitions: essays, music, art, oratory, debate, poetry, science, it didn't matter. And as the community watched and provided support, Roosevelt students began to hold their own, pulling in their share of first prizes and superior ratings.

Athletics at Roosevelt

Roosevelt also competed in athletics, although not with the white schools in Gary, because that was forbidden until 1942. Instead, the teams went to other black schools wherever they could be found—in Indiana, Arkansas, Texas, North Carolina, Virginia, and Missouri. While Mr. T. was developing poetry and debating clubs, music and art activities, and college preparatory courses, he was also making sure that Roosevelt had football, track, basketball, and swimming teams. (There was an indoor swimming pool and showers in the main building.)

Athletics was a key to capturing community support. In Pittsburgh, Atlanta, and Memphis, and throughout entire states such as Texas and Ohio, many blue-collar, working-class people loved and closely followed high school athletics because their sons, other relatives, and neighbors participated. Gary was no exception, and Roosevelt athletes, like those elsewhere, enjoyed great popularity. If they developed self-discipline and set high standards for themselves and their teams, they could become a positive influence on the entire student body in all its activities. Athletics were important for another reason: since the teams and their fans could not compete in Gary, they had to travel to other cities and states to meet their opponents, and Roosevelt would be on public display. It was no wonder that Mr. T. was a keen supporter of the athletic program.

In this rough steel town, some students were as old as the teachers and often considerably larger. The members of the male coaching staff were among the relatively few men on the faculty, and it was the coaches, therefore, who assumed the responsibilities as general disciplinarians. In the beginning, the coaches had a difficult time. They were all locals, reared in Gary, graduates of local high schools, and well known. They had all been outstanding high school and college athletes. If racial segregation and discrimination had not been so rigid, several would likely have become professionals.

None of this mattered much to the students who saw them only as disciplinarians, enforcers of strict rules of behavior. Tires on cars were slashed, windows were broken, and threats were made—sometimes in anonymous letters, some in veiled but menacing comments. On more than a few occasions, physical confrontations resulted, but the coaches and physical education teachers stood their ground and backed each other up, knowing full well that as long as they acted in the best interests of the students, they would have the support of the principal. Mr. T. stood shoulder to shoulder with his coaches and his teachers, against angry parents, rowdy students, and central office administrators.

The system paid off. Over the years Roosevelt produced one graduate after another who not only became star athletes but who earned one or more academic degrees. Athletic dynasties were created at Roosevelt. One family dominated the center position on the football team for years, until the last Dowdell graduated. It began with Cleveland Dowdell, and continued through Glen, James, Claude, John, and then Albert. Actually, Claude and John were twins, and only one could start at center! The battle for the position was furious, brutal, and persistent. Claude finally won and John became the starting tackle. Roosevelt was not admitted to the Indiana High School Athletic Association competition until 1942, but by 1980, the school had attained All-American status ten times. By 1990, it had produced eleven state championships in boys' track and field—nine of them in succession.

During the Great Depression, going to college or, for that matter, even finishing high school was out of the ordinary for most young people, especially if they were poor and black. Somehow, Mr. T. and his faculty and coaches made students get down to the business of learning, exploring and believing in their own potential. Disciplined behavior followed, but (as is always the case in good schools) this was the result not of rules and enforcement of the rules but of the enthusiasm and respect students and their parents had developed for the school and its activities. Nowhere was this more apparent than in the support generated by the athletic teams. Over two decades, as its facilities improved, Roosevelt slowly built outstanding teams in football, track, basketball, swimming, wrestling, golf, cross-country, and tennis.

In the beginning, there was little money, but every resource was tapped and everyone was eager to help. The faculty pooled their own meager funds and purchased a bus. It wasn't really a bus; it was a converted Ford, welded together in sections and looking very much like a modern stretch limousine. It was enough to transport the teams to games in small "colored" community centers or wherever they could play their games. Food, gasoline, lodging, uniforms, and other amenities were sometimes paid for from the paltry receipts from the games; more often than not they were provided by interested faculty, parents, or community organizations. The athletes had to depend upon the kindness and hospitality of black citizens in the communities where they played. There were no public accommodation laws in those days, nor any inclination to overturn racial barriers.

In later years, especially after Ethel Pannel and Ida Coleman arrived at Roosevelt, the old Ford was replaced by a legion of buses filled with boosters and supporters. In Indiana and especially in Gary, high school athletics are unlike athletics in any other place in the U.S., particularly when it comes to basketball. Then the unique phenomenon known as "Hoosier Hysteria" takes possession of students and adults alike. By the late 1950s, when Roosevelt teams traveled to distant points inside and outside the state, boosters went with them—not 100 or 200 fans, not 500, but as many as 1000 students, all on school buses, supervised by teachers, all dressed alike in white shirts or sweaters, and all having a good time singing, talking, joking, and jiving. This was Roosevelt on display and, from the very first trip, the deportment of the fans was as much a credit to the school as were the astounding successes of its athletic teams. Not once in the more than ten years that Ethel Pannel was in charge of the boosters did the school receive anything other than the most complimentary telephone calls, letters, and telegrams from mayors, police chiefs, superintendents, coaches, citizens, and parents alike. They simply couldn't believe it. After all, the students were all black, weren't they? Didn't they attend an all-black school? Weren't they poor and from Gary?

These boosters were not specially selected, nor were they all able to afford the trips and the tickets. Ethel and Mr. T. saw to it that every student who wanted to go could go. Bus companies competed for the business from Roosevelt and Ethel drove a hard bargain, keeping the price down so that even the poorest student could attend. For active supporters who could not afford the total price, there was a fund to underwrite the cost. Free tickets were available for indigent students.

At one point, all of this activity got Ethel embroiled in a major battle. The company which obtained the contract for Roosevelt's charter buses was not the local, privately-owned bus company. There was a simple reason. The local company charged too much, and using their buses would have raised the price for students. The local company resorted to political influence, pressure, a whispering campaign, the threat of a legal suit, and ultimately accused the other company of using unsafe equipment and unqualified drivers, a number of whom were women. Ethel stood her ground and Mr. T. backed her. The local bus company finally lowered its prices and became competitive, so Roosevelt began to use its buses as well.

Roosevelt's Achievements

Through it all—the tough times and the good times—coaches, teachers, assistant principals, and the principal counseled their charges, listened to them, argued with them, soothed their damaged egos and wounded pride, applauded their triumphs, and spurred them on to the next hurdle. Tough stuff to pull off, but it worked. Being at Roosevelt began to mean something; the "Velt" was special. Beginning in 1962, when all the city recreational facilities closed by 9:00 p.m. because of a lack of supervisors, the lights were left on until midnight at the Roosevelt basketball courts and the playground. Such was the respect for the school that there were no break-ins, no vandalism, no graffiti. Nobody walked on or abused the front lawn or foliage either.

Over the years, the dropout rate was gradually reduced, and one by one, Roosevelt graduates began to take their places on college campuses. In 1933, when the first group of thirty seniors graduated, only six went on to college, but throughout the thirties, Roosevelt sent students to the University of Chicago and Big Ten universities, as well as to Hampton, Fisk, North Carolina A. & T., and Howard. As the years passed, Roosevelt graduates found their way to more than 100 colleges and universities across the country.

Roosevelt didn't just send its graduates to college; it kept in close contact with them and tried to help them succeed. Students were carefully placed on some campuses; success was important so that additional students could be sent year after year, especially if scholarship assistance was available. Revenues from school shows and athletics were used to help defray the cost of transportation to and from college interviews. It became the general rule and practice to prepare all varsity athletes for college entrance whether they had this in mind or not. Because Roosevelt athletes were so outstanding, college scholarships were almost always available to some institution. Mr. T. believed that as many as possible should get enrolled, because even if they stayed only one year the experience would enrich their lives. In many instances, all that was needed was an opportunity to go to college.

Mr. T.'s dream for Roosevelt was becoming a reality, but like all such endeavors, there were failures as well. The education wasn't always as good as it should have been. Many students couldn't read at "grade level." Not everybody graduated, and not all who had the ability to go to college decided to or were able to do so. Sometimes, the shrinking violet or the slow starter or the different learner wasted a few years or got lost in the shuffle. Roosevelt had its shortcomings, but it was also a symbol of achievement and a source of pride to the students, to the faculty, and to the black citizens of Gary. Mr. T. had made certain of that. The things he did for Roosevelt were important in and of themselves, but they were also gestures, examples of power with which an oppressed and poor black community could identify and in which they could participate, however vicariously.

In the days before Black Power, Mr. T. was its apostle and Roosevelt was its temple in Gary, Indiana. The walls of the principal's office and the walls in the corridors were lined with photographs and paintings of black men and women of achievement. Mr. T. used them to help his students develop a clear awareness of their black identity, long before anyone had heard the slogan "black is beautiful." In the early 1960s, students, faculty, and alumni paid for a life membership in the NAACP for Roosevelt, one of several purchased for the school. Student leaders in the civil rights movement at Indiana University, Southern University, and Harvard, to name a few, were graduates of Roosevelt.

Roosevelt was unique, because it represented the entire black community of Gary. Most blacks sent their children there, and in fact most of them were alumni themselves (if they had lasted through high school). It had more college-educated Negroes on its staff than any other local institution, and its teams, its band and orchestra, its musical and drama groups, were sources of pride to all black Garyites. There were few opportunities elsewhere, so the championships, the awards, the degrees, were important to everyone.

In the early years (the 1930s and 1940s), graduation from high school was a special event, and usually the conclusion of formal education for most Americans, white or black. Roosevelt graduates were intensely loyal, returning to the school for their fifth reunion and every one thereafter. This tradition continues today, and it is not unusual for 90 percent of a class to attend reunions for the first ten or fifteen years. As the number of alumni increased, the program changed from a dinner to a full day of activities, then to several days at different sites, including the Playboy Clubs and McCormick Place Convention Center in Chicago.

I look forward to attending my 50th reunion in 1997.

CHAPTER III
LIFE ON CAMPUS AND IN THE MILITARY

Higher Education for Minorities Before 1965

African Americans have always encountered obstacles in their quest to obtain an education. From the time of the arrival of the first slaves in Jamestown in 1619 to the publication of The Bell Curve *in 1994, arguments have raged about our intelligence and indeed our status as human beings. The story has many chapters: enforced illiteracy to make sure that plantation workers did not rebel against their masters; segregated and unequal schools to keep free Negroes in the lowly places assigned to them by white society; exclusion from colleges, universities, and professional schools through outright proscription, quotas, or lack of financial aid.*

Despite the barriers—which sometimes included harsh penalties for those who chose to ignore them—many blacks succeeded in acquiring an education. Those who did not served as convenient proof that the entire race was intellectually inferior, lazy, and gifted only with a talent for rhythm and dancing. In fact, the idea of black inferiority was so deeply entrenched that relatively few whites could see the absurdly circular nature of their argument: prevent minorities from getting an education, then blame them for being stupid (or later, in the early days of the civil rights movement, announce that no qualified blacks could be found).

Fortunately, not everyone subscribed to this kind of racist outlook, and in the period following the Civil War progress was made by and on behalf of the newly freed slaves. Both government and private sources contributed to the establishment of Negro schools in the south, and the first of the "historically black colleges and universities" (HBCUs) were founded: Howard, Hampton, Atlanta, and Fisk. As I noted in the chapter on Mr. T. and the Roosevelt School, the importance of the role played by the HBCUs in African American life can hardly be overestimated.

Although many began as agricultural or industrial training schools, by the end of the 19th century they were providing the vast majority of professional training available to blacks—and continued to do so until well into the latter half of the 20th century.

Notwithstanding the passage of the 13th, 14th, and 15th amendments to the Constitution, the federal government did little to forward the cause of black higher education. When federal land was granted for public colleges (under the Morrill Act of 1890), those established in southern and border states were designated for blacks only to prevent them from attempting admission to white institutions. Separate facilities were given the blessing of the Supreme Court in the Plessy v. Ferguson decision of 1896, and educational segregation at every level was practiced throughout the country until the Brown decision of 1954.

Nevertheless, African Americans continued to pursue education for themselves and their children, recognizing that it was our only ticket to security and status. My family may have been unusual in that one parent was a college graduate, but it was like countless others in its insistence that we all go as far as we could and in its willingness to make any sacrifice toward that goal.

My years at Roosevelt gave me tremendous advantages. By the time I graduated in 1946, I was ready and eager to move on, begin college work, prepare for my future career. Good grades, participation in a variety of extracurricular activities, and friendship with many remarkable teachers had equipped me with self-confidence, a wide range of interests, and the determination to succeed. I had decided that I wanted to attend a predominantly white institution—Indiana University—rather than a black college or university, and I was looking forward to new academic and social challenges.

Unfortunately, my academic record and enthusiasm were not enough. I simply did not have the resources to pay for college, even the comparatively inexpensive fees charged by Indiana. My scholarship would pay about half the tuition, nothing else. My savings would cover room and board for one semester. My parents could provide no financial assistance. Instead of enrolling in classes at Bloomington, I went to work full-time in the Gary steel mills.

From June through most of January of the following year, I worked in the open hearths and in the blast furnaces. "Full-time" meant six or seven days a week, ten or twelve hours a day. In February 1947, I entered Indiana University for the second semester. Until then, Negroes had lived off campus in boarding houses, apartments, or fraternity houses, but I was one of the first eight men to be admitted to Rogers Halls, a new dormitory complex.

It soon became clear, however, that I needed to earn some real money in order to remain at the university. So at the end of the semester, it was back to the mills. From June 1947 until September 1948, I worked at U. S. Steel—again full-time— and occasionally gigged on the weekends, saving every cent I could. I also attended classes at Indiana's local extension, then known as Gary College.

Finally, I was ready to go back to Bloomington and stay there. At that time, there were two Negro fraternities on campus, but I chose not to join either one. With a group of friends, I joined the Indianapolis graduate chapter of Omega Psi Phi and—without the approval of Indiana University—we established a new chapter, Zeta Epsilon. We pulled a fast one with the house. We found one for sale in an all-white residential area. It was perfect: close to campus, not far from downtown, and beautifully maintained. We talked to the owner, made a down payment, and told him that the national office would purchase it for us.

My friend and mentor, Milo Murray, a graduate of Bowdoin College and Harvard Law School, arranged for us to attend the fraternity's national convention in Chicago and for me to give a speech on the floor of the main assembly. We all worked on that speech, but I was chosen to deliver it because I was our chapter president. After the convention delegates heard me describe the history of racism on campus and the restriction on the number of minority fraternities and sororities, they exploded in applause. They voted, without dissent, to purchase the house for us. I still have the photograph of that conference: it is remarkable because the members were like a "Who's Who" of Negro America, and because it shows how completely segregated things were at that time. There is not a single white face to be seen in that hotel dining room.

Within three weeks, the house had been purchased, and we moved in time for the second semester. With a national charter, a fraternity house in a good residential neighborhood already paid for, and a chapter whose members all had good grades, the University finally had to recognize our existence. We joined the inter-fraternity council and proceeded to hold our own academically with all the other organizations.

I still had to earn money, so I ran the laundry and dry cleaning concession for my fraternity house, earning a 10 percent commission on the dry cleaning and 15 percent on the laundry. My own clothes were free. During Christmas vacations, I worked in the U.S. Post Office in Gary and made good money. In the summers, I worked in the steel mills and made better money. Things got easier each year.

I was a pretty good vocalist, and I sang with one of "Lish" Henderson's bands and—when no one else was available—filled in as a saxophone player. Indiana has a world-class music school, and people who had entered college with me to major in music were so far ahead in their knowledge and technique that it was embarrassing to try to play with them. Med Flory of Super Sax was one of my classmates.

The Special Merit Scholarship which I had earned was good for only one year, so I began to look for other sources of student aid. When I found a listing of the LaVerne Noyes scholarships for the children of World War I overseas and combat veterans, I took my father's discharge papers and went to the student aid office to apply.

The clerks acted as if I were out of my mind. "These are for children of World War I veterans," one said. Another asked if my father had been white. It was inconceivable to them that a Negro could have fought in World War I. I had to prove that my father had fought in France, had been honorably discharged with an excellent character rating—and was, in fact, black. Finally a supervisor came over and signed the papers and I was awarded the scholarship. It was worth $70.00 a year—not much, but almost enough to pay a full year's tuition in the 1940s. I took between eighteen and twenty-five hours a semester so that I could finish as soon as possible. (The more hours you took, the fewer semesters of room and board you had to pay.) It wasn't that hard, because I loved the work and, after getting around the rigid rules, took more than half of graduation requirements in history, political science, and sociology. I was on the dean's list every semester and graduated with a better than "B" average.

It was no great secret that you had to be better than your white counterparts to earn the grades they received, or you had to be so superior that there was no question in the mind of the professor or other students that you were superior. For students like Andrew Spencer, Mary Ethel Lane, and John Ward, this was not a problem. Andy, an all-state high school basketball player, was awarded a Phi Beta Kappa key in his junior year. He received only one grade of "B+"—because the professor told him he needed the experience of receiving something lower than an "A." Andy went on to become an outstanding surgeon, one of those who managed to overcome the quota system for Negroes and Jews at Indiana University's medical, dental, and law schools. Mary Ethel made Mortar Board and graduated with honors at age twenty—but couldn't get into any medical school, white or black. She had three strikes against her: she was young, female, and black. Women's Medical College in Philadelphia finally admitted her, and she is now a distinguished physician in New York. John, who was also Phi Beta Kappa, earned a law degree and completed all the requirements except a dissertation for a Ph.D. in political science. Incidentally, he was and is totally blind.

The rest of us knew that you usually had to earn an "A" in order to get a "B," or earn a "B" to get a grade of "C." There were exceptions, but most students of my era will tell you there weren't many. It wasn't until after World War II that Negroes were first admitted to many honor societies at Indiana University. One of my favorite professors, a sociologist, pulled me aside after class and told me that I was his best student and he was going to give me a "B." I knew exactly what he meant and was glad to receive the grade. I knew I had earned an "A."

The grading disparities were not always obvious. It was easier for an instructor to shade grades in essay examinations than in those which called for a single right-or-wrong answer. Some professors were known for their standards, standards all students were held to equally. There was Kistler in history, Byrum Carter in political theory and political thought, Hire in physics—names I remember to this day. About some other professors, however, there was a message which was passed on to each generation of students: avoid them if you can; if you can't, then do the work, keep your mouth shut, and try to remain invisible. Despite all this, many of us managed to graduate with respectable averages, averages good enough to get us admitted to schools like Berkeley, the University of Illinois, and the University of Chicago. A fair number of my classmates became distinguished contributors to their fields.

Campus Activism

World War II ended in 1945, but the racial wars in the U.S. did not. Many of my classmates were veterans—non-commissioned officers, pilots, combat officers—and they had become men before their time. Those who were married came to campus with their wives and families and lived in trailers set up by the university. Many attended college only because of the GI Bill benefits; otherwise, they could not have afforded it.

If they were Negroes, however, veterans who had fought for their country could not live in the dorms, had to sit in the balcony of the local theater, could not arrange for visiting parents or families to stay in the local hotel, could not get their hair cut in downtown barber shops, and could not eat in downtown restaurants. These restrictions did not begin to ease until 1949 or 1950, and then only after persistent protest and demonstrations.

The Gables, which was immediately off campus and fabled as the location where Hoagy Carmichael wrote "Stardust" during his student days at Indiana University, had a life-size photograph of George Taliaferro, the black athlete who led IU to its first Big Ten football championship. But George could not eat a hamburger there because he was Negro. Neither could he live on campus when he enrolled in 1945; he rented an apartment over a garage belonging to a physician in town. In 1947, there were 14,700 students at Indiana; the Negro enrollment was approximately 250-300.

Bloomington is in the southern part of a very conservative state. Its attitudes were more like those of Kentucky, more southern than northern. At one time, it was almost impossible to be elected to statewide office without Ku Klux Klan support or at least its tacit approval. Negroes had been lynched in Indiana as recently as 1931, and there were small towns where your life was in danger if you were still there when the sun set. In earlier years, legend had it, signs to this effect were actually posted at the city limits. I never saw such signs, but we knew which towns to avoid, even in daylight.

I did see handwritten signs on campus announcing KKK meetings. They were regularly taken down by Negro students, who were not intimidated. Fraternities and sororities were segregated by race and religion. There were no Negro teachers or professors. Whatever progress had been made could be traced directly to Herman B. Wells, president of the university, holder of two degrees including one in law from Indiana. The scion of a very wealthy family, he lived with his mother, never married, and was thus free to devote all his time and energy to the university. He also served for many years on the board of trustees of Howard University.

President Wells had ended segregation in the cafeteria in the Union Building in 1945. From that time on, agitation began for eliminating some of the most humiliating vestiges of racial discrimination. That agitation, along with quiet diplomacy, resulted in an agreement to permit Negro women to live in dormitories on campus. Opening Lincoln House as a separate facility for Negro females was a first step: the dorm was segregated, but it *was* on campus. Until this agreement, Negro women lived off campus in Darden House and other locations. Campus housing for Negro men had been made available in 1946, and I was among the first to move in, along with two other students from Gary. Over the next two years, we concentrated on getting the movie theaters to permit Negroes to sit anywhere they wanted, to get restaurants to serve Negroes, and to get the local hotel to admit Negroes who were visiting. I was very active in this movement to change the campus and the town.

There was a chapter of the NAACP on campus and most of the members were white. In fact, during one period, even the president was white. A World War II veteran, he had come from a small town and had never seen a real live Negro until he entered the armed forces (at least that is the story we all believed). Hansel Crimiel Hall was another veteran, a U.S. Air Force officer, a lifelong member of the Republican Party—and a Negro. He actually ran as a Republican for a seat on the Gary city council. He didn't win, but he made a respectable showing.

Hansel was very vocal on racial issues, active and unafraid, and a strong ally in our struggle for equality and racial justice. He and Clarence Currie, another Roosevelt alumnus and my best friend, participated in our sit-ins, public protests, and organizing activities. Our strategy was simple. Since the state of Indiana prohibited segregation in certain public facilities, we would go to restaurants or movies in groups of three—two whites and one Negro, or two Negroes and one white. We would tell them it was the law to serve us, and if they refused they had to close the establishment.

It wasn't just the city of Bloomington, however; in many ways, the campus was not much better. Although there were Negro fraternities and sororities, they did not have houses on the frat "row" on campus. There was literally no minority representation on any of the student organizations, although University-sponsored social activities on the main campus were open to all students. Some of us made a special effort to have Negroes attend all of these social activities so people would become accustomed to our presence. I occasionally played or sang with Ulysses Henderson's jazz groups, and it was always good to see black faces in the audience or on the dance floor.

One of the most offensive activities on campus was the spring festival, when white members of sororities and fraternities dressed up in costumes, put on skits, and generally acted like adolescents for about a week. Each year, at least one fraternity would have members dressed as "Hottentots," with big red lips, blackface, bones through their noses, a southern dialect, and rolling white eyes. Some white women put on bandannas, speaking and acting like "Aunt Jemima." Racial slurs were shouted, and obscene remarks were directed at black women when they walked across campus. Attempts to convince the fraternities and sororities to cease and desist were futile, and there were several incidents which could have escalated into racial confrontations and fistfights. Although there was no evidence that the university condoned these insulting and provocative activities, the dean of students was unable or unwilling to stop them.

There was a strong feeling among minority students that we needed a voice. Repeated efforts to forge agreements with white organizations to support Negro candidates had been unsuccessful, despite the fact that these organizations sought our backing in closely contested elections. We resolved to find some way to get our views heard, particularly on issues of fairness and justice. One day, looking through an old copy of the regulations governing elections for student government, I found an obscure rule which provided for a "minority representative" in the Indiana University student senate. Earlier versions of the regulations contained this stipulation; the current edition did not. When I shared it with Clarence Currie, Hansel Hall, Jim Dowdell, and a few other activists, we agreed that the provision was out-of-date and probably not meant to apply to Negro students: there had been precious few attending the university prior to World War II. It was there, however, and I decided to take advantage of the earlier version.

I filed a letter with the dean of students, declaring my intention to seek the position in the upcoming election. The dean was a retired Marine Corps colonel—tall, handsome, erect, tough as nails, and admired and loved by almost every female on campus. He didn't like my running under this banner, and he refused to let me run unopposed. He insisted on placing announcements in the student paper, and three other candidates— none of whom had been active or outspoken on the issues—entered the race. To this day, I believe at least one was personally solicited and encouraged by someone in the dean's office. I appointed Hansel Hall and Clarence Currie as my campaign managers. I won the four-way election, trounced my opponent in the runoff, and became the only minority member of the Indiana University student senate. The senate floor became my platform for attacking the issues of racism on campus.

It should be noted that others were involved in this fight in their own way. George Taliaferro, star halfback on the football team, and Bill Garrett, first Negro to play on the basketball team (and, I believe, the first Negro to play Big Ten basketball), also spoke out about campus discrimination. Taliaferro told the owners of the Gables that he would be back again and again until they served him.

We decided to put the issue of African burlesques and other demeaning behavior on the front burner; no more quiet negotiation. I would introduce a resolution condemning the practices on the floor of the student senate. Resolutions had to be submitted by five o'clock on the day of the meeting, which was held later in the evening. I worked with Clarence, Hansel, and others to craft the statement, but we waited until the last moment—five minutes to five—to present a copy to the student government office. There was little time for the opponents to get together and plan a strategy to oppose it.

When the senate was convened that evening, everybody was there, no absentees. After routine business, resolutions were introduced. As I read ours, the air was tense and the silence overwhelming. When I finished, there was no discussion. Not one senator spoke against it or for it. It was passed unanimously. I didn't know at the time that the local and regional press had been notified to come to the meeting because there might be fireworks. They were all there. They were not disappointed.

Colonel Shoemaker, the dean of students, rose to his feet, glared at me and then at the rest of the senate, and proceeded to castigate me for introducing the resolution. He said that this was one of the darkest days on campus, that I was jeopardizing all the gains that had been made by "my people" over the past few years, that this was not the way to remove prejudice or stop discrimination. Through this resolution, he said, I had set race relations back in important ways, and I was performing a disservice not only to Negroes but to decent people everywhere on campus. He then scolded the student senators for passing the resolution unanimously. It was a sad day, he said. Then he sat down with great dignity. Nobody in the room moved, but they all looked at me, some of them apprehensive and perspiring.

I had been prepared for this argument from other students, but not from the dean. I began my response by expressing my respect for Colonel Shoemaker as a dean and as an experienced leader and serviceman. I then proceeded to tell him what it was like from the black students' perspective. I pointed out that we had made complaints over the years and that quiet attempts to reach a reasonable compromise had failed, making this public action necessary. I reminded him that among the people offended by the behavior we condemned were men who had recently been fighting a war for democracy, risking their lives—only to return home to this kind of insensitivity and racism. I said that the progress about which he had spoken in such glowing terms was long overdue. In a state university supported by taxes from all of the citizens, no distinction should ever have been made between blacks and whites in dormitories, in eating facilities, in anything.

In closing, I respectfully disagreed with his statement that the student senate should be ashamed. In fact, I said, he and the members should be proud that this body had passed, without a dissenting vote, a resolution that reaffirmed the dignity of all students and recognized that harmonious relationships on campus could not develop until practices which were offensive and demeaning to some students ceased.

I left the meeting and was headed across campus to my fraternity. I heard footsteps and then Dean Shoemaker's voice calling my name. He asked whether I would agree to have my remarks deleted from the official records and would refrain from talking to the press who "had come to the meeting to record controversy." Shoemaker said that if I agreed, he would do the same and would say nothing else about the issue. This would be for the good of the university, he added. I acquiesced, and walked off into the evening.

Although the press had been there, and the event was reported in the paper the following day, there was no follow-up, no interviews with either of us. The other student senators were happy to put the incident behind them. You need to understand that this was 1949, not the 1960s. Nobody gave much of a damn about Negro complaints, especially on this southern campus in a conservative state. I still have the original of the resolution which was introduced on that date.

Each year, President Herman Wells invited the officers and members of the student senate to his home for dinner and a social. Naturally, I went and was the only Negro in attendance. The president's mother was a lovely person, gracious, witty, and very sensitive. She made a special effort to make me feel welcome and comfortable. So did the president, but his mother spent a fair amount of time talking to me and encouraging me to keep up the good academic work. I heard her message loud and clear. It was the same message given to me and others who were active in civil rights: keep your grades up; don't give anyone an excuse to throw you out of school.

We knew what we had to do to make it in this environment. One could easily ask why, if there was this much discrimination and prejudice, did I or others like me choose to attend Indiana University rather than one of the HBCUs, where most of our peers went during the 1940s and 1950s. The answer is not simple, but it is not all that complicated either. During my youth and early adulthood, most of us perceived our responsibility as twofold: to ourselves and our families, and to the Race. We were Race Men. That meant, in its simplest terms, that we had to do well, to succeed, so that there would be opportunities for the Negroes who would come after us. We had an obligation to be above reproach, not to "mess up," so that other—no, all—Negroes would not be blamed for our shortcomings and failures.

Rarely did people say this to us directly, but we all knew what was expected from us by our parents and peers, and by those who had gone before us and paved the way. It may not have been fair to place that burden upon our generation, but that was the way it was—and most of us did not view it as an unreasonable demand. We looked at it more as a challenge. Perhaps by our success, we could open up opportunities for others. And to be honest, there was also an element of competitiveness in each of us. Many of us chose this predominantly white environment precisely in order to compete. We never accepted the assertion that Negroes were intellectually inferior and unable to excel. We had had experiences which gave the lie to those myths of superiority. We knew better. Being at Indiana gave us a chance to slay those dragons of prejudice and discrimination, to demonstrate our excellence, even our superiority.

Our activism did not go unnoticed, either on campus or in the city of Bloomington. Those of us who were most visible were advised by our friends that we were jeopardizing our own futures, that we were being placed on un-American activity lists and labeled as subversives. There were threats from fraternity bullies and anonymous warnings from members of the KKK and other yahoos. We usually didn't pay much attention to them, but at one point we notified the national office of the NAACP through Milo Murray, the attorney who had earlier helped our fraternity chapter. Thurgood Marshall came to Indianapolis on a bus and met with the campus activists in the local Negro YMCA. (Although the capital was fifty miles from Bloomington, it was safer to hold our discussion in private, far away from our opponents and critics.) Marshall assured us that the university had been put on notice that the NAACP was monitoring our activities. We were not alone.

One night as I walked home, I noticed a car slowly moving up the street behind me. In Bloomington in the 1940s, if you were black and by yourself, you always watched your back. About a block from the fraternity house, the car pulled over and a man on the passenger side got out. I could see he was a policemen, even though he didn't have on his hat, just the rest of his uniform. He was smiling and friendly as he asked me if I lived nearby. I said yes, and pointed to the house on the next corner with the neon fraternity sign outside. "Oh, you're one of the new ones," he said. By this time the car had pulled around the corner, blocking the view of the intersection. Very quietly and with smooth unhurried motions, the cop had his gun out of his holster and in my face, right under my nose. He kept smiling and said evenly, "See how easy it is? I could blow your head off and leave your stinking black ass out here on the street and nobody would ever know who did it. Watch your ass! I'll be keeping my eyes on you, and I'd better not see you around here making trouble."

I had never been that frightened before; I have never been that frightened since. But I didn't panic; I didn't cry or shake. I didn't lose control of my bodily functions. I don't know how I did it, but I looked him in the eye and didn't say a word. He put his gun away, got in the car, and drove off with his partner. The car was unmarked. I didn't get a license number, but I remembered the face. I looked for it at every demonstration or rally. I searched my mind for where I had seen that smiling son of a bitch before. I never saw him again. I didn't tell anybody about that incident for more than a year. My mother didn't hear about it until I went into the service, where far worse things happened, and I never told my father.

I was never afraid of dying again. I knew from that day forward how quickly, how quietly, how easily and unexpectedly death could come to anyone, but especially to those who rocked the boat. It was then that I began to form my own philosophy about standing up for things you believe in. Be sure you feel strongly about them personally. Be prepared to stand alone; don't expect support or assistance. Be prepared to accept the consequences alone. The support may indeed be there, but don't count on it. An experience like that helps you choose the things you are willing to die for.

But I also enjoyed my undergraduate years: I was not in a blue funk and seething rage all the time. Our fraternity-house neighbors were no trouble, even though we were the first and only black people to live in that area. We made special efforts to keep the lawn mowed, the walks clean, and the house in excellent condition. We were not loud or profane. We didn't act like typical college students, especially on weekends. Still, people knew we were there.

I attended all the football and home basketball games, where I cheered the teams. We were quite proud of Bill Garrett on the basketball team, and of George Taliaferro and the many other Negroes who made the football and track teams. Even the gymnastics team had a "brother" from Cardozo High School in Washington, D.C. He was the only one and, I believe, the first. We had our fraternity and sorority parties and dances; we went on picnics, and we held intramural competitions in many sports. I dated some good-looking, smart, and interesting co-eds from Indianapolis and South Bend. When my mother sent me magnificent boxes filled with goodies—salami, cheese, cookies, crackers, or candy—we all shared with one another. In the middle of the night after a long evening of studying, these "care packages" were especially appreciated. It wasn't all tension and struggle: we had fun as well.

I actually enjoyed many of my classes, whether the professors were fair or not. Most of my work was in history, political science, and sociology, subjects I truly loved. Amazingly, my teachers at Roosevelt kept up with my progress and my activities. When I made the dean's list or was elected to office or won a scholarship or prize, I would get little notes not only from my parents but from teachers like Mrs. Duncan or Mrs. Beckman. When I returned home during vacations, I might see a teacher or neighbor who would say they had read about me in the paper and tell me to keep up the good work. My brother's friends would occasionally warn me to watch my back and be careful with my activism.

Until I was a senior at Indiana, I had not given much thought to what I would do after graduation. Everybody seemed to assume that I would become a lawyer (although it was never really discussed with me), so I vaguely planned on attending law school in spite of the fact that I had no money and had developed some doubts about a career in law. Then, as I was looking for a course which would give me a couple of credits, I saw one listed as "Education as a Field of Study," taught by a doctoral candidate named Jack Elzay. Jack's course emphasized the power of education in enabling people to exercise control over their lives, especially important in a democracy—and I was hooked. I gave up the idea of being a lawyer, dealing with injustice on a case by case basis, and took some extra hours in education, including student teaching. When I left the university, I was a duly certified teacher.

Later, when I returned to Gary and Roosevelt, some people expressed disappointment with my decision. They had hoped I'd be not only a lawyer, but maybe a judge. There were so few opportunities for blacks in those days that young people with intelligence and determination were expected to undertake careers which would advance the race. Juanita Kidd Stout (who later became the first black woman to sit on the Supreme Court of the Commonwealth of Pennsylvania) attended Indiana University law school while I was an undergraduate. She was there to earn a master's degree in law and, as far as I can remember, she was the only Negro doing so at that time. I met her and her husband, who was also at Indiana University pursuing a doctorate in chemistry. What I didn't know at the time was that A. Leon Higginbotham, Jr., now chief judge emeritus of the U.S. Court of Appeals in Philadelphia, had experienced racism worse than ours at Purdue, another state school which trained architects and engineers. It was the technical and agricultural part of the Indiana state system. Leon changed his major from engineering and left Purdue to attend Antioch University and, later, Yale Law School.

As it happened, there were no jobs available in education in 1951 when I graduated from college. Moreover, the graduate fellowships and internships which became common in the 1960s and 1970s were scarce then, and almost non-existent for black Americans. I returned to the steel mills and was told—by people with only high school diplomas or even less education—that I could have my old job back. I actually had as much or more working experience than some of the straw bosses or assistant foremen. My college degree made no difference. Blacks qualified only as laborers.

When I raised the question of fairness and a good record with the personnel supervisor, he told me that he was just following orders. Maybe some day, things would be different. I asked him about the men who had fought in the war, only to come back to the same dead-end jobs. He just looked at me. He wasn't hostile or defensive; he just kept telling me what a fine record I had (and my father as well), implying I would always have a job if I didn't mess up. I decided it was time for me to do something else.

My experience was not unique. Rosewell Bibb had attended Indiana after the war, earning a degree in business and then an MBA. But while his white classmates became bankers, financiers, or managers in industry, Rosewell was a social worker and a business entrepreneur on the side. Others with similar qualifications settled for jobs in the post office, which offered a decent salary, benefits, decent working conditions, and security. The post office was a veritable intellectual hot house in those days, staffed by black lawyers, chemists, engineers, biologists, and teachers. Most spent their entire lives in the post office. It was the same all over the country. Even jobs as clerks, lab technicians, tellers, and teamsters who drove bread and bakery trucks were reserved for white people and denied to black Americans. In my home town, it would be years before Doc James, and the Oldtimers' Club that he founded and led, would begin to organize against these practices and change them through the political process and the threat of mass action.

·

*M*ilitary Service

Segregation in the armed forces had continued during and after World War II. Prejudice and discrimination were rampant, despite the heroic feats of many black fighting men, particularly the special group of pilots, the 99th Pursuit Squadron, who became known as the Tuskegee Airmen. Nowadays, when an African American, Colin Powell, has already served with distinction as chairman of the joint chiefs of staff, it may be difficult to imagine how rough things used to be, even for the heroes.

President Truman ordered the military to desegregate in 1948, and his action was a direct result of an incident involving someone I knew—my former Roosevelt teacher, Q. P. Smith. Smith and another black, Chappie James, were among the first to be admitted to the segregated training program for black pilots, established (reluctantly) by the air force at Tuskegee Air Base in 1941. They were both six feet, two inches tall (the maximum height for pilots) and weighed 198 pounds (two short of the limit of 200). Both were pilots in the European conflict. James went on to become the first black four-star general, in charge of the North American Air Defense Command. Smith was booted out of the military.

In April 1945, the two men and a large group of other pilots flew from Fort Knox, Kentucky, to Seymour, Indiana. When they landed at the local air base, they went to the officers' club for drinks and dinner—only to be ordered out by the base commander, Colonel Robert Selway. When they protested, he informed them that "trainees" (defined as officers with no overseas experience) were not permitted in the club. Smith bitterly reported later: "Here I was, sitting next to a man who'd had half his face blown off in combat in Italy, and they were calling us trainees?!"

Selway persisted, however, demanding that they all sign a form consenting to the club's segregation rule. Most of the men agreed to sign, but Smith and 98 others refused. On their way out of the club, they were immediately arrested by an MP who told them he had orders to shoot to kill. They were court-martialed and sentenced to twenty years in military prison for disobeying an officer's orders.

The pilots who had signed the form pooled their money and arranged for Thurgood Marshall to appeal the verdict, and once again Marshall came to the aid of blacks who were the victims of unfair and illegal practices. In Washington, he brought to the attention of senior military officials the outstanding records of the dissenting officers, obtaining their release from prison and honorable discharges. The story received national and even international publicity—and led directly to President Truman's desegregation order.

Many years later, I met Q.P. Smith's son in Arizona, where I was the speaker at a banquet. I started to tell him about this incident, but he interrupted me to say that he already knew the story. During a tour of the Air Defense installation near Denver, he had heard it directly from General Chappie James, who was then the commanding officer. "Your father might have had my position," said James, "if it had not been for that incident."

I enlisted in the United States Air Force in August 1951. Entering the service was not unusual for the Watsons: my father had fought in World War I and my brother Herman had attempted to enlist in the navy in World War II. He was declared physically unfit because of a minor heart murmur, but my brother was convinced the navy simply didn't want black people: they had tried to talk him into going into the army before they rejected him. Almost every one of his buddies had been turned down by the navy for one reason or another. (Filipinos were accepted—and then restricted to serving as waiters or stewards.)

My ambition was to become the world's greatest jet fighter pilot. During my high school years, I had been thrilled by the exploits of the 99th Pursuit Squadron: the Tuskegee Airmen had been sent to the Mediterranean in 1943 and had performed magnificently. Not one of the bombers they escorted was lost, and the very people who had once questioned the ability of blacks—any blacks—to fly were soon asking for, if not demanding, the 99th as their escorts. (It is incredible that the contribution to the war effort of these amazing men was not acknowledged publicly until 1995, when a documentary about them was shown on cable television. The film wasn't really adequate, but it helped me recall how much I had been personally inspired by these courageous flyers.)

Although I had completed two years of college ROTC and had earned a baccalaureate degree, I could not get a commission. So I enlisted as an airman with the intention of going through Officer Candidate School, then flight school. I went through basic training at Lackland Air Force Base in San Antonio, Texas. It was badly overcrowded and we lived in tents, using portable showers and temporary latrines. My flight consisted of a few people from the midwest, but most were from Kentucky, West Virginia, and scattered other southern locales.

Because of my ROTC training, I already knew how to drill, and soon I was commanding the drill sessions under the supervision of Sergeant Ford, our instructor. A tall, muscular, career airman from upstate New York, Ford was a good dude who treated us fairly, although he took no shit from anybody, including officers. Rumor had it that he loved roller skating and fighting—and had been busted more than once for kicking somebody's butt off base or insulting some officer.

About two-thirds of the way through basic training, Sergeant Ford told me that I could no longer drill the recruits—even though our flight was winning most of the competitions between units. He was clearly embarrassed about having to give me this information. It turned out that the order had come down through his captain from the group commander, a colonel, who had said: "No nigger is going to drill troops in Texas as long as I am in command here." I was livid. "Does this mean that I am not a full-fledged airman?" I asked my sergeant. "If so, does this mean I can do only those things black airmen are allowed to do?" He answered that he was just following orders. He left my tent, red as a beet and obviously pissed that he had had to deliver this news, instead of his captain, who obviously agreed with the order. I was more than livid: I was also pretty worried, because I knew that this same colonel would be the one to interview me for admission to OCS or to flight school. You could not go forward without the approval of your squadron and group commanders. I had already been assured of a favorable recommendation from my squadron commander, so this colonel held my future in his hands.

I immediately consulted my old friend, Clarence Currie, one of the smartest people I have ever met in my life. Clarence was equally talented in science, mathematics, social science, the humanities—you name it. He could have chosen any field he wanted and done well in it. He was a pre-medical graduate who did not get into medical school because of the quota system which limited the number of blacks and Jews in each class. At any rate, we talked, and I told him what I was going to do: I would participate in everything the flight did except drill, because I had been denied full participation.

I would also write to the NAACP and Thurgood Marshall; to Milo C. Murray; and to the *Chicago Defender* and the *Pittsburgh Courier*. After I wrote the letters, I sealed them and put stamps on them (so that anyone tampering with them would be violating federal law), and left them in plain sight on my bed every morning after I made it. I sent the letters to Attorney Murray and the NAACP, and I gave Clarence copies of the others, along with instructions to mail them if I were arrested or court-martialed.

The stand-off went on for three days. Nobody bothered me when I refused to drill, but my buddies warned me I was going to be court-martialed and dishonorably discharged. I informed them that President Harry Truman had issued an executive order which the Air Force was violating. On the fourth day, Sergeant Ford came in with a big smile on his face and told me to line the troops up and take them for close-order drill. That's all he said. I assembled the flight and we went out and really showed off. We also won the competition.

When I was interviewed by the group commander, I was shocked. He couldn't have been nicer. He told me he would give me a strong

recommendation and that I should be in the next OCS class. While waiting for my OCS class to start, I was assigned to instructor's school, graduated at the top of my class, and taught academic subjects to new basic
trainees. In OCS, I became the second-ranking officer in my flight
(Charlie) and graduated on time, fully expecting to enter flight training
and become a jet pilot. But a funny thing happened on the way to flight
school: I found out that I was color-blind, which eliminated any chance of
flying jets. I was twenty-two years old and had never known I was color-
blind—or, rather, color-deficient. I confused blues and grays at the upper
end of the spectrum, but I had no problem with basic colors.

After OCS and my aborted pilot dreams, I was assigned to the
Department of Defense Information and Education School on David's
Island off New Rochelle, New York. I loved it. There were only a few
blacks there, one of whom was A. Q. Carrol, a former Tuskegee Airman,
a re-tread from World War II who was (according to him) the first black
POW, shot down over Italy. He had graduated from Howard University
and desperately wanted the necessary training to become an air force jet
pilot. He never made it; he became a military police commander.

When I completed my work at the school, I was assigned to Kelley Air
Force Base in San Antonio, Texas, and appointed group training officer.
My responsibilities included seeing that all scheduled training for
enlisted personnel and officers was carried out, and I reported directly to
the group commander, a full colonel. My top non-commissioned officer
was a career master sergeant of Chinese background. He knew everything
there was to know and we worked out a very comfortable relationship.
Together, we ran a tight ship and stayed out of each other's way. We both
developed good reputations among the veteran career personnel, including the group commander.

Over the course of my tour on the base, I became friendly with all the
civilian workers in the commander's office. I mention this because San
Antonio in 1952 was a very different place from the tourist attraction it is
today. The theaters, movies, restaurants, hotels, and just about everything
else were segregated by race. Restrictions applied to both Negroes and
Mexicans. There were movie houses owned and operated by Negroes, and
restaurants and hotels owned by members of both groups. There were some
"black and tan" clubs where the races mixed, but they were few and far
between, usually frequented by individuals accustomed to a different
lifestyle: servicemen, musicians, gamblers, very rich young white people,
and assorted others. On the air force bases, officers' and enlisted men's
clubs were integrated, while on army installations, such as Fort Sam

Houston, there were separate clubs for Negroes and whites. On buses, local residents segregated themselves—Negroes in the rear—but servicemen ignored this custom and sat anywhere they wanted. The contrast between life in the military and life in San Antonio and its suburbs was striking.

When my orders came to report to the Northeast Air Command headquarters in Newfoundland, the civilians in the group commander's office gave a going-away party for me. It was held in an apartment building in New Braunfels, a beautiful nearby suburb which was mostly German, middle-class, and all-white. There were about twenty people at the party, including military personnel from the base, but we all wore civilian clothes. It was a great evening, starting about seven and ending about nine-thirty.

When I left, the hostess and her daughter accompanied me to the lobby to wait for a cab. As we stood talking in the all-glass foyer, I noticed a group of about ten white teenagers on the other side of the avenue, watching us and gesticulating. As the cab approached, the two women said good-bye and gave me a hug and kiss. The group became extremely agitated and started to cross the street. It suddenly occurred to me that I could be in deep trouble. Fortunately, the taxi driver was just arriving. Seeing what was happening, he drove his cab in front of the group, made a U-turn, pulled up in front of the building, and reached back to open the rear door. He never stopped, just slowed enough for me to dive into the car. Then he took off, with the white teens behind him, yelling insults and shaking their fists. The driver didn't say a word, just kept speeding. I told him where I wanted to go and, when we reached our destination in the business area of the Negro neighborhood, I thanked him and gave him a very big tip. After I was out of the cab, the white driver, about thirty-five years old, smiled and told me to enjoy the weekend. He had probably saved me from a serious beating or worse.

I had wanted to go to Korea or Europe. During this period I thought that I might pursue a political career when I was discharged, and I knew that military service overseas would be a definite asset. Instead, I was requested by name to go to the Northeast Air Command in St. Johns, Newfoundland, where I became the assistant personnel officer at headquarters. Soon thereafter, however, I was assigned to Goose Bay Air Base in Labrador, where I became the chief of the personnel services section. This base was run jointly by Canada, Denmark, and the United States, and had an international and multi-service force. I loved it, especially in the non-American sector where I encountered no racial prejudice. I was a bachelor, and there were a number of single women from other countries on the base. This so disturbed certain people that they arranged for a black female officer to be assigned and made a point of trying to get us together.

I formed a band on the base because there was no entertainment in this remote location, where precipitation reached 140 inches a year, most of it snow. My group consisted of two air force officers (trombone and alto saxophone), three enlisted men (piano, bass, and drums), and me (tenor sax and vocals). Officers were not supposed to fraternize with enlisted men, but we had a ball. Our skills and knowledge varied widely, but since we were the only game in town, we played every weekend. Just before I left, we played for Christmas on the American side and for New Year's Eve on the Canadian side. The latter gig was wonderful! There was a big crowd, because Canadians who were married had their families with them, as a condition of their being assigned to this hardship base. We played all the standards and chestnuts, including some we had to learn on stage. As the night wore on, the party got better and people requested still more tunes. By the time it was over, my horn had been stuffed with money several times. I had sung almost every song I knew and made almost four hundred dollars. Fortunately, the piano player, a Chicano from Los Angeles, was very good and knew most of the tunes. He was a real musician.

One day, as I was sitting at my desk, an intelligence officer came to see me. The Criminal Investigation Division offices were in my building, so I knew the agents and what they did. He told me that this was a formal interview and he would be taking notes and recording part of it. He then asked all kinds of questions about organizations I had belonged to as a youth and a student at Indiana University. He wanted to know if my parents or brother were communists and what my feelings were about this country. I gave him a lesson in patriotism, telling him that my father was a combat veteran of World War I, that my brother had volunteered for service in World War II, and that I had volunteered for Korea. I also pointed out that my right to engage in civil rights activities was guaranteed by the Constitution.

Some weeks later, I got a telephone call from my mother. She was in Indiana, and I was in Labrador, and how she figured out how to reach me, I will never know: we were not permitted to call home and relatives could not call the base except in an emergency. She asked, "Are you in trouble?" She had heard from several people that the F.B.I. was making inquiries about me, even asking my elementary school teachers about my interests and character. I assured her that everything was fine, that I was being investigated for top secret clearance.

A month or so later, after my jazz group had finished playing at the officers' club, the CID agent who had interviewed me asked if he could buy me a drink. He had been sitting at this table and drinking for a long time. I sat down, he ordered, and we chatted for a few minutes. Suddenly he said, "Lieutenant Watson, you are a hell of a guy. I couldn't find anyone in your home town who would say a bad thing about you. You have a lot of friends. People really think highly of you." Then his eyes watered and his voice cracked a little. "I'm sorry I had to do this to you, Lieutenant. I was just doing my job." It turned out that this was one of the investigations of people who had belonged to "subversive organizations," who were communist sympathizers or associated with "fellow travelers." Those were crazy times, remember: the days of McCarthy and Cohn, red hunts and the like. Apparently, my civil rights activities and political activism had attracted the attention of the wrong people.

Colonel Lammons, the base commander, was one of the "Wonder Colonels" from the Class of 1936 at West Point (at least that is what we were told by other officers). When he took over, he ordered me to clean up the mess in personnel services, regardless of whose feet I had to step on. This involved retrieving, from the homes and offices of favored officers and non-coms, equipment intended to boost the morale of regular servicemen: tape recorders, record players, radios, records, even furniture. I did the job, with his backing, and it resulted in one officer's forced transfer stateside and discharge.

Lammons promoted me and gave me his bars, which I still have. He tried to talk me into staying in the air force, saying that I would likely become a general because the services were changing and there would be new opportunities for blacks. He was right, and he was also right about the fact that a non-pilot would eventually reach the rank of general in the air force. I declined his offer to go regular and to stay with him. When the Korean War ended, I took advantage of the early out and returned to civilian life.

The University of Illinois

After my stint in the air force, I had planned to enroll at the University of California at Berkeley and pursue my doctorate. But when I got home, I found that my father was seriously ill with cancer and was awaiting admission to a veterans' hospital. My mother had been unable to get my father into the hospital where black veterans were apparently sent, because there were so few openings. She had written to the regional officers to no avail. As soon as my mother told me about this, I called the person in charge of the local VA to say that I would be down the next day to see what was causing the delay. I also noted that I was very angry and disappointed that a combat veteran of World War I had been treated this way, while his only surviving son was serving overseas in another war.

When my mother and I got to the office, they were waiting for us. I was in full dress uniform, mad as hell. After a brief consultation, we were told that my father was being assigned to the veterans' hospital in Waukesha, Wisconsin, and would be transported there within two days. He was in the hospital by the weekend, taken by a close friend who owned several funeral homes and had a fleet of vehicles, including ambulances. The doctors said that my dad had no more than six months to live and suggested that I delay going to Berkeley if I wanted to spend some time with my father. So, instead of going to California, I enrolled at the University of Illinois. With my family, I visited my father every weekend. Within six months he was dead. I received the news during one of my final examinations. He was only fifty-six.

I had entered the University of Illinois a week or so after taking my father to the hospital. I signed up for a full load of classes, including a course in the Civil War and Reconstruction, a continuation of my history major. This class was taught by J.B. Randall, a noted Civil War historian and a dedicated racist who attempted to hide his views by using humor. Throughout the semester, he made jokes about darkies and tried to paint the picture of slaves as childlike and happy, better off under slavery than as free men and women. I was having none of that crap, and every time he made a remark or cracked a joke, I responded. It got to the point where the class expected us to clash and try to out-maneuver each other. It was all so very lighthearted, but deadly serious—and everybody knew it.

There were only two other blacks in the class: one was probably smart enough to know that grades could be affected by student relationships with the professor; perhaps the other student didn't take offense at Randall's jokes. But I didn't give a damn. Sure enough, I always did very well on the objective parts of the examinations when the answer was clear. On the essay exams, however, I never did quite as well. There was just enough difference to make my grade average a "strong C," which as any graduate student knows is the same as failing. I still didn't give a damn. All my other grades were "A"s, which made the "C" stand out like a sore thumb. My advisor and one of my professors asked me about it, but they just smiled, apparently knowing about Professor Randall. As a matter of fact, the dean called me in and told me he had arranged a graduate assistantship for me that would pay a stipend as well as my tuition. I was sent to be interviewed by my new boss.

The University of Illinois Institute for the Study of Exceptional Children was known all over the country for its research on and treatment of exceptional children. It was headed by Dr. Samuel Kirk, a respected and well-known scholar who later won the first John F. Kennedy Award given by the president for work with exceptional children. Kirk's assistant was Professor Kolstoe, another scholar of impeccable reputation. I was interviewed by both and given an office where my job was to work on the statistics involved in their research projects and other assignments.

After that first interview, Professor Kirk never spoke to me again, even when I passed him in the hall and spoke directly to him. His office was almost directly across the hall from mine, but he acted as though I did not exist. His colleague, Professor Kolstoe, was not only cordial, but went out of his way to be collegial and to make suggestions about things I could read or observe to learn more about the research I was working on. I remembered this experience years later, when I saw the televised ceremony of Professor Kirk receiving the presidential award.

I finished my master's degree in a year and decided to stay on and pursue the doctorate at Illinois. Midway through my third semester, the dean called me in and informed me that the University would not award a Ph.D. in any field of education unless the candidate had had at least a year of experience. Although I had taught in the air force and had been group training officer for an air force base, this was not considered "experience." My graduate test scores placed me in the top five percent, and my grades in history, psychology, sociology, and education courses were all "A"s, except for three courses, one of which was the Civil War and Reconstruction course I mentioned earlier. Yet I was advised—told, actually—to go out and get a year or two of experience before I could return and finish the degree, probably as a teaching assistant.

Although I had no interest in leaving the university at that time, I did apply for a teaching position in my home town. Miracle of miracles, a position was open at Roosevelt, my alma mater.

CHAPTER IV
MY EARLY CAREER AND MARRIAGE

In the autumn of 1955, with two degrees in hand and my military oblig-
ation completed, I returned to my hometown of Gary. It was the era of the
so-called "silent generation." The Korean conflict had been concluded in
1953, and the following year the Army-McCarthy hearings had virtually
ended the anti-communist hysteria of the House Un-American Activities
Committee. Although the cold war continued to dominate foreign affairs,
the country seemed to be settling down and faring well under the grand-
fatherly supervision of President Eisenhower.

The calm did not continue. In fact, two events in 1954—one which took
place thousands of miles away and the other in the nation's capital—con-
tained the seeds of nearly indescribable pain and controversy. The first
was the defeat of the French at Dienbienphu and their departure from
Vietnam. I'm certain that most Americans paid little attention to this
news, could not have located the country on a map, and had no idea at
all that it would ever have any significance for the United States. The
other event—the result of many years of effort by NAACP lawyers such as
Thurgood Marshall—was the unanimous U.S. Supreme Court decision,
Brown v. Board of Education, banning segregation in the public schools.

The battle to defeat the separate-but-equal doctrine laid down by the
Court in 1896 was long and arduous. The strategic framework was estab-
lished by Charles Hamilton Houston, dean of Howard University law
school. Although he did not live to see the victory (he died in 1950), his
contributions were incalculable, ranging from the reform of legal educa-
tion and the training of many young lawyers for the civil rights battles, to
personal participation in the step-by-step assault on educational discrim-
ination and continuing inspiration and guidance to the Legal Defense
Fund staff. For black people—and all who believed in the ideals set forth

in the Constitution—the Brown decision was an incredible triumph, but it was soon apparent that the war against racism in education was far from over. The reaction of many whites was immediate, noisy, and violent.

Not many months after I had moved back to Gary, the battle for the civil rights of all Americans began in earnest. A quiet Negro woman who commuted every day to her job as a seamstress in a Montgomery, Alabama, department store, refused—simply refused—to move to the back of the bus to make way for a white passenger. When Rosa Parks was arrested and jailed on December 1, 1955, it was as though someone had tossed a match in a tank of gasoline. The long struggle to end segregation moved out of the courtrooms and into the streets. On December 5, the Rev. Dr. Martin Luther King, Jr., youthful pastor of the Dexter Avenue Baptist Church, announced that Montgomery Negroes would henceforth boycott public transportation. (A year later, the U.S. Supreme Court upheld the decision of a federal panel which had declared that bus segregation was unconstitutional.)

The remainder of the 1950s—which some remember nostalgically as an era of relative tranquility— was marked by conflict and controversy. Eisenhower was kept busy stopping war (in Egypt, over the Suez Canal) and starting one (in Lebanon)—and had to send federal troops to enforce school integration in Little Rock, Arkansas. The cold war took a deadly turn when Russia launched the first earth-orbiting satellite in late 1957 and the U.S. followed suit in early 1958. Castro took over Cuba in 1959, and U-2 pilot Francis Gary Powers was shot down by the U.S.S.R. in 1960. This was the background against which my first few years as an educator unfolded.

The War on Poverty and the War in Vietnam

The 1960s began with the excitement of Camelot, as Americans eagerly responded to Kennedy's challenge to "do something" for the country. Despite the fiasco of the Bay of Pigs adventure and the terrors of the Cuban missile crisis, there was pride in being an American, renewed confidence that problems could be and would be solved, an almost religious enthusiasm to enlist as a volunteer for the New Frontier. But less than three years after his inauguration, Kennedy was assassinated. Millions of people still remember, with startling clarity, where they were when they learned that the unthinkable had happened, that the president was dead.

Lyndon Baines Johnson, who succeeded Kennedy, was and is a hero to many blacks and other minorities. Whatever his faults or foibles, he *stands with Lincoln as a president who led a campaign to rid America of its ancient bondage to slavery and racism. In 1967, President Johnson appointed me to the National Advisory Council on Education Professions Development, on which I served for a time as vice chairman. One of my most treasured memories is of the reception given by black presidential appointees when Johnson announced that he would not run for re-election. It was wonderful. LBJ promised that he would come for a few minutes to thank us, but he stayed for at least 45 minutes. Lois and I were scared to death. In this room at a Washington hotel were many of the outstanding black American leaders: Thurgood Marshall, Roger Wilkins, Clarence Mitchell of the NAACP, Whitney Young of the National Urban League, Louis Martin (a special White House assistant), Robert Weaver (Secretary of Housing and Urban Development), Kenneth Clark, Benjamin Mays, Marian Anderson. What if someone had thrown a bomb...? But it was a love-in. Johnson was very comfortable, and so were his appointees. I saw him several times later, after he left the White House. Shortly before he died, he addressed a conference at the LBJ School at the University of Texas, reiterating his belief in equal opportunity and his desire that the school be a center for preparation of the next generation of minority leaders for government service.*

Even the most ardent admirers of Johnson agree that he conceived the Great Society with its astonishing array of domestic programs in order to assure his own place in history and to erase the opprobrium of being called an "accidental president." (Previously, for instance, he had not been known for his sympathy with the civil rights movement.) But the fact remains that his formidable knowledge of the legislative process, experience in Congress, and political skills were responsible for the passage of the landmark Civil Rights Act (1964) and, in 1965, the Voting Rights Act and the Elementary and Secondary Education Act. He announced the War on Poverty and established the Office of Economic Opportunity. He created the Department of Housing and Urban Development. And he initiated the Head Start program, still considered perhaps the most successful component of the Great Society.

Much of the credit for passage of these bills, as Johnson himself acknowledged, was due to Adam Clayton Powell, the black Congressman from Harlem who served eleven successive terms. Like King, he was the son of a well-known minister, succeeding his father in the pulpit at the Abyssinian Baptist Church. Throughout the Depression years, he was active in relief and civil rights activities, and in 1941 he was elected to the New York City Council. He became a member of the House of

Representatives in 1945 and quickly established a reputation for his vocal opposition to segregation in Washington. Appointed chair of the House Education and Labor Committee in 1960, he became the most powerful African American in Congress, helping to pass such important pieces of legislation as the Minimum Wage Bill, the Manpower Development and Training Act, the Anti-Poverty Bill, the Juvenile Delinquency Act, the Vocational Education Act, and the National Defense Education Act. The 48 social welfare laws with which he was associated involved the expenditure of some $14 billion.

One promising proposal after another, all intended to improve the lives of the poor and assure minorities their rightful place in American society, were planned and implemented. But a somber, and ultimately tragic, theme was developing in counterpoint to the heady and optimistic march of national progress: Vietnam. Johnson had inherited the question of what to do about that little-known part of Southeast Asia from the two previous administrations: Eisenhower had helped to establish the unpopular Diem regime in the south, while Kennedy at first supported Diem and then encouraged his overthrow.

Johnson certainly was not eager to pursue the war, but like Kennedy before him he believed that if he did not, his political life would be threatened by accusations of being soft on communism, of "losing" Vietnam the way China had been "lost." Less than three months after announcing the Great Society, he asked for, and was granted, authority to "take all necessary measures...to prevent further aggression." The Gulf of Tonkin Resolution was endorsed almost unanimously by the Senate in August 1964. Following Johnson's landslide election later that year, the disastrous escalation of the war in Vietnam began in earnest. Winning had become a matter of national pride, the country was told, but it was soon America's turn to learn that it could not have both guns and butter.

From Peaceful Protest to Urban Riots

Resistance to the war, particularly by potential draftees and by those who deplored the diversion of national resources from domestic programs, was inextricably entwined with the on-going and dangerous struggle against segregation in the south. Young people across the United States joined in protests against the war, poverty, and discrimination; soon they were also challenging the policies of their own colleges and universities, which were viewed as collaborators with "The Establishment" (government and business), and defying authority in general. Sometimes it did not seem to matter what the cause for demonstrations was: the threat of nuclear annihilation, the plight of the oppressed, the constraints of traditional morals. Student sit-ins and marches, hippies and drugs, Eastern religion and sexual freedom, rock and roll or folk rock seemed to have taken over the country, and all contributed to the older generation's horrified impression that the youth of America had collectively gone off the deep end. It should be noted, however, that most of the young people involved were white and middle-class: the youth revolt was based on college campuses where few poor minority students were to be found.

African Americans had a more serious and more focused agenda than many of their white contemporaries. They were fighting for the elementary freedoms which white people took for granted: the right to vote, the right to live where they chose, the right to a decent education, the right to be treated as a human being. I have already described the northern segregated society in which I grew up. Although racism was usually more blatant in the south, it was an ever-present reality in the north. All persons of color have their own stories of how they were affected from childhood on by the recognition that they were objects of contempt, hatred, and fear. Some were taught to go along with the system and avoid confrontation; others were encouraged to pursue their personal goals regardless of the difficulties their ambition engendered. In the 1960s, black pain and frustration boiled over: neither the law nor nonviolent protest appeared capable of rectifying what Gunnar Myrdal had termed the "American Dilemma."

Almost immediately after the Brown decision in 1954, furious southerners had formed White Citizens' Councils to resist not only school integration but all attempts to abolish the Jim Crow laws which governed every aspect of southern society. In 1957, Martin Luther King, Jr., who had led the Montgomery bus boycott, organized the Southern Christian Leadership Conference to counter the threats and violence with peaceful demonstrations, but even as the term "civil disobedience" became familiar, so did the names of many cities throughout the south where marches and sit-ins were attacked not only by angry mobs but by the police.

Angered by the white backlash and impatient with the slow pace of efforts to reduce poverty, some African Americans opted for militant action. Beginning in 1964, violence regularly exploded all over the north, as hundreds set fire to cars and buildings, looted local stores, and engaged in pitched battles with police in New York, Chicago, Newark, Detroit, Philadelphia, and numerous other cities. The worst riots occurred *following the assassination of Martin Luther King, Jr., in April 1968; in Washington, D.C., troops were called out to guard the White House. Philadelphia was a notable exception, for reasons I will describe later.*

Some people then and now have pondered the irony of the fact that the uprisings in northern ghettos started immediately after the passage of the 1964 Civil Rights Act and the initiation of the War on Poverty. Certainly, President Johnson was both appalled and puzzled that the unrest continued, despite his avowed sympathy with civil rights. For instance, in his speech to Congress in March 1965 urging passage of the Voting Rights Act, he had condemned the bloody events in Selma and concluded with a dramatic enunciation of the anthem of the civil rights movement, "We Shall Overcome."

But the black reaction should not be so difficult to understand. Hopes of a new era of justice and progress had been raised by court decisions, federal programs, and public statements, but they had eroded into bitterness by the opposition of white racists and the diversion of federal funds to the war in Vietnam. Ten years after the Brown decision, the good things that had been promised seemed as elusive as ever.

***

It really did seem too good to be true: just after I had been told by the University of Illinois that I needed classroom experience, I learned that Roosevelt had an opening that I might be able to fill. What a privilege it would be to return as a teacher to the school that had meant so much to me! Of course, I had to have a formal interview, even though I had spent almost half my life at Roosevelt. I had not seen Mr. T. since leaving Gary four years earlier to enlist in the air force. He was clearly beginning to age, but he was just as I remembered him: courteous, quiet, and very much in charge. By the end of our conversation, I had been given a two-part assignment, beginning in September 1955: social studies teacher for grades 8 and 9 and counselor for grades 7 through 12.

I loved teaching—American history, civics, and geography—but I found that I liked the informal contacts with students even better. Within the next couple of years, I became a full-time counselor, obtained certification as a guidance supervisor, and was appointed chairman of Roosevelt's guidance department. There was no doubt that I was a popular person on campus, but then I had several advantages. First, I was a native of Gary and a Roosevelt alumnus—which meant that I knew many of the students and their families very well and understood their background and experience. Moreover, as one of the youngest members of the faculty and administration, I shared many of the students' interests and attitudes.

Perhaps the fact that I was single made it possible for me to do the things I did with students. I was free to devote as much of my time as I chose to their activities. I attended every basketball and football game, traveling with the teams to games and track meets on the road. I attended and then helped to chaperone every talent show, play, and public performance. I got to know students by name, knew their interests, and this enabled me to encourage and counsel them. They began to believe that I was truly interested in each one, not just the stars, the visible ones. They believed it, and it was true.

During the second semester of my first year, I heard a loud disturbance outside my ninth-grade civics classroom on the third floor, where most senior classes were taught. Stepping into the hall, I saw two of the largest boys fighting, surrounded by a large crowd of fascinated and frightened students. Some were cheering them on. These guys were enormous, both over six feet tall and one weighing over two hundred pounds. Without thinking, I plowed into the crowd, grabbed one of the combatants, threw him into my classroom, and yelled for the fight to stop. A teacher across the hall—shorter then I was, but older—grabbed the other student and got him into his classroom. We quickly dispersed the crowd, and Timuel Black, the other teacher, brought the second student into my room, which was empty. As the students sat there glowering at each other, I told them they were a disgrace to the football team, on which both played varsity, and to the school.

Mistaking their size for maturity, I said, "You are seniors and should be setting an example." They were not seniors, but I didn't care. I told them that if I ever heard of them fighting and disgracing the team and the school again, I would see to it that they were not only removed from the team but suspended from school. They were stunned at my outburst, considering my size and the fact that I was new to the school, I guess. Then it dawned on them that I was not going to report them to the principal and seek disciplinary action. I then told them to leave my room, go to the study hall, and act like Roosevelt students, not hoodlums.

The word spread quickly throughout the school: this new guy took no crap, had taken on two of the biggest and toughest students in the school, Haywood Turnipseed and Lethenius Irons. Equally important to them, I later learned, was that I was not afraid to act on my own. I was not afraid of the principal, either. And, in their eyes, I was fair to students.

In December 1959, Mr. T. stopped me in the hall and asked me to drop in before I left the school. It was the last day before the Christmas vacation, and I had stayed late to check the building and get ready for the break. "Mr. Watson," he said, "What I am about to tell you is strictly confidential. Our junior high school principal is about to be appointed as principal of Froebel School, and I am recommending you to take his place here." I was flabbergasted. Mr. T. continued, "Yes, I know that many other people want the job. They have seniority and experience which you do not. One applicant even has a doctorate and has already served as a high school principal elsewhere. But you are my choice, for several reasons: you care about students, you have good relationships with them and your peers, you have high standards and expectations, and you know the school and this city. Besides, you have done something other than go to school. You have worked in the steel mills, been in the service, and done other things."

Mr. T. concluded the conversation by saying that the board of education would be meeting the following Monday to act on this and other recommendations. I was in a daze when I left his office, but there was nothing to do but go home and wait. Several days later, I got the news: I had been appointed principal of the junior high school and assistant principal of Roosevelt. (My predecessor was also a Watson—Dr. William H. Watson—but we were not related. At the same board meeting, Dr. Watson was indeed assigned to Froebel and thus became the second black high school principal in Gary's history.) Some time later, Dr. Alden Blankenship, the superintendent of schools, asked me why I had not applied earlier for an administrative position. "When Mr. Tatum recommended you," he said, "I checked your credentials and found out how highly qualified you are." It may sound naive, but I could only tell him the truth: I had assumed that the superintendent, who had access to everyone's files, would know when a person was ready for more responsibility, and besides, I thought I was too young to be a secondary principal.

My appointment could have caused some difficulty at Roosevelt. There were, in fact, teachers there who had more experience; a number of them had taught me, some in junior high and a few in elementary school. Fortunately—and this is a credit to their professionalism and to the fact that they knew and respected me—nothing untoward happened. The junior high faculty accepted the appointment with pride and open arms. They gave me their complete support and told me they did so because I respected teachers and teaching and loved the students. I left on a Friday as their teaching colleague and returned after the holidays as their principal. It was an exciting time. I added algebra, French, and Spanish to the junior high curriculum. Students who successfully completed two years of a foreign language could enroll in the next year when they entered high school. The same was true of algebra. Some of the high school teachers resisted this, but our junior high graduates held their own, and opposition vanished.

The junior high school moved into its own new building a few years later, and Robert Jones became the principal. I elected to stay on as assistant principal of Roosevelt High School. Mr. Tatum had retired and been succeeded by his long-time assistant, Warren M. Anderson. Robert Jones replaced me when I went to the University of Chicago, and on Mr. Anderson's retirement, he became Roosevelt's principal.

Lois

After I returned to Gary, I met and dated a number of attractive women, women with intelligence and character who would have made good wives, but it looked as if I would remain a bachelor forever. In fact, that was the rumor that circulated among some of my peers. I was supposed to be too cool to get married, or too wrapped up in my career, or too close to my mother, with whom I still lived. None of it was accurate; I just hadn't met the right person. Another factor contributed to the notion that I might become a perpetual bachelor: after my father's death, I had purchased a new home and moved my mother and sister into it. Furthermore, I had sent my sister to school; there was no reason for her to be denied a college education because her father and older brothers had died prematurely. These events led some to conclude, mistakenly, that I would forever be tied to my immediate family, especially my mother.

One Wednesday evening, we had the monthly junior high school PTA meeting in the school cafeteria. Mildred Logan, one of the science teachers, was there with a friend. Since the meetings rarely lasted longer than an hour, the two of them had planned to go out with friends afterwards. In the course of the evening, Mildred introduced me to Lois Lathan, a new elementary teacher at Drew School.

The only way I can describe meeting Lois is "unreal"! Lois was gorgeous, but she was different. She looked you in the eye when she talked to you; she was confident without being arrogant about her looks. We actually had a brief conversation about her choosing to come to Gary from St. Louis, Missouri. Her black, contoured suit was a knockout. I remember to this day exactly what she had on and how she looked. I was cool, but I was floored. I knew that I needed to find out more about this young lady.

The next day, I visited Mildred Logan's classroom to observe her teaching. After class, I asked, in my most professional manner, the telephone number and address of the young woman she had introduced me to the previous evening. She gave me the number and I went about my business. It turned out that Lois lived across the street from Roosevelt with her aunt and uncle. Mildred also lived there. The aunt and uncle had no children, so they rented rooms in their large house to single teachers who came to work in Gary.

I called Lois that evening and asked her for a date on Friday. She agreed to go out with me. The date was quiet: we went to a movie, had dessert and coffee afterward, and talked. That was it. Neither of us dated anyone else after that. There was one major difference between us: I was ten years older than Lois. Yet we had many of the same interests, we shared the same set of values. We even wanted some of the same things out of life. We were aware of the age difference and we talked about it. It didn't seem to matter.

I asked Lois to marry me before Thanksgiving vacation, and we were formally engaged by Christmas. She went back to St. Louis to visit her parents over the holidays and was quite ill with the flu, so it was not until her return in January that I gave her an engagement ring. During spring break, I went to visit Lois's parents. Her father was not too pleased about the impending marriage because of the age difference, but her mother was very nice and welcomed me with open arms. As I suspect most mothers will, she had investigated my reputation in my hometown and was convinced that I loved her daughter. After 34 years of marriage, I still call Mrs. Lathan "the world's greatest mother-in-law." She is a remarkable woman. Mr. Lathan eventually got over his apprehensions and decided that I truly loved Lois enough not to mistreat her or take advantage of her. He learned that I could be the kind of husband any father wants for his daughter.

We were married on July 1, 1961—the same day restaurants and hotels in St. Louis were finally desegregated and opened to black people. We had made reservations at the newly opened Diplomat Hotel/Motel. After the reception, we had dinner in the restaurant without incident. The next morning, we left for New York, where we spent our honeymoon. We stayed at the Henry Hudson Hotel and spent the next ten days seeing Broadway plays, such as *The Best Man*, *Rhinoceros* (with Zero Mostel) and *To Be Young, Gifted and Black*, eating in great restaurants, and enjoying all the best jazz. Birdland was still open, along with all of the other jazz sites in the Village and Harlem.

When we returned to Gary, we lived in my mother's house until we found an apartment, a difficult thing to do because there were few rental properties available to black people. There were wonderful apartments in the Horace Mann neighborhood, along Fifth Avenue downtown, and in the Miller and Marquette Park areas. Any white person who could afford the rent was welcome, but they were not available to any black person, regardless of income, credit history, education, employment record, or marital status.

The same was true for homes in these areas: they were not for sale to black people. I cannot tell you how angry this made us, especially those of us who had been born and reared in the city. Tolleston, the area where we lived, had just been "broken." In fact, when I moved there with my mother and sister after my father died, we were among the first black people in the neighborhood. I had purchased the home from Michael Sowochka, head of the local teamsters' union, a union which even after the Korean war excluded blacks. (Later, under Sowochka's son, who succeeded him, blacks were admitted to membership. The pressure was on, from non-union businesses who hired black drivers and from the burgeoning local civil rights movement being led by Edward "Doc" James and a younger more active group.)

We finally found an apartment in a building owned by Spike White, a Roosevelt graduate who was a teacher and coach in the public schools. We rented a third-floor, two-bedroom walkup and began married life on our own. The neighborhood was still integrated, but only because the remaining white people could not afford to move away. We were regularly treated to the sounds of one man beating his wife. Another couple, professional burglars who used to live in the area where I grew up, cussed each other out after drinking binges. The wife was in a wheelchair, paralyzed after being shot by someone intending to kill her husband. She had saved his life and she never let him forget that he was responsible for her condition. Amazingly, he stayed with her, took care of her, and did no more than cuss her back. It was a lovely environment for newlyweds— forced on us because of the racially restrictive housing market which was still legal in those days. Transportation was a problem: we had only one car, but we worked in schools on opposite sides of Gary. After a year of having to make daily arrangements for rides with colleagues, friends, and me, Lois insisted on having her own car and we bought a used Rambler.

Within three years, we had saved enough to buy our own home—something Lois desperately wanted. We designed the house, getting ideas from magazines and existing homes. We then contracted with one of the largest builders in the city. In 1964, we moved into our first dream house: brick and stone, with three bedrooms, two-and-a-half baths, large living and dining rooms, full eat-in kitchen, two-car garage, full basement, fireplace, study, and large front and rear lawns on a half-acre lot. It also had a large front porch, a common feature of midwestern houses during that period.

From the beginning, Lois and I had agreed to postpone having children until we had completed our graduate education and were more secure financially. More importantly, we agreed that we wanted to be free to spend a lot of time with our children during their formative years. We both knew parents who were very successful but had little time to spend with their children at critical periods of their development. Lois continued to work as a full-time teacher/librarian in the elementary schools, while attending evening classes and full-time summer sessions at Purdue University. She received her master's degree in library science in 1966, one year before I completed my Ph.D. at the University of Chicago.

Chicago

The University of Chicago was probably the defining educational experience of my life. I had loved Roosevelt, and it had prepared me for college and graduate school, but Chicago was something else entirely. It is difficult to describe the atmosphere, full of intellectual energy and excitement. The students were bright and well-educated, and the place crackled with ideas. Classes were exciting, but the discussions in the student lounge, talk over a brown bag lunch in the office, arguments in the cafeteria or in the Beehive, a local hangout and jazz club, could be equally stimulating. The debates which took place regularly in the theological school were legendary. I met the Rev. Jesse Jackson when he was a student there and to this day, even though neither of us is from the city of Chicago, he still calls me "homeboy."

What I liked most of all was the lack of rigidity. You were told what the requirements were to earn a degree and then it was up to you to decide how you wanted to jump those hurdles. You could choose almost any course in any department or division, you could probably get in, and you would find students from six or eight different major programs. Professors from many disciplines routinely served on dissertation committees, sometimes just because the topics interested them or students asked them. I was always a good student and received good grades, but it was at Chicago that I received an education. I worked harder than I had ever worked in my life and, despite some bad times which are a part of being in graduate school, I enjoyed it tremendously. I will always be

Bernard C. Watson at eight

Home of my mother, Fannie Mae Browne, in Talladega, Alabama

In eighth grade

My maternal grandmother, Amanda,
and Aunt Birdie

My sister Helen

My parents, Homer and Fannie Watson

My sister Dolores

My brother Homer

Graduation from Roosevelt High School, 1946

Clarence Currie and
Bernard Watson
Senior Honor Society

Playing the saxophone

Some of my friends at Indiana University in 1949, discussing civil rights protests

My best friend,
Clarence Currie

As an officer in
the U.S. Air Force

"Bebop Watson & the Hungry Five" at Goose Bay Air Force base in 1953

Roosevelt High School, Gary, Indiana

grateful that a university like that exists. It was an ideal setting for a person like me who hates regimentation, prescribed courses, and not having the freedom to educate yourself.

I went to the University of Chicago primarily because of the influence of Dr. Haron Battle, one of my early mentors. He had earned his Ph.D. there and suggested that it would be a better choice for me than Harvard, which I was also considering at the time. The Staff Associate Program in the Midwest Administration Center was the premier program for graduate students in the Department of Education, Division of Social Sciences. It was highly competitive, accepting only six or eight persons a year of the 120 applicants from the United States and Canada. I was appointed a staff associate in 1965, and in return for a stipend, tuition, and fees, I worked as a research or teaching assistant twenty hours a week and took a full load of graduate courses.

Barbara Sizemore and I were the first and, as far as I know, the only blacks to enter the program. Barbara was an exceptional person, much brighter than most of the other students although they included Phi Beta Kappa, *magna* and *summa cum laude* graduates of Harvard, Yale, Syracuse, and premier Canadian universities. Barbara had graduated from Northwestern University at age nineteen, *summa cum laude* in classics. She was beautiful, cultured, and dressed as if she had stepped out of *Vogue*. Appearances can be deceiving, however, because Barbara was dedicated to improving the education afforded black children.

She had been a spectacular elementary school principal in the Chicago public schools and, because of this, Dr. Benjamin Willis, the superintendent, prevailed upon her to take on a tough public high school on the south side. Barbara agreed to do so—against the advice of everyone who knew her at the university, as well as people in the community. We all knew that Dr. Willis could not be trusted to live up to his many commitments of resources, staff, and autonomy. Barbara left the program, took over the school, and did an outstanding job. True to form, Willis went back on his word.

Barbara did not obtain her Ph.D. at Chicago until 1979. During her career, she became the superintendent of the Washington, D.C., public schools, was a professor at the University of Pittsburgh, and is now the dean of the School of Education at DePaul University in Chicago. I have met few people who have the intelligence and intellect she possesses. I have also met few who burn with such righteous anger over the injustice of denying black children, regardless of their socioeconomic background, the very best education possible.

I went to Chicago on a mission. I knew why I was there, and my priority was to learn everything I could, to drain every ounce of learning from that incredible faculty, to absorb as much as humanly possible from the diverse student body with whom we had daily contact. I entered the program in the summer of 1965; I intended to be out of there with my degree in 1967. Of course, everybody thought I was deranged when I said this—nobody finished a doctorate from Chicago in that time—so I didn't mention it again. My plans, however did not change. I remained focused. Lois and I had dinner together every night. We would talk an hour and then go our separate ways to study or work. We said good-bye after juice every morning. On weekends, we might go to a movie or to dinner or to a club with friends.

As a staff associate in the Midwest Administration Center, one of my major projects was leading a team of graduate students to study teacher strikes in Indiana and Michigan as examples of the new militancy among teachers and administrators. Under Professor Luvern Cunningham, director of the Midwest Center, we published the first major paper on this phenomenon. I subsequently published my first article in a professional journal and authored my first chapter in a book. I also participated with other graduate students in a major study of the Blue Island, Illinois, public school system which was struggling with racial integration and educational reform. A special privilege was co-teaching a graduate course with Frank Chase, former dean and chair of the school and department. And it was a great honor to meet and talk with Professor Allison Davis, a black scholar who spent most of his career at Chicago as a principal investigator in landmark research with W. Lloyd Warner, Havighurst, and others.

Of all the outstanding individuals I came to know at Chicago, Luvern Cunningham was unique. Vern was my mentor and remains a very close friend. He was the person who introduced me to the world of consulting. He asked me to serve with him on a search team engaged to assist an Illinois community college in finding a new president. Vern and I met with the board and were very excited about the challenge. As was Vern's habit, he wanted to engage the very best brains to help him carry out his responsibilities. The two leading experts on community colleges were professors of higher education, one at Berkeley and the other at Michigan State. After talking to both, Vern decided to bring in the one from Michigan State for consultation, and arranged for the three of us to meet at the O'Hare airport restaurant.

Vern and I arrived about six o'clock. Our colleague was already there; he had had a couple of drinks and was a little flushed. We ordered dinner and after the amenities began to discuss the project at hand. After about ten minutes, the professor turned to me and said, "I have heard a lot about you, nice things . You are doing well and are smart, but you are still just a nigger, you know." Poor Vern turned red, then purple, he was so shocked. I was pissed also, but I knew this kind of thing could happen when white people have too much to drink. The man was clearly drunk by this time; his speech was slurred and his eyelids at half mast.

But he wasn't through. "You don't mind me calling you a nigger, do you?" he said. The place was packed with people waiting to be seated. Vern started to tell him he shouldn't be using that kind of language and that we should proceed with our discussion without personal references. Vern was struggling for words, embarrassed for me and wondering what my reaction was going to be. I was cool—pissed, but cool. I had several choices: knock this old white man on his ass and create a big scene; ignore him; get up and walk out of the restaurant; try to carry on a civil conversation with a person who was obviously out of it. Instead, I said, "Let's finish eating and get out of here. People are waiting and you have a plane to catch back to Michigan. Just keep your mouth shut and don't use that word again." He shut up, and we finished within ten or fifteen minutes. By this time, he was nodding and, as Vern paid the check, I kicked that SOB under the table. In those days, I wore boots during the winter, and I knew that he would wake up in the morning with a badly bruised and sore leg. He did, as I learned later from Vern. The Michigan State professor thought he had hurt it himself by bumping into something.

On the way home, Vern was a nervous wreck, apologizing for the evening, telling me he had never been so embarrassed in his life, thanking me for not making a scene. He had been truly traumatized by it, an occurrence common or at least known to most black people my age or older. Years later, Vern and I were together at an American Association of School Administrators conference in Atlantic City, when a white superintendent of an overwhelmingly black district said to Vern and five other white professors, "God, am I glad to see all of these white people." It was out of his mouth before he recognized that I was with the group. Everybody was embarrassed, but Vern was the only one who immediately spoke up— "Shame on you! You ought to be ashamed of yourself, talking like that."—before I walked away. These, and scores of other incidents, as well as the stands Vern has taken on tough issues, led Barbara Sizemore to give him the nickname "our blue-eyed soul brother."

During my two years at Chicago, I did more than course work. I learned about faculty politics and how to deal with them without losing sight of my own goals. The chairman of my dissertation committee was a sociologist, a former faculty member at Harvard, but he was only an associate professor. Everyone else on my committee was not only a full professor, but a superstar. Yet Dan Lortie was the best person for my topic, which involved theory and organizational issues he knew most about. Dan was a great guy, a man at home in a jazz club or a tavern, on a street corner talking to neighborhood residents, or in a high-powered discussion of competing intellectual viewpoints. I was very comfortable with him, and we remained friends after I left.

I was invited to his home several times, but there was one evening I will never forget. Dan had asked all his graduate students and their spouses to dinner. When Lois and I pulled up in front of his apartment building not far from the university, I noticed a couple on their way out who had stopped to stare at us. Maybe their attention had been attracted by my car—a red Mustang with wire wheels and sprint stripes—but I had that all-too-familiar sense of racial antagonism. In those days, many African Americans had developed a kind of third eye or a third ear, and we just knew when racial animosity was at hand. At any rate, the couple got into their car, and as Lois and I started across the street, the driver gunned the engine and tried to run us down. Fortunately, we weren't hurt, but Lois was very upset. To me, it was just one more incident.

In my first summer, I was part of a program which brought students to the university for an eight-week session designed to give them alternatives to becoming leaders of the most powerful gang in the neighborhood, the Blackstone Rangers. I also got to study Chicago politics, particularly how the Daley machine could identify, recruit, entice and co-opt potential opponents.

I became the first black person to win the Finis E. Engleman Award, given by the American Association of School Administrators to the outstanding young administrator of the year. It was the same year the late Leonard Bernstein received the American Education Award from the same organization. When we saw each other at the cocktail reception preceding the dinner and award ceremony, we winked and burst into laughter at our private joke. We both recognized that it was time for a black person and a Jewish person to receive these awards. Later, we chatted about it.

Near the end of my study at Chicago, I was offered a very exciting position—a joint appointment as an assistant professor at Northwestern University and assistant superintendent of the Evanston School District. It seemed ideal to my professors, who had helped to arrange it, and to both universities, which were trying to forge stronger ties between theory and practice. It seemed ideal to Lois and me as well; we could remain in the midwest and close to our friends in the Chicago area. My meetings with Northwestern representatives went very well; they were excited about my joining them. My meetings with the superintendent were a disaster. He was arrogant, and he thought he knew whatever needed to be known about black people, racial integration, and school reform. It quickly became clear to me that neither I nor the university could work easily with this man. I declined the position, to the disappointment of Northwestern and to the surprise of the superintendent. I believe he thought I should have felt honored to have an opportunity to work with him.

Later, I was asked to meet some people in Atlantic City about the possibility of going to Philadelphia as part of the leadership team of Dr. Mark Shedd, a relative unknown who had recently been appointed to head the Philadelphia public school system. I had never heard of Dr. Shedd, but the educational reform movement in that city, under the leadership of school board chairman and former mayor Richardson Dilworth, had been in the news for some time. I spoke with Richard deLone, one of Shedd's assistants and a former *Philadelphia Bulletin* reporter, and agreed to visit Philadelphia to discuss possibilities.

Most of my professors and colleagues at Chicago were dubious. They wanted me to remain in the area and looked forward to the prospect of my becoming a powerful central office administrator in the Chicago public schools, with strong formal and informal relationships with the university community. The two people I trusted most (other than Vern Cunningham) had other advice. Frank Chase told me that he didn't know Mark Shedd, but he did know Richardson Dilworth and his record. If I went to Philadelphia, he said, I would learn more from Dilworth in five years than from anyone else in ten or twenty years. Dan Lortie, my chairman, did know Shedd, having taught him at Harvard. He echoed Frank Chase, telling me that the chance to work for and learn from Dilworth was a once-in-a-lifetime opportunity.

After several visits to the city, including one with Lois to check things out, I accepted the offer to become part of the new Shedd team. Lois and I sold our house, packed up our belongings, and set out for Philadelphia in July 1967. I had completed my Ph.D., she had completed her master's degree.

CHAPTER V
SCHOOL REFORM IN PHILADELPHIA

Ferment in Education in the 1960s

The public schools became the focus of national attention in the wake of two events: the 1954 Supreme Court announcement that segregated schooling was no longer acceptable, and the Russians' successful launching, in 1957, of the first space satellite, thus issuing a critical challenge to the quality of American science and mathematics.

In response to Sputnik, Congress quickly passed the National Defense Education Act, a multi-million dollar, multi-faceted effort to restore U.S. superiority in the space race, and public anxiety was quickly allayed when the United States managed to launch its own small satellite only a few months after Sputnik. The impact of the Brown decision was permanent, its consequences far more traumatic. The desegregation mandate was fought—state by state, and school district by school district—throughout the United States, on the streets and in the courts. Busing became the legal remedy of choice in many areas, but even in its early stages it was obvious that it could not by itself create equal educational opportunities for black children.

Integration efforts often meant disruption and hardship for black students and their teachers, not least because of the underlying assumption that their schools could not possibly be as good as or better than white ones. Black schools were closed, the staff reassigned, and black children forced to make long bus trips to schools where they were unwelcome and considered inferior. Because of their travel schedule, some black students were unable to participate in extracurricular activities (thus further alienating them from their new classmates), while others found that they were excluded from honors classes, popular clubs, and elective positions in the "integrated" schools. Unfortunately, many people, both black and white, mistakenly confused racial integration with quality education. The 1967 Civil Rights Commission report, entitled "Racial Integration in the Public Schools," helped to reinforce the idea that the Supreme Court had mandated that blacks and whites share classrooms, and that any other solution to the deficiencies of minority education was precluded. As one historian wrote, "Unable to imagine the possibility of a good school that had more blacks than whites, the commission's report was uniquely a document of its time, which could not extricate itself from the very racism it so passionately denounced."

Meantime, radical—and frequently conflicting—ideas about school reform began to emerge. The panic about restoring rigor to public school instruction had barely died down when a dramatically different approach to education was introduced—or, perhaps more accurately, reintroduced—with the publication of A. S. Neill's Summerhill in 1960. Inspired in large part by the theories of John Dewey, Summerhill was a small English school which prided itself on giving children almost total control of the pace and content of their learning. "Open education" or the "new progressivism" found a warm response among many teachers. The Summerhill idea was reinforced by a series of articles, some years later, by Joseph Featherstone, who described the British "infant schools" as models of informal, experience-based learning; Charles Silberman's book, Crisis in the Classroom (1970), popularized the idea further and extended it to high schools. Many of the experimental schools begun in the 1960s (including some in Philadelphia, which I will mention later) were based, in whole or in part, on the Summerhill philosophy, although some people expressed doubt about its relevance to poor and minority students.

Another prescription for reform, however, did attempt to address the needs of the disadvantaged. In 1962, Frank Riessman published The Culturally Deprived Child, in which he advanced the theory that poor children failed because of fundamental cultural dissonance between themselves and their teachers. Teachers should understand and accept lower-class differences, advised Riessman, and changes should be made in both methods and textbooks to make them "relevant" to students outside the middle-class norm. The idea of "cultural deprivation" evoked a different proposal, which was almost humorously antithetical to Riessman's: instead of trying to change the schools, perhaps the children themselves needed to be changed. Their families could not, or at any rate did not, prepare them properly for school, so someone else should try to do so. Thus *was born the idea of "compensatory education," which would prepare "culturally deprived" children to compete with their more privileged peers. It served as the rationale for Head Start, a federal program for pre-kindergarten experiences for young children from low-income families.*

Integration continued to be a controversial topic, although it was a virtual impossibility in many districts, where minority students constituted the vast majority of the public school population. In any case, many African Americans came to agree that it was insulting to think that their children could learn only when seated next to white students. As a result, "community control of the schools" became another of the myriad ideas for reform. In theory, of course, this concept was fundamental to the American system of public education—but it seemed to work much better in small, relatively homogenous towns than in cities of great size and diversity. Many urban districts, including Philadelphia, experimented with giving parents and community residents more of a voice in their schools. By far the most extensive attempt was in New York City. The city's board of education agreed to the election of community boards in three demonstration districts (one school, I.S. 201, became the symbol for them all); the teachers responded with a two-month strike in 1968; and the state legislature ended the venture the following year. The controversy continues.

Educational renewal was intimately connected to—indeed, it could not be separated from—the highly-charged political and social atmosphere of the day. The problems seemed overwhelming, the recipes for reform were numerous, the arguments about what to do were heated. In trying to sort out my recollections of the period from the late 1950s to the early 1980s, I decided to develop an outline of the dilemmas we faced and the recommendations that were made: in the 1960s, Philadelphia's school system tried them all.

❧❧

Philadelphia had become famous in the 1950s for the "renaissance" which had taken place under the leadership of Joseph Clark and Richardson Dilworth, two patricians-turned-politicians who had wrested power from the corrupt and uncaring Republican machine. Clark served as mayor from 1952 to 1956 before going on to the U.S. Senate; he was succeeded by Dilworth, who resigned in 1962, half-way through his second term, in order to run for governor of Pennsylvania, an election which he lost. The reforming zeal which had accomplished remarkable feats of urban planning and renewal—among them, the creation of a modern downtown center and the renovation of the colonial area around Independence Hall—became focused on the Philadelphia public schools.

Throughout the 1920s, the Philadelphia system was considered second to none, and middle class families often moved into the city to take advantage of the good education it offered. But with the Depression came cost-cutting and retrenchment, and the school system inevitably began to deteriorate. In 1934, the board appointed Add B. Anderson its secretary and business manager, a position which carried authority equal to that of the superintendent. For nearly thirty years, Anderson ran the school system almost singlehandedly, controlling the budget, purchasing, and school custodians, and the board was more than willing to go along with Anderson because he never caused them any trouble, least of all about money. In 1951, the Greater Philadelphia Movement studied the schools and concluded that they were doing their job, and the Chamber of Commerce stated that no new taxes were necessary for their support.

But not everyone was as satisfied with the schools as the GPM. In 1957, the first cracks in the educational facade began to appear. A new board member, the wife of a well-known real estate tycoon, announced that she was not at all satisfied with the way educational affairs were conducted or the reliability of the information dispensed by Anderson. Within months of taking her seat, she was calling for a "renaissance" of the public schools comparable to the one that had revived the city. Her investigation revealed for the first time many of the school system's inadequacies and became the basis for the largest school tax increase in decades.

Soon after, the Citizens Committee on Public Education hired as its executive director a young man named Robert Blackburn, and as it turned out he was an inspired choice. Bob (who became and remains one of my closest friends) had graduated from Oberlin College, but he had spent his junior year at Hampton Institute, where he was the only white student among 1,500 blacks. Passionately committed to improving both human relations and minority opportunities, Bob saw the job with CCPE as a way to forward both causes. Fortunately, he also had a well-developed sense of humor—a trait which would serve him and others well in the battles which lay ahead. One of his strongest allies was Bill Wilcox, the executive director of the Greater Philadelphia Movement, who persuaded GPM to undertake a new study of the schools. In a complete reversal of the earlier report, the 1962 edition had almost nothing good to say about their condition. With even the GPM advocating change, it became "respectable to criticize the school board." In a curious coincidence, 1962 was also the year in which Add Anderson, the symbol of scrimping and secrecy, died.

Under increasing pressure from a variety of groups—the NAACP and the teachers' organizations, as well as the Citizens Committee and the GPM—the board was forced to respond. It hired Dr. William R. Odell of Stanford University to undertake a comprehensive survey of the school system and established a Special Committee on Nondiscrimination to study the problems of de facto segregation in the schools. In a hitherto unimaginable flurry of activity, the board appointed a new superintendent, Dr. C. Taylor Whittier, planned a multimillion-dollar capital campaign, and called for dramatic increases in school funding.

But it was too late. The reform groups, spearheaded by Blackburn and Wilcox, had formed an Educational Home Rule Assembly in Harrisburg, the state capital, to hammer out a new "constitution" for the Philadelphia schools and get it approved by the state legislature. After many months of energetic effort in both Harrisburg and Philadelphia, the educational supplement to the Philadelphia Home Rule Charter was placed on the ballot and endorsed by Philadelphia voters in May 1965.

The members of the board of education must have often wondered how their formerly respected positions and routine jobs had become so perilous. As if they didn't have enough to contend with, the years from 1962 to 1965 were also fraught with criticism from the teachers and their demand for a collective bargaining agent. An election was held in early 1965, more than 95 percent of the 10,000 teachers voted, and the Philadelphia Federation of Teachers was declared the winner. The very next week, one of the PFT leaders, Celia Pincus, was in Washington, testifying before a Senate subcommittee—which included, to his embarrassment, Senator Clark—on the miserable conditions in many Philadelphia schools. When she was chastised by the president of the school board for "going public," she retorted that she had said the same thing to local authorities many times over, and nothing had been done. Superintendent Whittier inspected all the sites she had mentioned, and found that she was entirely accurate.

A key provision of the educational home rule charter was a new method of selecting school board members: the mayor was to appoint a thirteen-member nominating panel, naming four individuals himself, while the other nine were to be representatives of categories of organizations defined in the charter, such as "labor union council" and "public school parent-teacher association." The panel's mandate was to provide 27 names to the mayor (and a second set of 27) from which he was obliged to select the new board of education no later than mid-September.

On September 3, the new board was announced. The key appointee was

Richardson Dilworth, an attorney and Tate's predecessor as mayor; it was widely held that he had been intimately involved in the selection process and had agreed to serve only if he were made president of the board. Dilworth, a silver-haired aristocrat then approaching seventy, was an anomaly. In private, he was shy, had a self-deprecating sense of humor, and was unfailingly courteous; in public he was a fearless crusader for reform as well as a ruthless politician. Out on the hustings, his candid comments evoked both cheers and fury, prompting the wry observation that he had obviously been born with a silver foot in his mouth. At his age, most people would have retired from public life, satisfied that their place in history was secure, but Dilworth was unique: knowing that his old friends and allies were increasingly concerned about the local schools, he began a new career as an educational reformer.

The other appointees to the new school board, in addition to the two holdovers from the previous board, included two blacks (a minister and an engineer), an official of a major union, an internationally renowned physician, and two lawyers. Perhaps there still exists, somewhere in the city archives, Mayor Tate's list of the 54 candidates and the relevant biographic data. It could not have been an easy task, particularly given the high degree of public and private interest in the matter, to select a group of individuals who would be seen as sufficiently diverse, intelligent, responsible, and well-informed about educational issues. In these days of hyper-sensitivity to what is "politically correct," it is interesting to observe how well the mayor managed to distribute the appointments across the spectrum of age, religion, ethnic group, and social class—although modern feminists would undoubtedly condemn the absence of more women. At the time, there was near unanimous approval, particularly for Richardson Dilworth, whose effectiveness as mayor boded well for school reform.

Dilworth moved with characteristic vigor to apply his city hall experience to the massive challenge of restructuring a system comprising 280 buildings and 275,000 students. Even before the new board took over, he had appointed a blue ribbon task force to study the major aspects of the system. Although school officials served on each committee, it was clear that recommendations would be largely coming from non-educators. When the reports were released in late 1965, they were greeted with widespread praise and expressions of support for the proposed reforms.

It was never easy. In fact, Dilworth was quoted as saying that "Trying to move a system like that is like trying to move a roomful of Jell-O." One of his promises—to make the board's activities more open and accessible—was implemented almost immediately: board meetings were televised and some of them were held in schools around the city rather than at 21st Street. But his most urgent task was to find a superintendent who was in sympathy with the burgeoning reform efforts, able to pull them all together, and who could build on the foundation being laid for the new era. Dr. Whittier (by all accounts, a fair and decent man) did not appear to meet those criteria. The board reached an amicable agreement with him, which allowed him to resign gracefully and cleared the way for the "visionary leader" Dilworth wanted.

There are various stories about how Dilworth found his man—Mark Shedd—and whether or not he was the first choice. In any event, Shedd's appointment was approved by the board in December 1966. At the time, he was the superintendent in Englewood, New Jersey, where there were fewer pupils in the entire system than there were in a single one of Philadelphia's large high schools. Born and brought up in a small town in Maine, he had later served as the superintendent of rural schools in Connecticut; as his critics pointedly observed, there was nothing in his background to suggest that he could manage—let alone reform—the fourth largest school system in the country. But Shedd was young and personable, he had a doctorate from Harvard's Graduate School of Education, and he was Dilworth's choice. Although his appointment was not effective until September 1, 1967, Shedd visited Philadelphia regularly during the preceding months in order to obtain first-hand knowledge not only of the schools but of the neighborhoods surrounding them. By the time his term officially began, he had developed the main themes of his program—decentralization, community control, a new "professionalism," a new emphasis on "affective development." He had surrounded himself with a number of bright, young assistants (who became known as the "Ivy Mafia") and project directors to help him implement his goals. And he had also made it clear that the system's negative attitudes toward black students (already well over half of the school population), its neglect of their needs and aspirations, and its failure to encourage and promote black educators would no longer be tolerated.

At Dilworth's recommendation, Shedd immediately appointed a young man named Richard deLone as his executive assistant. DeLone had spent the previous two years covering education for the *Philadelphia Evening Bulletin*—his first job after graduating from Harvard and earning an M.A. at Berkeley. He was in his mid-twenties, tall and attractive (although he always looked somewhat disheveled), with indefatigable curiosity and an interesting combination of idealism and cynicism. DeLone's familiarity with the school system, as well as his reporter's brash indifference toward protocol and status, were enormously helpful to the incoming superintendent from the small town in New Jersey, but many people then and since have debated whether Shedd should have relied so heavily on the advice and opinions of his fearless but inexperienced aide. One observer darkly suggested that deLone "created" the Shedd image and Dilworth supported it.

Once Shedd took over the school district, deLone became the most powerful figure at 21st Street: the man who guarded access to the superintendent, who wrote all his speeches, who frequently made decisions on his behalf. Together with the other members of the Ivy Mafia, deLone encouraged innovative people and programs, making no secret of their scorn for the oldtimers, whom they held responsible for all the failures of the public schools. In some circles they were both hated and feared. The net effect was the creation of parallel lines of decision-making, formal and informal power structures, which both confused and angered many people throughout the system.

Mark Shedd retained several high-ranking members of the previous regime, but in May 1968 he announced that in order to save $3.5 million he was going to eliminate 381 positions, from the associate superintendent level down. Many of these positions were unfilled at the time, but needless to say this action created shock waves. Some people termed Mark "ruthless," but others called his decision "a hopeful sign."

As it turned out, deLone's career with the school district was relatively brief. In December 1967 he wrote a memo, intended only for discussion within the inner circle, in which he suggested that "Madison Avenue techniques" be used to raise public awareness of the financial needs of the schools. Six months later, Bill Ross (the labor representative on the board and no friend of either Dilworth or Shedd) unveiled a copy of the memo and gleefully read it aloud at the June board meeting. Expressions of shock were heard from the mayor and numerous other individuals—who by this time were hostile to almost everything Shedd stood for—and deLone's attitude was termed cynical, stupid, and sinister. A few months later deLone went off to work with Graham Finney, the former deputy superintendent for planning, as staff to the Commission on Decentralization and Community Participation.

By then, Rick deLone and I had developed a close relationship. He spent many evenings in my apartment discussing everything, but especially issues of race, class, and education. Rick died—much too young—in 1994. He was one of the least prejudiced people I have ever met, a decent human being who cared about people. As I noted earlier, it was

Rick who sought me out to discuss the possibility of my becoming part of the Shedd administration. Because I had gained national recognition when the American Association of School Administrators chose me as the 1966 winner of the Finis Engelman Award, my name had come to the attention of deLone and others at the School District of Philadelphia. I don't think it is immodest to say that I was considered an ideal candidate. I had had ten years of experience as a teacher and principal in Gary, Indiana; I was on the staff of the highly respected Midwest Administration Center of the University of Chicago; I was about to complete my work for a Ph.D. from the University; and I was black.

After a number of conversations and visits to the city, I accepted an appointment, effective July 1, 1967, as director of innovative programs, a position which placed me in charge of special programs funded by Title III of the 1965 Elementary and Secondary Education Act, magnet schools and community schools, and a myriad of other recent and disparate initiatives, such as the Intensive Learning Center, the Pennsylvania Advancement School, and the West Philadelphia mini-school. One of my early discoveries, as I became acquainted with the intricacies of the system's personnel practices, was that the title of "director"—to say nothing of the salary—was completely inappropriate for such heavy responsibilities. Within a few months of my arrival, I was made associate superintendent for innovative programs, reporting to the deputy superintendent for planning, Graham Finney.

Philadelphia was the first school system in the country to have a planning office. Its initial function was to draft the "Comprehensive Program for Innovation," the district's application for ESEA funds, and, once those were received, to supervise the establishment of these projects. It also included the Office of Research and Evaluation, which was responsible for gathering and analyzing testing, demographic, and other data, and the Office of Development, which coordinated program development with school building construction.

Graham Finney, once characterized as someone who "reminisced about the future," was a person with restless curiosity, keen intelligence, and the ability to grasp the inter-related factors and wider implications of a specific assignment—to see the big picture, so to speak. He had come to Philadelphia to work under internationally renowned Edmund Bacon (who played a key role in the municipal renaissance of the 1960s) in the city planning office, where he was involved in analyses of the consequences of urban renewal, such as manpower studies. He subsequently moved to the Philadelphia Council for Community Advancement to become its executive director, a post later held by Wilson Goode before he was elected as the first black mayor.

Recruited by Richardson Dilworth in 1965 to assist with the facilities planning aspect of the new school board's task force, Finney stayed on to supervise the drafting and implementation of the capital program and was appointed deputy superintendent for planning in 1967. From his experience in Bacon's office, he knew that the comprehensive plan for the city contained no allocations of land for school buildings, but throughout the arduous search for appropriate sites, he was well aware that where schools were located could either reinforce segregation or promote integration. Moreover, he understood that, in his phrase, "buildings drive programs": planning for new schools must first involve intensive consideration of new instructional practices, innovative programs, and alternative uses. Graham and my friend Dick Gilmore, who headed the administrative wing, were two people—perhaps the only two—in whom Dilworth had absolute confidence: he trusted them because of their intelligence and integrity, and possibly also because he felt more comfortable with people like himself who were not professional educators.

I became deputy superintendent for planning in November 1968 upon Graham's resignation (about which I will say more later). The staff was comprised of a motley group of people who prepared position papers on policy questions and served as consultants to local schools and community groups engaged in developing new programs. A few were experienced veterans of the school district, while others were brand-new to education. Like the "Ivy Mafia" in the superintendent's office, the latter group had degrees from first-class institutions, were extremely intelligent, had little patience with old-timers and bureaucratic wheel-turning, and were (in some cases) all but bereft of common sense. Some staff members had simply been transferred to the planning office when they did not fit in well in other branches of the administration.

The only black staff member was from a prominent Philadelphia family and had attended an Ivy League school; she knew little more about poor African Americans than her colleagues did. But there were also a few "real people," like the young man who had grown up in Kensington and knew the streets. He earned a law degree from the University of Pennsylvania but remained an activist, practicing public interest law and living in a poor, non-white neighborhood. Another person who comes to mind was an architect and planner, always calm and competent. Because she had always wanted to work with children, she went on to obtain a doctorate in early childhood education.

The Project Approach to Reform

In the l960s, as I indicated earlier, education throughout the United States was the focus of immense creativity and serious controversy. Everybody agreed that the schools were far from perfect—and disagreed on everything else: the problems, the causes, and the possible solutions. The reports from the Odell team and the board's own task force had produced ample evidence of what was wrong in Philadelphia, and a number of recommendations for reform. At the same time, more than one department of the federal government (particularly the Office of Education, which was administering the l965 Elementary and Secondary Education Act) and several large foundations were eager to dispatch large sums of money to bring about the New Day. Given the quantities of data and dollars, to say nothing of the sheer size of the city school system and the rising expectations of the community, the parents, and the teachers, it is no wonder that the Dilworth/Shedd administration appeared to be on a somewhat erratic course. It was rather like trying to build a bicycle and ride it at the same time.

Knowing that it would be impossible to turn the entire system around overnight, Mark and his advisers decided to develop or adopt a number of small-scale programs which they hoped would demonstrate desirable educational philosophies and practices, and thus serve as catalysts for change. Most of these programs were developed before I arrived and I therefore had little say in their purpose or structure, but since they were assigned to the planning office, they became my responsibility.

A theme which ran through many of them was the notion of a "curriculum of concern." In this view, the traditional emphasis on rules and facts had bored and ultimately alienated students and was therefore to blame for their poor achievement. The way to turn them on (a favorite phrase of the day) was by replacing old-fashioned "cognitive" education with "affective" education—focusing on the students themselves, their life experiences and emotions and values. Freeing classrooms from rigidity and repression was a goal which certainly appealed to Rick deLone, and it quickly became a rallying cry for numerous youthful rebels of the l960s.

Affective Education. The high priests of affective education in Philadelphia were Norman Newberg and Terry Borton. Newberg was a local freelance theater director who had developed a summer drama program for the Friends Neighborhood Guild, while Borton had studied education at Berkeley and written a *Saturday Review* article about his experiences as a student teacher in Richmond, a nearby blue-collar town.

He had come east to study at Temple University, but was sidetracked when he met Newberg and began working in his drama project. Rick—at that point still a *Bulletin* reporter—was so impressed with their ideas that he helped to get them federal funding and jobs with the school district. Together they worked away at curriculum development, teacher training, and spreading the gospel of relevance.

Intensive Learning Center. The school district had acquired an old factory building at Fifth and Luzerne Streets with the intention of using it as the site for developing and testing some educational innovations which could then be observed by teachers and perhaps replicated in their own schools and classrooms. The first program to open at Fifth and Luzerne was the Pennsylvania Advancement School (see below), and the second was the Intensive Learning Center. In 1968, it opened with a student body of 160 second-to-fourth graders; the following year it expanded its age range and its population. Students were selected from five nearby overcrowded schools for a two-year stay at the ILC, where they were assigned to one of three ungraded "houses" for instruction using computers, the discovery method, or a blend of the two.

Parkway Program (School Without Walls). Philadelphia's Benjamin Franklin Parkway, sometimes compared to the Champs-Elysées in Paris, is a magnificent avenue stretching from City Hall to the Art Museum and lined with various cultural institutions. During the heady days following Mark's official arrival, when the atmosphere crackled with new ideas, several of us were having a lunch meeting in the planning office, which overlooked the Parkway. Someone said "Why not use the Parkway as a school?" The proposal came from Cliff Brenner—former newspaperman, press secretary to Dilworth when the latter was mayor, and currently Dilworth's administrative assistant—who spelled out his thoughts in a lengthy memo to the deputy superintendent for planning, Graham Finney. Instead of constructing another expensive high school, why not schedule classes in the museums and other buildings along the Parkway and invite students from all over the city to attend? Science at the Museum of Natural History and the Franklin Institute, math classes at a big insurance company, literature at the Free Library.

The memo was dated November 13, 1967. Four days later, the new school administration found itself in the midst of a major crisis (which I will describe below), triggered by police reaction to a black student demonstration at board headquarters. Discussions of the Parkway proposal were necessarily postponed, and by the time it was made public the following February, Cliff had left the school district. The idea was received with widespread applause, but several of the institutions mentioned in the memo indicated that they were not committed to participation or had not even been contacted about it. Rick deLone quickly became the program's sponsor, but said that it should be planned by an educator. In short order, a person who had headed one of New York City's decentralized districts was identified, and John Bremer's appointment was approved by the board at its June meeting.

The first unit of the Parkway Program opened in February 1969, the students having been selected by lottery; two additional units began later that year. That it ever got off the ground is remarkable, considering Bremer's own list of the difficulties he encountered—little documentation of the proposal or its underlying philosophy, his own unfamiliarity with the city and the school system, no funds, halfhearted support from Shedd, the departure of Finney and deLone in the fall of 1968, and the waning enthusiasm for reform. Nevertheless, Bremer was a great success as a speaker and had no difficulty attracting parents, students, teachers—and the Ford Foundation. Bremer was eager to expand quickly because he feared that city hall would take over the school district and close down experimental programs such as his. Friction between him and Shedd had been increasing, and Bremer resigned in mid-1970, a few months after one of his schemes was eliminated by the superintendent. Like some of the other radicals who participated in the reform era, Bremer was both impatient and arrogant.

Pennsylvania Advancement School. This program had been established in North Carolina as an 11-week residential experience for seventh- and eighth-grade underachieving boys. Made possible by the state governor's blessing and a $500 thousand grant from the Carnegie Corporation, the school was a much-publicized laboratory for innovative teaching methods which, it was hoped, would spread throughout the state's educational system. After only a few years of operation, the school was in danger of closing because the political climate had changed—but just then Mark Shedd visited it, and was so impressed that he invited the director, Peter Buttenwieser, scion of a wealthy New York family, to bring the school and its staff to Philadelphia.

PAS, as it then became known, encountered difficulties almost from the start: renovations in the factory building were far from complete; the students, all of whom were in trouble at their home schools, were bused in from across the city; the PAS staff was almost all white and totally unprepared for dealing with the poor, minority, city children who constituted the student body; many teachers were anarchists in their approach to curriculum planning and could not bear the notion of lesson planning.

Although PAS garnered national publicity, local appraisal was less favorable: most students returned to their home schools with even more hostility to conventional education, and the lavish PAS budget was a sore point with many people, in and outside the school system. Because PAS had its own board of directors, it could and did operate independently—at least until problems arose. Then PAS was only too pleased to become my responsibility again!

Numerous other projects and programs were launched during the brief period between the final years of the old board of education and the departure of Shedd and Dilworth in 1971. Unfortunately, few succeeded in inspiring the hoped-for renewal of the schools, while many of them created antagonism and attracted critics both in and out of the school system. Not long before I left the school system in 1970, I was asked to speak to a group of 400 teachers and parents who were gathered to review and recommend alternative education programs. After warning them not to seek change simply for the sake of change, I told them exactly what I thought: "At least 90 percent of what passes for innovation is junk." By then, I had had plenty of experience on which to base my opinion.

One innovation which was an exception—it not only lasted but has been widely expanded—was the academy program. Deputy mayor Charles Bowser and I were concerned about the sad state of vocational training, which all too often was a dead-end track for young people judged incapable of academic learning and which seldom led them to jobs in the real world. We conceived the idea of installing in a regular high school an "academy" focused on a specific occupation, run by experts in the field, and equipped with the latest technical machinery and tools. The first one, the Applied Electrical Science Academy at the old Edison High School, was spearheaded by an executive of the Bell Telephone Company and Stuart Rauch, chairman and CEO of the Philadelphia Savings Fund Society—and very effectively run by a man who happened to be an Episcopal priest from the Netherlands. Today, there are similar academies in several high schools, training young people for up-to-date jobs: the Automotive Academy, more than half a dozen Business Academies, the Environmental/Horticulture Academy, the Health Academy, and three Hotel, Restaurant and Tourism Academies (one of which is located very near Philadelphia's new convention center).

From the start, Mark managed to exacerbate the fears that many people had of educational innovation and change. Even before he took office he had challenged the principals to become more "relevant" and "responsive," and his relations with them became so strained that at one point they threatened to join the teamsters union. There was widespread jealousy of the special attention and funding which the new projects attracted. Anger and suspicion were aroused by the Ivy Mafia and other newcomers who seemed committed to doing away with the conventional establishment altogether, as well as by Shedd's lack of attention to either the good work or the grievances of many who had toiled for years in the repressive old system. Celia Pincus, an outspoken leader of the teachers' union, expressed the concern of many, many people when she said she was tired of special little projects and was still waiting for a reform which would improve education for all Philadelphia's students and teachers.

Although there were various attempts to explore decentralization and introduce a measure of community control, they were episodic in nature and frequently influenced by political considerations. Graham Finney became so concerned about the lack of a strategy for approaching these issues that he decided in November 1968 to resign as deputy superintendent for planning and take over leadership of a school district commission to develop an orderly plan for system-wide change—one which, he hoped, would avoid the violent controversies which had surrounded the New York City experiment with its community school districts.

I was more than a little surprised that Graham, with whom I had worked so closely for almost eighteen months, gave me no warning of his impending departure. In fact, I first heard about it when a member of the board of education came to my office to tell me that Mark had announced the resignation, said he intended to initiate a search to fill the position, and reported that Dr. Watson would serve as "acting" deputy (without the deputy's salary) but would not himself be a candidate. The board member, Henry Nichols, wanted to know my reaction. I was furious! It seemed as though my credentials, the knowledge of the school system I had gained, my loyal service in one crisis after another, had all been ignored, and there was only one thing to do—to confront Mark with what I considered were his demeaning and devious actions. I stormed into his office to let him know that I wouldn't "act" for anyone and that he had no right to make these announcements without any discussion with me. He quickly reversed himself and said he would recommend my appointment as deputy superintendent for planning—but my relationship with him was never the same. My mood was not improved when, after my appointment was official, a delegation from Graham's office came to me to offer their assurances of loyalty and assistance—"even though you are not a planner"! The delegation consisted of young, inexperienced, privileged, Ivy

League graduates who were having their first exposure to poor urban youth and ordinary minority people. Most had never attended public schools.

Racial Issues

When the new school board took office, the school district's student population was 60 percent black, and its administrative staff, including principals, was almost 100 percent white. Moreover, although the Brown decision had ended legal segregation in education more than a decade earlier, few Philadelphia schools were integrated, and most of those attended by black children were characterized by deterioration and decay. It is quite likely that the combination of government pressure and reforming zeal (by white liberals, mostly) for the "culturally deprived" would eventually have effected some improvement in the educational prospects of black students, but happily, by 1965, black rage had boiled over and was making its own demands for equity. Minority staff members, community leaders, and the students themselves became crusaders—and in the process angered or terrified the white citizens of Philadelphia.

During the period between Mark's appointment and his taking office, he paid special attention to the problems in black schools and communities. In conversations and speeches which were widely reported, he promised that he would address minority concerns as quickly and effectively as possible. In some cases, the response was literally explosive. There was an enormous variety of demands and proposals and experiments—too many to describe in detail here—but perhaps the following paragraphs will serve as illustrations. With few exceptions, the calls for change were clustered in three areas:

1. Minority teachers and administrators wanted a chance to compete for promotions, and an end to unfair employment policies and practices;
2. Minority community members wanted better education for their children—and a voice in deciding what shape that would take;
3. Minority students wanted teachers who cared about them and a curriculum which taught them about their past as well as preparing them for their future.

This is, of course, a vast simplification of an extremely complex phenomenon: the emergence of a hitherto oppressed group to insist on the equality of opportunity which had supposedly been theirs for one hundred years. Affirmative action was just beginning to make its way into law and regulation; federal anti-poverty funds required community participation in determining how they were to be spent; both Martin Luther King and Malcolm X were urging an end to subservience and passivity. Added to the turbulence resulting from the clash of old and new administrative styles, the introduction of innovative programs, and the often condescending attitude of new school system personnel, the struggle for recognition of the legitimate demands of African Americans placed almost intolerable strains on the new school board and administration.

Before describing my experience in these three racially-charged areas, I must recount the events of November 17, 1967. They occurred less than three months after Mark took office, and they polarized not only the school district but the entire city. In fact, the suspicion, distrust, and outright hostility which were generated that day made all the subsequent activities of the school district infinitely more difficult and complex. The way it was handled became a political issue and ultimately led to Shedd's resignation, as well as the early departure of some of his key staff members, myself included.

Shedd's announced commitment to improving inner-city schools, and particularly to meeting the demands of students for a more relevant curriculum, quickly provoked reactions. His challenges to city-wide gatherings of principals and (later) teachers had already made many of them nervous and angry, and his policies became an issue in the fall mayoralty campaign. In contrast to the critics who feared change and wanted to continue doing business as usual, many blacks (and white liberals) were jubilant and determined to press their case.

Following a skirmish over curriculum at Bok Vocational School and a sympathy demonstration at the police administration building, things began coming to a head. When leaflets were distributed at ten largely black high schools, urging students to attend a rally at the board of education offices in support of a list of demands for educational change, it was clear that planning for a response by the school district was urgent. Principals were told to make every attempt to keep their students in school, a communications headquarters was set up next to Mark's office, and we discussed the situation among ourselves and with members of the police department's civil disobedience squad for many hours. Mark wanted to avoid a violent confrontation—and even hoped that the rally would result in a fruitful dialogue with representatives of the participating students—but Lieutenant George Fencl, head of the civil disobedience squad, insisted that some plainclothesmen were essential and would be backed up by uniformed police, nearby but out of sight of the demonstrators. Fencl was an eminently fair-minded person, widely respected by radicals, activists, and labor; he knew all the leaders by sight and by name. It was rumored that his promotions were held up because he was "not tough enough, not enough of a cop," but later a substantial cash award was established, to be given annually to the member of the police force who best exemplified the ideals by which he acted.

November 17 dawned bright and clear, and students began arriving at 21st and the Parkway around 10 o'clock. They were gradually joined by others until there were—estimates vary—between 2,500 and 5,000 teenagers, chanting and marching around the building. The kids were cheerful and the atmosphere was festive, rather like a football rally. Along with several white school district officials, I went outside to assess the situation and identify the persons authorized to negotiate. The late state representative, Dave Richardson, then just nineteen years old, was one of the leaders (it was on that day that we began a close relationship which lasted until his untimely death). At 11:30, Mark invited a delegation of students into the first-floor board room to begin a discussion of their demands: courses in Afro-American history, permission to wear African garb in school, and more black teachers, principals, and athletic officials. Nothing revolutionary, really—and several were already in the process of implementation by the school authorities. I was one of the several black administrators and board members who participated in the deliberations.

Outside, the students continued their march. Here again, accounts vary, but apparently Lt. Fencl thought that the situation was deteriorating and that the demonstrators were getting out of hand. Shortly after noon, just as we had reached agreement on eleven out of the thirteen student demands, the police riot troops were ordered into action and, directed by commissioner Frank Rizzo, began charging into the throng of students with billy-clubs swinging. Most of the people in the building watched helplessly but some of us—white and black alike—ran out to try and stop the melee. Security officers blocked us, advising us to remain inside lest we make the situation worse.

Frightened and angry, the students were forced in the direction of center city, only a few blocks away, and—quite understandably, I think—some of them damaged shop windows and cars along the way. When most of the students had gone, Freddie Holliday and I decided to leave the building. Exiting first, he was grabbed by one policeman with such force that he went headfirst down the stone steps and the sleeve of his overcoat was ripped out. Another cop came after me and desisted only after Bill

Meek yelled "Dr. Watson" in his loudest voice. By the end of the day, twenty-two persons had been injured and almost sixty arrested. Dilworth and Shedd, furious at the precipitous action of the police, did not rest until they had arranged to get all the students out of jail and ordered school buses to take them home, accompanied by school district personnel.

The city was divided overnight between those who were appalled by the brutal police actions and those who loudly supported Rizzo's successful quelling of the black student "riot." Journalists had a field day. Some citizens called for the resignation of the police commissioner, others for the dismissal of Shedd and Dilworth. Community Legal Services filed a suit against the police commissioner, but that case was dismissed by Judge Van Dusen; however, no students were ever brought to trial. For my colleagues and myself, the days and weeks after November 17 were harrowing; we were convinced that we were being followed and our telephones were tapped. Outside the windows of the planning office, we saw plainclothes detectives in an unmarked police car, sitting and watching for many months.....

It is interesting, but futile, to speculate on what might have happened, had the negotiations continued and the student representatives been able to report that their demands had been heard. We did our best to fulfill their perfectly sound requests, but no one could erase the bitter memories of police attacking young people or undo the evil miasma of racism which had been let loose in Philadelphia. In the months following, tension increased, and ultimately, when Frank Rizzo was elected mayor, he carried out his campaign promise to get rid of Mark Shedd.

Staffing Patterns and Policies

Nowadays, it is hard to imagine how difficult it was for black people to become principals and administrators in school systems during the period prior to the 1970s. There were few black principals, almost no black central office administrators, and literally no black school superintendents, except in the dual system of segregated schools in the south, where they were "superintendents of the colored."

When I arrived in Philadelphia in 1967, Robert Poindexter, the executive deputy superintendent, was the ranking black administrator. Poindexter had been a successful principal who was appointed an auxiliary district superintendent in 1963. When a group of black ministers, led by the Rev. Leon Sullivan, stormed a board meeting to insist that something be done to improve achievement in black schools, Bob was appointed to head the effort. With the aid and encouragement of board member Elizabeth Greenfield and teachers' union leader Celia Pincus, he created the Educational Improvement Program. Bob personally selected 60 master teachers from all over the city to train other teachers in effective methods with minority children, and the program was so successful that it was singled out for praise in the Odell Report. He became executive deputy superintendent under C. Taylor Whittier, Shedd's predecessor, but unfortunately, during the Dilworth/Shedd regime he was never given the responsibility or the respect which he deserved.

Philadelphia, like most public school systems, was permeated with racism. In earlier years, Jews had had experiences which were uncannily similar to those later encountered by African Americans. In the 1930s, when the system was dominated by Germans, Jews could not be appointed as principals, even when they scored at the top in the examination, nor were they considered for physical education positions. The first ones to become principals were assigned to the then-separate special education schools, and when Dave Horowitz became the first Jewish district superintendent, he was asked whether, since there were very few Jews in the area, he thought he could get along with the "others."

At the time of my arrival, Dave was the deputy superintendent for instruction and the highest ranking Jewish administrator; Dr. Ezra Staples, assistant superintendent for curriculum, was second. The Italians were represented by Mike Marcase, associate superintendent for facilities, and Matt Costanzo, a district superintendent. Next to Bob Poindexter, Thomas Watkins, director of non-certificated personnel, was the ranking black until I became an associate, then deputy, superintendent, and Dick Gilmore was appointed director of finance and later deputy superintendent for administration. There was a club for every racial and ethnic group: The Emerald Society (Irish), Sons of Italy (Italian), Educators Roundtable (black), and B'nai B'rith (Jewish).

For years, the personnel department maintained two lists of teachers and administrators, one white and one black, and assignments to schools were based primarily on race, not on qualifications or experience. Only through the unremitting efforts of Floyd Logan, founder of the Educational Equality League, were the dual lists abolished in 1938, but progress for blacks was painfully slow. Tanner Duckrey became the first black district superintendent; James Duckrey, his brother, and Marechal-Neil Young were the first junior high school principals. When Dr. Ruth Hayre was assigned to the all-girl William Penn High School in 1955, she became the first black high school principal—and immediately began to cause trouble by raising standards, requiring more rigorous courses, and demanding higher achievement. Prior to her arrival, little was expected of the predominantly minority student body.

Nevertheless, the school system continued to resist black progress. All tests for open positions or promotions had two parts: written and oral. It was the oral section of the test which tripped up minority candidates. Even when they scored exceptionally well on the written portion, their scores were not as good on the oral, which was administered and graded by those who already held sway in the school system. This way of doing things was reinforced because most minority staff members did not pursue advanced degrees, especially the doctorate. Convinced that another degree would do them little good, many people of talent and ability stopped far short of their potential.

Black coaches did not have a chance to coach varsity high school athletics. Even officials for athletic events were selected on the basis of race: very few, if any, black officials were "able" to pass the test until the late 1960s. John Chaney, now the well-known coach of Temple University basketball, was appointed during the Dilworth/Shedd era.

Fortunately, acceptance of the status quo was vigorously challenged by many tireless fighters for equality: Floyd Logan, who was still active when I came to Philadelphia; attorney Sylvia Meek, the education director of the Philadelphia Urban League; Cecil B. Moore, who frequently appeared before the board of education to issue threats of protests or legal suits. There were others who helped to open up the system. Two whom I especially admired were Celia Pincus of the Philadelphia Federation of Teachers, a feisty critic of the blatant discrimination against black students and educators, and Paul Vance, who organized the Educators Roundtable to promote opportunities for black advancement.

Paul Vance was frequently embroiled in controversy because of his outspoken criticism of both union contracts and administrative policies when he felt they ran counter to the interests of black students or teachers. In 1968, for instance, he advocated placing experienced teachers where they were most needed—which was clearly in poor, minority schools—although the contract limited involuntary transfer to first-year teachers. The following year, the board began moving black teachers to white schools as a desegregation maneuver—which Paul termed a "sham." Even worse, these teachers were replaced by (as Paul described them in a letter to the board) "poorly prepared, young hippie, draft-dodging, marijuana-smoking white hustlers," who were bent on "corrupting and further destroying the minds of our young people." The superintendent reprimanded him for his intemperate language, but Vance was only saying out loud what many others thought about the undue number of "hairy barefoots" who had briefly invaded the system, only to leave when it suited them.

Under the terms of the 1965 educational home rule charter, the board had been given the authority to appoint five percent of the staff without regard to civil service requirements and testing, and this proved to be a potent weapon against the racist processes of the personnel office. Dilworth issued an ultimatum—find more minority candidates—and the personnel department miraculously did so. Taylor Whittier is credited with the initial assault on racism, and his successor, Mark Shedd, began sending some people to Harvard and encouraging others to go back to school.

After I left the school district, I was able to make a small contribution of my own to helping black educators advance, through my participation in a Rockefeller Foundation program. It was established in response to a complaint that was common in the 1960s, not only in Philadelphia but throughout the country and in almost every occupational field: "It is impossible to find qualified minorities. Although there are now opportunities, blacks do not have sufficient education or experience for more responsible positions." Of course, no mention was made of biased tests, infrequent promotions, and other deterrents to youthful ambition. The argument was laughable in its circularity. "Under segregation, we kept you from becoming qualified. Now the rules have changed and we want to employ a black person—but we can't hire you because you don't have the proper experience!"

The program which, more than any other, broke the back of that argument, at least in education, was the Rockefeller Foundation Superintendents' Training Program. It was the brainchild of Charles Smith, an associate director at the foundation, who had earlier worked for Doc Howe when he was U.S. Commissioner of Education. Chuck Smith had also been a teacher, elementary school principal, and job corps supervisor and director. The program was elegant in its simplicity. Minority candidates (black, Latino, Asian, Native American) were recruited from all over the country. They could be assistant principals, curriculum specialists, principals, assistant directors, counselors, but all would have to have some experience, talent, appropriate education, and ambition.

After rigorous screening, up to ten individuals per year were selected for the program. Following an intense orientation period, they were given six-month assignments in each of two school districts where they worked for the superintendent or one of his key assistants. These assignments included exposure to a variety of functions and opportunities to interact with the board of education. Funds were provided to permit the interns to attend important conferences, such as the annual convention of the American Association of School Administrators, and—most important—each one received a handsome stipend to cover personal and family expenses.

A unique feature of the program was that each intern was assigned to his or her own mentor, an experienced educator. I was one of the two Rockefeller consultants who, in effect, worked *for* the interns. We were available 24 hours a day, seven days a week by telephone. We visited our interns at least twice a year in their assigned cities and school districts. We spoke with their supervisors to make sure the interns were having a good experience, and we helped the interns to interpret that experience. If necessary, the interns could meet with us at other times. The Rockefeller Foundation program was the most effective and efficient one with which I have ever worked.

Dilworth and Shedd's greatest legacy to the school system of Philadelphia was undoubtedly their insistence on equal opportunity—a legacy which culminated some ten years later when Dr. Constance Clayton was appointed superintendent, the first black and first woman in that position. When I met her in 1968, she was a "collaborator"—not a high-level position—but later she earned a national reputation as an associate superintendent for early childhood education, a program she pioneered with Milton Goldberg in Philadelphia.

Unfortunately, by the time that Dilworth and Shedd left the school system in 1971, a number of black educators had preceded them. Was the exodus caused by disillusionment with the "reactionaries," as board member Henry Nichols charged, or was it a result of the excellent opportunities in Philadelphia which prepared them for higher positions elsewhere? Actually, each case was different.

Marcus Foster, for instance, had been an outstanding principal of Gratz High School (although when his appointment was announced, a delegation of teachers and administrators had protested it at a board meeting) before becoming associate superintendent for community affairs, heading the office formerly known as intergroup relations. In the aftermath of the November 17 affair, his office was under increasing attack and he knew that his days at the school district were numbered. He came to me to seek advice. It happened that I had twice been recommended for and declined the superintendency in Oakland, California, but the chair of the search committee, who was president of the Spencer Foundation, had urged me to recommend a suitable black candidate. While Marcus was in my office,

I made a couple of telephone calls, to the Oakland board of education and the chair of the search committee. A few days later, Marcus flew to California and after an interview was offered the position. When we next met, I advised him to take his own immediate staff with him, to ensure loyalty in his office. Foster accepted the job and moved to Oakland, taking his secretary and Bob Blackburn along with him.

Gratz seemed to be a particularly effective springboard for minority advancement: Freddie Holliday, a member of Shedd's inner circle of assistants, succeeded Foster as principal of Simon Gratz High School before moving to Ann Arbor, Michigan, as deputy superintendent, then to York, Pennsylvania, and later Cleveland as superintendent; Oliver Lancaster, who became the principal after service as one of the field agents in the intergroup relations office, departed for the superintendency in Hempstead, New York. Sam Woodard was yet another. He had worked in my office as director of a successful program of making small grants in response to applications from principals and teachers, but I knew he wasn't happy in Philadelphia. For one thing, he had hoped to become superintendent of the Model School District, an idea which never materialized, as I will describe later. When Woodard announced that he was leaving for a professorial position in Illinois, the local newspapers quoted him as saying this was because of continuing racism in the system.

Paul Vance, who left to become executive deputy superintendent in Baltimore (and later superintendent in Montgomery County, Maryland) put it this way: "The talent was there all along. It just wasn't generally recognized." In 1976, a *Philadelphia Daily News* columnist wrote about Philadelphia's black educators—those who had moved on to better positions and those still in the system who were regarded by administrators as "tabbed for future prominence." He commented:

> In fact, black educators have not just sprouted like weeds in Philadelphia, only to be plucked away by other hands. There's nothing mystical about the increase in qualified black talent. It was planned that way... Watson is at the group center. Several, including [Strawberry Mansion Junior High principal] Gillespie and preschool specialist Dr. June Hairston Brown, credit him with helping their careers. Bernie is the sole remaining chief player from Mark Shedd's administration. Many of the younger folk still look to him for leadership and advice.

By the time that column appeared, I had been at Temple University for six years. I left the school district in mid-1970 for Temple's College of Education, where I had been asked to establish a graduate program in urban education.

Activism in the Black Community

Philadelphia is a city of many and diverse neighborhoods. In the 1960s almost all of them were constantly engaged in frenetic activity. All over the city, there were community organizations which were active and outspoken—in the Northeast, North Philadelphia, Mantua-Powelton, South Philadelphia, West Philadelphia, and Germantown—not to mention the numerous national or citywide organizations which kept the pot boiling. The civil rights movement was very much alive and the concept of community empowerment was thriving.

I spent a lot of time in the community. Paul Vance introduced me to the legendary attorney, Cecil B. Moore, who upon meeting me said, "Now you listen, you little——, we've heard about you and your reputation. You're supposed to be black but we'll see. We'll be watching your——. Glad to meet you and welcome to Philly." I really liked Cecil: he was what he was, and he made no apologies for it. The rambunctiousness that angered or irritated many people had just the opposite effect on me: Cecil B. Moore was a man with *style*, and I respected him for his courage and honesty. Charles Bowser, who was deputy mayor under Jim Tate (Dilworth's successor), and I established a relationship which lasted through many political campaigns and many summers at Martha's Vineyard. I respected him for his honesty and courage, but most of all for his ideas.

I think with admiration of many individuals whom I met in my first years here, and in Appendix III. I have listed those who were particularly prominent in the fight for educational equality, along with others who helped to create a political consciousness among Philadelphia's African Americans. Although Shedd had widespread support among Philadelphia black leaders, my knowledge of people and organizations in the black community was invaluable to his administration as attempts were made to implement its promises to improve the conditions of education for poor and minority children. The task was infinitely more complex than it might once have been. The school district could no longer simply impose its decisions on a given neighborhood: it had to work closely with newly-liberated residents who had strong views about what they wanted, although sometimes little or no experience in negotiation and compromise. I remember many of the struggles in which we engaged.

One particularly ambitious project, which ultimately came to naught, was the creation of a "Model School District." As the name implied, it was intended to be a showcase for many of the most promising innovations in education, as well as the first entire district under the at least partial control of the community. (At that time, the Philadelphia school system was divided into eight districts, each headed by a district superintendent, although most decisions remained firmly centralized.) A task force was appointed to study the possibility, and by September 1967 the committee had issued a report recommending that a large central portion of the city become the "Model School District." The area designated was enormous, reaching from North Philadelphia to well below city hall, and from river to river, but it was soon reduced in size, while retaining the essential element of "feeder patterns" (i.e., groups of elementary schools "feeding" junior highs which, in turn, would send their graduates to the same high school). This concept, like many others, has been re-introduced and is now known as "clustering."

Not much was done about the Model School District until interest in the idea was rekindled in the aftermath of November 17. Since the target area had been changed, it was decided to conduct a survey to determine local views on decentralization and educational priorities, but the survey was embroiled in controversy from the start. Operation Feedback, as it was termed, trailed on for a couple of years under the aegis of Area Wide Council, but in the end the Model School District was quietly abandoned. One might wonder why the opportunity for a louder voice in educational affairs should have been allowed to slip away or even actively opposed by local residents. Many apparently felt that the board of education was trying to evade its own responsibilities, asking them to undertake tasks for which they were not yet prepared; when failures occurred, as they almost certainly would, the board could then figuratively shrug its shoulders, say "I told you so," and blame the community for its insistence on taking over.

North City Congress, headed by attorney Alvin Echols, was an organization which offered legal, financial, and other kinds of professional service to community organizations. In a brilliant critique of the 1967 report on the Model School District, NCC provided a somewhat different explanation:

> ...the School District wants community involvement in, and support of, the existing evolutionary educational process which it feels is basically sound...The community wants revolutionary change and improvement in an educational system which it feels is somehow basically unsound... MSD, when brought to the community by Dr. Mark Shedd...was a vaguely articulated concept. In real fact, it was two phrases—'administrative decentralization' and 'community participation'—tied together by publicity... In general terms, the School District wants to change the style in which education is delivered, while the community wants to change the product—education—which the School District delivers....

There was another attempt at creating a new district, although for quite different reasons. With vigorous support from a white member of the board of education, plans were made to divide District 4, the largest of the eight, into two districts: one containing the white neighborhoods on its western fringes, and the other comprising largely black areas. Joe Lapchick, Jr. (son of the famous St. John's University basketball coach) was recruited from Harvard to head the new district—but that idea, too, died aborning. Dr. Ruth Hayre, the district superintendent, out of whose territory it would have been carved, would simply not allow it to happen. Nor would her constituents—the parents, churches, and community organizations in the area—who saw the idea for what it was, a blatant attempt to segregate black and white schoolchildren.

In many neighborhoods, the residents simply wanted to have the local school building available for other uses. In fact, one of Dilworth's task force recommendations was that some schools be designated as "community schools," and federal funding was obtained for this purpose. In the fall of 1966, four elementary schools (Childs, Locke, Ludlow, and McMichael) began staying open after regular hours to offer recreational and educational programs, counseling, and health services to neighborhood residents. The situation at a fifth school, Hartranft, was complicated by the fact that the building was scheduled for replacement in 1968. Since community schools constituted part of my "portfolio," I not only supervised the four schools which were going smoothly but became involved in the battles over plans for the new Hartranft. It soon became obvious that a separate building would be needed for the variety of activities desired by neighborhood residents, but planning meetings were marked by controversy and often competition among rival "spokesmen" for the community. As if local jockeying for power were not enough, the Hartranft group also found itself in arguments with bureaucrats in Washington. Eventually, both the school and the community center were built, but many people, including me, were nearly worn out in the process.

The Clarence Pickett Middle School in Germantown had been intended as the first community middle school in Philadelphia. First an ad hoc and then a regular advisory board had been organized, and construction had begun, by the time Paul Vance was appointed principal/planner in 1968. Paul was perhaps the most militant black in the area, certainly in the school district. He was very active in the local chapter of the NAACP under Cecil B. Moore, and he had participated in the eight-month-long picketing of Girard College in 1965. As a native Philadelphian, Paul knew the schools intimately—he had attended three, he had been a teacher for nine years, he had served in the curriculum office "downtown," and he had been an auxiliary principal. Quite possibly, it was this intimate acquaintance with the school system that aroused his ire and prompted his frequent public denunciations! In 1965, he was appointed principal of a largely white elementary school complex in Germantown, Cook-Wissahickon—and to everyone's surprise, in that racially sensitive period, he quickly became a favorite with teachers and parents, and they were rather distressed when he moved on to Pickett.

Paul Vance became a member of my staff during the planning phase of the school, and I came to know him very well. Somehow he never seemed to have as much difficulty working with his community board as some of the other school district personnel, both black and white. Pickett opened in September 1970, only a few months behind schedule, and at the time it was considered an excellent example of innovative school architecture.

Student Demands

In the months and even years that followed the events of November 17, 1967, the schools were frequently the scene of student unrest, demonstrations, and confrontations between school staff and students or members of the community. On one occasion, Bob Poindexter and I were called to restore order at Overbrook High School, and I personally had to take over two high schools when their administrators lost control. These incidents were not unusual. Tensions, often racial in nature, existed at South Philadelphia High School, Bartram, West Philadelphia, Olney, Edison, George Washington, and a number of junior high schools.

Bok Vocational High School was the focus of a particularly alarming battle. It was attended by black students from all over the city. One day, residents of the white neighborhood through which they passed began claiming that they were causing trouble en route and threatened revenge. Hundreds participated in "white power" marches. Because the situation seemed to be growing out of control, both Bok and South Philly were closed (when they reopened the black students attending Bok were bused in and out under police escort, a practice which continued for years). The mayor considered declaring a state of emergency. In Harrisburg the governor announced that he was ready to send in the state police and the national guard. (Amidst the conflict, some 400 South Philly seniors—half black and half white—took a trip to Washington and reportedly had a great time.)

Police monitoring of a wide area, and occasional arrests, gradually quieted the community, but it was grimly amusing to learn that the white militants held the mayor, the school board president, and Cecil B. Moore equally responsible for the problems in South Philadelphia. Not so entertaining was the running battle with the mayor, who tried to capitalize on outbreaks of racial tension—in or outside the schools—by threatening to have city hall seize responsibility from the board of education.

Benjamin Franklin was one of the two high schools I had to take over. It was something of a dumping ground for black male students from all over the city, a trade school with a limited curriculum and low standards; its graduates were not expected to attend college. Most of the staff members were white, and some were by turns hostile, condescending, contemptuous, and afraid of their students. One teacher told me that he was very well-educated—indeed, he had studied at the University of Padua—but that he could not teach these young men because they were inferior, incapable of understanding government and history. I was so enraged by this man's attitude that I told him that I would bet $100 that I could teach his course and that the students would understand and learn. He refused my challenge. These "inferior" students were furious about the kind of education he represented, and fascinated by their own heritage. Many were members of the worst gangs in the city, but in school they were absolutely loyal to a fellow student named Ronald White, electing him president of the student body.

Ron was intelligent, articulate, and the beneficiary of advice and support from a number of adult activists: members of a public housing tenants' council, Bill Meek and Walter Palmer of Area Wide Council, Mattie Humphrey, Ed Robinson. There were even a few faculty members on his side. When the board of education held a meeting at Franklin, Ron told the members about the inadequate curriculum, the lack of black administrators, the poor condition of the building. Nothing happened, and the students decided to protest by occupying the school overnight. When they emerged the next morning, there was no sign of trash or damage—thanks to Ron's leadership.

The situation simmered for several days, with support from community leaders. When Mark Shedd asked someone to go to the school and manage the situation, I volunteered. When I got there, the principal was locked in his office, while teachers, students, and parents were milling around in the halls. I informed the principal that I was taking charge and asked him to stay where he was until the end of the day. I didn't want his presence to inflame the situation. He was not a bad person or a bad principal, just out of his element in those turbulent times. After conferring with the coach and several teachers, I heard about Ron White, including the fact that although he was not a big dude, he had once headed one of the largest and most feared gangs in the city. Ron was smart and cooperative. What he told us about the school was confirmed by other students, teachers, and a number of parents and community leaders. Over a three-day period, we waited it out until a new assistant principal was assigned. At the end of the semester (and after consultation with school students and others), the principal was replaced by Leon Bass. Dr. Bass, who had led some of the first American troops into Buchenwald at the end of World War II, stayed at Franklin for many years and under his administration, the school met many of the student demands.

One battle which Ron did not win was the one to change the name of his school. He and the other students began to chafe at being associated with Franklin, who, whatever his other virtues, was a slaveowner. One day, after several weeks of planning, new Malcolm X banners, T-shirts, sweatshirts, and caps proclaimed that Ben Franklin High had become Malcolm X High. The principal, Bass, had insisted on a secret ballot, and Malcolm had won by a more than two-to-one vote, but only the board of education could make the change official. The scene at the board meeting, as described by newspaper columnist Claude Lewis, was the stuff of high drama. A white Franklin teacher testified, then Ron White, and finally Leon Bass—but to no avail. Lewis wrote:

> ...a negative decision had been reached in a back room long before the public meeting. Somehow the board reasoned that it was better for a school for blacks to be named after a white man who traded in slaves than to rename it for a man who established a sense of pride and self-respect for millions. This kind of reasoning is precisely why students—white and black alike—are rebelling all over this nation....

Ron went on to Wesleyan University in Connecticut (on full scholarship), from which he graduated in three years, and then earned a law degree from the University of Pennsylvania. I'll never forget the day he made a special trip to Philadelphia in order to warn me not to continue visiting certain housing projects. With the rising drug activity, he told me, they're just too dangerous and you might get killed. Today, Ron is an attorney, married to a physician, and the father of three children, one of them a law student at Harvard.

I found myself back at Ben Franklin the day after Martin Luther King, Jr., was assassinated. Along with Ed Robinson, Mattie Humphrey, Rose Wiley, and other community leaders, I roamed the halls trying to get a sense of how the students were reacting. At noon, there was an assembly: every seat was filled, people were standing two-deep along the walls or sitting on the floor. After several speeches, Mattie came up to me and whispered: "It's up to you now, Bernie. We have to keep these young men in the building. It's on you now." I knew what she meant. Rumors had been circulating that the students were going to move downtown and trash center city, and the police were mobilized in buses near the school or watching the building from across the street. Some students were ready to explode with rage at the King murder; some police officers were nervous, frightened of black male students who belonged to the biggest, baddest gangs around. It was a recipe for disaster, one which could be much worse than the chaos at the school board building the previous November.

I walked to the microphone, every eye upon me. The silence was profound, yet full of tension and threat. As I looked out at all those young men, I saw pain and uncertainty, hurt and vulnerability, behind their masks of harsh, fierce anger, and I paused to stay in control of my own emotions. Then I said something like this:

> ...They say a man ain't supposed to cry. But, as any one who has heard the blues knows, it's all right. Sometimes you have to do it in the darkness and privacy of your bedroom. Sometimes, when you are with the only person you trust, the one you know will always be there. But sometimes it's all right to let it out, because the pain is so great that you can't hold it in and you need to let people know that you hurt. This is one of those times. They have killed our leader, a man who believed in peace, who hated violence. They did it, and we hurt... I want to scream, I hurt so bad, and I know it's all right to cry....

A sigh swept the auditorium, as the tension was transformed into a blanket of mutual support. Amen's came from those on the stage, and then there was attention. I talked for about ten minutes about how to handle our pain, our anger: we would not let "them" goad us into dishonoring what Dr. King stood for; we would continue the struggle, knowing that you could kill a man but not an idea. I told them how good it felt to be able to share my grief with them, that we needed to cling to one another, that we could be in control of our destiny. I thanked Ron for inviting me to speak and sat down to a standing ovation.

Ron was immediately on his feet, in charge. He gave instructions on how the building was to be vacated and he reminded them of their responsibility. The students departed in perfect order—and the waiting police did not have the slightest excuse for action. I was so proud of those young men. They knew they were in control of the situation that day. I sat in front of the building until every student and teacher had left. I could barely control my anger and my tears.

Germantown High School was another "hot spot." The late David Richardson (until his death a senior member of the Pennsylvania House of Representatives and two-term president of the National Council of Black State Legislators) had always been involved in the Germantown High School area. He wanted to improve the school, but his methods—such as trespassing on school property without permission of the principal—sometimes got him in trouble. Yet what he was fighting for was what the school needed: better discipline, more supportive teachers who had high expectations of students, mutual respect between teachers and students, student input into school decisions, Afro-American studies. He was one of the people who encouraged the students to protest. One day, they took over the school: the student leaders retreated to the "crow's nest" on the top floor, and the rest of the students roamed the halls and grounds, doing whatever they wanted to do. The principal and vice principal had completely lost control (although the vice principal had some influence).

By now, I was the designated hitter. When I was dispatched to the school, I took Al Sessions with me. Al was a big, bright, articulate, funny man who had lost an arm while serving as an officer in the U.S. Army—and he was a magician with young people. I had recruited him to my office from Wanamaker Junior High School in North Philadelphia, and we had become friends because of our shared interests in jazz, sports, books, ideas, and students. Together, we had to take the school back and get classes started.

When we arrived at Germantown High, Inspector Tommie Frye of the Philadelphia Police Department was on the scene. He had restored order, but classes were not being attended and the air was filled with tension. Frye briefed us, told us who the student leaders were and where they were headquartered. He was disgusted that principals and teachers could not handle a school like this, where the students were decent and had certain advantages. He didn't think their demands were outrageous, but he felt that they were not going about them in the proper way.

After reporting to the principals' office and informing them that we were now in charge, Al and I went to the "crow's nest" to meet with the student leaders. Our first agreement was that we would listen, that no spectators would be allowed in the meeting, and that everyone would be treated with respect. After two hours or so behind closed doors, we agreed that no further progress could be made until classes resumed. Within ninety minutes, Inspector Frye had cleared the grounds, the student leaders had emptied the halls, and the regular schedule was restored.

Al and I resumed our meeting with the student leaders, and by the time the school day ended, we had worked out a joint plan to address grievances. The two of us then met with some of the teachers, the administrators, and the counselors. One teacher, a union representative and a coach, was very helpful in this process. He had excellent rapport with both students and teachers. Although he was white and racial tension was an underlying factor, this did not affect his relationship with the leaders of the student body. He was very popular. Since Germantown was one of the magnet schools which reported to my office, I already knew some of the staff members, like the retired police detective who lived in the neighborhood, whose children had attended the school, and who was well-liked by the students.

Later that afternoon and evening, Al and I conferred with Dave Richardson, members of the Young Afro Americans, the Reverend Nichols (a black school board member whose church was next to the school), and other knowledgeable people. When the day was over, we told Inspector Frye that we would not need a police presence the next day, but that it would be helpful if they were on call. The students generally respected and liked Frye, unusual for a police/student relationship at this time.

The following morning, Germantown opened on time and without incident. Al and I stayed at the school for a week to work through the details of our agreement with the staff and students. We never needed the police again. Within a week or so, things were not only back to normal, the school was better because of the increased sensitivity and know-how which the students and staff had acquired. One unanticipated outcome of this incident was the good relationship I developed with Inspector Frye, who provided sound advice and who offered to drive me around the city to observe schools and neighborhoods which were potential trouble spots. He was the only black police inspector at the time.

In the fall of 1969, trouble arose at West Philadelphia High School when the Black Students Union, supported by a community group, Citizens for Progress, demanded the transfer of a white social studies teacher who, they claimed, was irrelevant and incompetent. (The school's principal, Walter Scott, was a white man who was very popular in the school and the community.) Quality education, not race, was said to be the issue, and school board member George Hutt agreed, noting that this teacher was merely a symbol for instructors throughout the system. The teacher's classes were boycotted, the school was surrounded by protesters and pickets, the principal recommended the transfer, and the union voted

9 - 1 to strike if the man were transferred. At the end of two weeks, Dilworth ordered an end to the boycott while the board and school officials discussed the question, but students continued their protest and the school was closed. The board decided to obtain an injunction against the demonstrators—and at Marcus Foster's and my urging—against a teachers' strike as well. In the midst of all this turmoil, we were in the final stages of a campaign to win support for a $65 million bond issue.

Angry debate continued, in the newspapers and at public meetings. When Shedd finally announced that the teacher would not be transferred, he was censured by both the union (for the delay in making the decision) and the protesters. But although there were further rumblings, the worst of the storm was over. With the help of a team from our intergroup relations office, led by Marcus Foster and Bob Blackburn, two lengthy sessions were held on successive days, first with student representatives and then with the entire high school staff, to obtain recommendations for improvements. Finally, in January, an "Atmosphere for Learning" workshop was convened: the superintendent, Mark Shedd, his cabinet officers, and nearly thirty other top administrators met with West Philadelphia staff, parents, students, and community leaders. Trudy Haynes, then reporting on education for KYW-Channel 3, covered the conference and its conclusions, and did so in a wonderful, sensitive way. She had contacts and was trusted.

I still have a scrapbook in which a member of my planning office staff placed newspaper clippings about the West Philadelphia High School confrontation. She also included notes of her interviews with three of the key players: the principal, the district superintendent, and Marcus Foster, the associate superintendent for community affairs. Reading them is a depressing experience and a poignant reminder of the many, many days I spent listening to angry people (on all sides), observing situations and discussing the best way to restore order and get on with educating students. "There were many times when the situation could have been defused," Foster is quoted as saying about West Philly. "It should never have developed in the first place." He could have made the same comments about the unrest in high schools all over the city, but there wasn't enough wisdom, patience, or vision to make that possible.

It still amazes me how truly obtuse people could be. For instance, the major foundations had "discovered" public education, especially for the disadvantaged, but their way of gathering information was exasperating and, at times, infuriating. The top people from several big foundations—Ford, Carnegie, and Rockefeller—who visited Philadelphia to discuss programs for poor and minority students were all white. Moreover, the people they wanted to talk to were all white: Peter Buttenweiser, Graham Finney, Mark Shedd, Rick deLone, John Patterson, and white board members. Not once did they spend time with Bob Poindexter, Ruth Hayre, Fred Holliday, or any of the other people who had first-hand experience with minority problems. It seemed never to occur to them to seek out people who actually knew something about the realities of urban education, about the anger and frustration which were beginning to boil over almost daily in our schools.

People like Paul Vance, who had been appointed principal of two white schools, Cook and Wissahickon, against the wishes of the residents, but who had won them over. When he was re-assigned, the parents at Cook-Wissahickon did not want him to leave and protested his departure.... People like Marcus Foster, who became principal of Gratz High School over the objections of the teachers and administrators and turned them into his allies and supporters. He went into the community, won the loyalty of both parents and students, and transformed the school with a lengthy series of innovations. But only after he won the prestigious Philadelphia Award for his work at Gratz did people begin to think he had something to say about urban education.... Those outside funders never talked to me, either—despite the fact that, of all the new people brought in by Dilworth and Shedd, I was the only one who had been a teacher, counselor, department chair, and principal, in addition to working with gangs.

Even good people who were trying to be sensitive to the new realities were often unintentionally insulting. I have on file any number of letters asking me to consider new positions, like one entitled "inner city consultant to the faculty" in matters of program revision. The qualifications included being black, knowing the ghetto, youth, intelligence, and the ability to communicate clearly with the members of an academic community. What especially infuriated me was the following sentence: "A regular faculty appointment is possible if the person has the appropriate academic credentials, but it seems more likely that a title such as "Lecturer" will be attached to the position." Was I over-reacting to see, between the lines, the implication that few blacks would meet the standards for a "regular faculty appointment"? Or, knowing very well the incredible pecking order in a university, to wonder just how sincere they were if they were expecting a "lecturer" to influence faculty thinking?

Times changed, of course, but the issue of race never went away. Although there was suddenly an enormous demand for African American "superstars" to remedy the years of smug superiority and unconscionable neglect of black concerns, it was a bittersweet reversal. Some of the letters I received implied that I was the only one who could possibly do the job the writers had in mind, but of course that was nonsense. There were many qualified blacks, and I was always happy to make referrals whenever it was appropriate.

≈≈

As I look back on my three short years with the school district, from the perspective of twenty-five years, I remember the words of a school district colleague who said, "The wonder is not that the schools work so badly, but that they work at all." Things were always moving too quickly. There was never enough time to ponder, analyze, discuss the problems and agree on the best, the most coherent and comprehensive strategies for solving them. Before we could even begin, a new demand or threat resulted in a call to battle stations. It was an era of constant, never-ending change—in Philadelphia, the nation, and the world. Change which confronted everyone almost daily and required immediate response. Change which brought confusion and conflict. Change which opened doors of liberation, and also brought death in the streets and in Vietnam into the family living room. Some developments aroused hope; others, despair. Some events were the fulfillment of lifelong dreams; others, the stuff of nightmares.

As I have reflected on those years, I have been struck by the enormous number of personal tragedies which later afflicted my colleagues. I do not offer any explanations, simply some observations. Marcus Foster, who went to Oakland on my recommendation, was assassinated by the Symbionese Liberation Army, already notorious for their kidnapping of Patty Hearst. His assistant (and my dear friend), Bob Blackburn, was seriously wounded in that incident. Bruce McPherson, whom I had recruited from the University of Chicago to serve as associate superintendent for policy planning and development, later took the superintendency in Ann Arbor, Michigan, and saw his school administration building burned to the ground by arsonists. A promising young teacher who had developed his own curriculum committed suicide after going to Ann Arbor at McPherson's invitation. Freddie Holliday, Shedd's only black assistant, took his own life while serving as superintendent in Cleveland. Many marriages were ruined and relationships soured. And people like my friend Ophie Franklin were advised to leave town or else place his family in jeopardy. There are many more examples.

Those years with the school district were exhilarating and exhausting, a never-ending test of energy and imagination. The fourth largest school system in the country was struggling to undertake long-neglected duties, to restore hope and vitality to the educational process, to repair and renovate curriculum as well as buildings. Hundreds of thousands of people were involved; millions of dollars were at stake. It would have been a Herculean task at the best of times. In that chaotic decade, national and local events conspired to make success all but impossible.

Nevertheless, for those of us in the inner circle, working with Mark Shedd was exciting. He regularly met with his cabinet and kitchen cabinet in his home, in restaurants over dinner, on trips to conferences. Richardson Dilworth, too, invited us to his home for private strategy sessions away from the ears and eyes of outsiders, and he sometimes regaled us with personal anecdotes about leading citizens and prominent Philadelphians. Dilworth insisted that we take time off because of our impossible schedule, and when he went away on one of his frequent vacations he would send us cards and brief notes. I still have a package of those missives, including one from Palm Springs in which he complains that the place was being invaded by 10,000 hippies.

Dilworth was an amazing man, whose self-deprecating good humor sustained us through more than one crisis. He was a fighter, a combatant who relished combat, a competitor through and through. His marine training and experience, coupled with his patrician upbringing and education, made him a formidable ally and a frightening foe. My advisers at Chicago were right: I learned more from this man in three years than I would have learned from anyone else in ten. The knowledge he imparted about this city and its people enabled me, an outsider, to place in context the major events confronting the school district, the citizens, my family and me.

What I resented, then and now, about the Dilworth/Shedd years was the fact that most of the people who came to Philadelphia to reform the school system really believed that it could be fixed in a few years. In spite of their good intentions, they didn't have a clue. We were facing the legacy of decades of discrimination, isolation, unequal allocation of resources, trained incompetence. Teachers and administrators, often through no fault of their own, knew little about poor minority youngsters: how to motivate them, what to expect of them, how to deal with wide variations in their backgrounds.

Many newcomers had grown up in an environment of affluence and comfort, even privilege, but their efforts were often destructive. Yet with their outstanding education and youthful zeal, they were certain they had nothing to learn from people whom they considered to be their inferiors. Perhaps most disappointing was their lack of staying power. When they tired of this interlude, they could and did walk away to begin another career and continue the ascent up the ladder of success. Having managed to avoid Vietnam, they could resume their lives, get a haircut and shave, trade in their sandals for Gucci loafers, and become bankers, lawyers, business executives, whatever.

I see that same mistake being made today, not by idealistic young people, but by a corporate community and political leaders who are unwilling or unable to sustain the long, arduous task of doing what is necessary to give this country's most disadvantaged youth, the poor, a real shot at education. The kind of education that will enable them to compete in the world of the 21st century, a world like nothing we have experienced before.

CHAPTER VI
POLITICS IN GARY AND PHILADELPHIA

Gary

For my generation, politics was not a hobby, something you participated in if you happened to be interested. In my family, voting was taken seriously. Too many black Americans could not vote, and too many had been brutalized or killed for trying to exercise their constitutional right. My parents felt that voting was a duty as well as a right and, as I matured and learned more about the history of this country, I began to understand why they felt so strongly about it.

In my neighborhood on the east side of Gary, we were familiar with the voting habits of each ethnic and racial group. The Democratic party, which dominated politics in the city, approached everyone, seeking their support for the endorsed slate of candidates. Because my parents had moved to Gary only sixteen years after the city was founded, they were well known in the neighborhood, and we knew all of the politicians, the elected officials, some of whom lived nearby, and those running for office. It was all very well organized, with certain groups dominating the political process. For many years, it was the Poles, with token participation by other groups. Vice and crime were organized just as efficiently. Blacks controlled the numbers rackets, called "policy" in those days—until it was discovered how profitable it was. Later, the black policy barons were assassinated, or they disappeared or retired or went to work for the new leaders in organized crime.

Although African Americans had comprised almost one-third of the earliest (1906) group of settlers in Gary, they had few elected representatives and much of their participation in public life was through patronage. Most of the city's officials were white, although an informal history of

Gary states that as early as 1922 there was an African American alderman, a doctor on the board of health, and a police officer (not an unimportant position in the Prohibition era). The real beginning of assertive black politics coincided with the organization of the Oldtimers Club by Edward "Doc" James, a labor organizer who later became the business agent of a teamsters union local. James threatened private firms with boycotts, pickets, and worse, unless they hired black truck drivers and clerks. His attempt to integrate the teamsters union was aided by the fact that independent trucking companies had begun to hire non-union black drivers. As I mentioned earlier, I purchased a home in Tolleston from Michael Sawochka, head of the local teamsters union. Sawochka's son succeeded him in this office and finally integrated the union.

When I returned from military service in 1954, I attended the University of Illinois. I had intended to enroll at the University of California, Berkeley, but physicians treating my father had advised me that he had less than six months to live. If I wanted to spend time with him, I would have to attend a university closer to home and to the veterans' hospital in Waukesha, Wisconsin. Within a few weeks of my arrival in Gary, I was enrolled at the University of Illinois.

One day, while I was studying in my apartment just off campus, my mother called to give me a message: the head of the Democratic party on Gary's east side had informed her that I was being slated for city council. I was to be the endorsed candidate. My mother said to expect a call from him. The call came through later that afternoon: I was told that I was a favorite son of Gary, a person who was from a family of loyal Democrats, who had grown up in the neighborhood, stayed out of trouble, gone to college, and served his country with honor. The party was therefore slating me for city council, which in those days was tantamount to election. He was honest, admitting that things had changed and it was time for a black councilman from the east side.

I thanked him, but said that I was not interested in elective office at this time. I told him that I planned to pursue further graduate training and was not sure when I would return to Gary. After a lengthy discussion, during which he failed to convince me to change my mind, he asked me who I thought would be a good candidate. I said that my choice would be the incumbent, David Mitchell, a Fisk University graduate who, it was said, could never be shut up. Not until later did I discover that the party leaders wanted me to run against him. Dave was a fine person, a good family man and active in his community, Ironwood, one of the newer sections of homes on the east side. About three weeks later, I learned that Dave had become the endorsed candidate; he was re-elected in 1955 and again in 1959. He died in his third term, and was succeeded by his wife, Jessie.

My final encounter with elective politics in Gary occurred in 1967, when Richard Gordon Hatcher was running for his first term as mayor. As the campaign progressed, it became obvious that Dick was a bona fide black candidate (the first) and a real threat to win the election, although it was still going to be a horse race. Hatcher's opponent was the incumbent, Alex Katz, a former judge and the first Jew to be elected mayor of Gary. He had been somewhat more open and inclusive, more liberal than previous mayors as far as the black community was concerned, and he had strong support among African Americans.

Dick Hatcher, on the other hand, was a part of the new politics. A practicing attorney, he had run for an at-large seat on city council and had won in his first attempt despite the fact that he had not been born in Gary and had not even lived there very long. In small cities like Gary, people tend to support natives or longtime residents, but Hatcher (who had grown up in Michigan City, Indiana) had not only won the councilmanic race but, through adroit political maneuvering, was able to get himself elected president of Gary's city council in his first year.

Clearly, Hatcher was not a person who could be ignored. As a lawyer, he had a measure of economic independence. He was a bachelor and had no family obligations. As a young man himself, he was popular with young people, particularly youthful black Garyites. Hatcher was an outspoken opponent of the Vietnam War and argued openly that U.S. Steel, Gary's major employer, should do more to clean up the environment and reduce the pollution caused by its plants. He also made it clear that he would not continue longtime political practices favoring certain groups and individuals, and he vowed that he would make no deals with organized crime. These positions, however, were only the tip of the iceberg.

Taking dead aim at what he perceived to be a long history of political corruption, Hatcher promised to discontinue the alleged practice of requiring ten percent of every contract awarded by the city to be given as a kickback to the Democratic party coffers. He also vowed that there would no longer be payoffs to council members and other designated power brokers. In other words, Hatcher was a serious threat to business-as-usual. He complained publicly about the absence of cabinet-level black appointees and the lack of city contracts with black businesses in a city which was becoming increasingly non-white. Hatcher's campaign was picking up steam, not only among the young and blue-collar black community, but among the professional, business, and college-educated groups as well, people who had rarely been openly involved in politics. Contributions came not only from Gary but from across the country. James Brown, "the Godfather of Soul," and others came to Gary to do benefit performances. Hatcher's campaign manager, Jesse E. Bell, a high school teacher at Roosevelt, ran a well-organized campaign and mobilized support.

During the campaign, I was completing the dissertation for my Ph.D. at the University of Chicago, although my permanent residence was still in Gary. On weekends, my wife (who was finishing her master's at Purdue University) and I would have long, leisurely breakfasts, enjoying the time we were able to spend together on Saturday and Sunday. One Saturday morning, after we had finished breakfast, the doorbell rang. I answered the door and there stood one of my longtime friends, about five or six years my junior in age. His parents owned a business in Gary and I knew his family.

John (not his real name; he died some years ago) came in, and we sat down on the sofa in the living room. I offered him a cup of coffee, but he declined. He was sweating, although it was cool outside, and he seemed nervous. His speech was halting, unusual for him. I told him to relax and I got him a glass of water. After a few sips, he calmed down and launched into a lengthy recitation of how long we had known each other, how I had encouraged and supported him as he participated in sports and attended college, how much he and others in the city respected and admired me— even white people from other sections of the city. It made no difference, he said, whether the people were white or black: I was considered one of Gary's own, one of its finest citizens.

I was perplexed: why was John going on like this? It was not like him, and it was embarrassing. After a slight pause, he said, "As you know, an outsider is running for mayor and he just might win. You," he continued, "should be the one who becomes the first black mayor of Gary. You grew up here. You have earned that right and you should run. People will support you over Dick Hatcher." John then told me that he had been sent by unnamed leaders of the Democratic party to convince me to run against Hatcher. Not pausing for a response, John opened his briefcase and presented me with copies of filing papers already completed. All I had to do was sign them and they would be taken to Crown Point, the county seat, in time to meet the deadline for filing. It was the last day for filing.

As I sat there dumbfounded, he showed me a list of planned radio announcements and paid political advertisements for newspapers. He told me that a friendly reporter had already written a story juxtaposing the hometown boy and the outsider who were competing to become Gary's first black mayor. Finally, perspiring even more profusely, John removed a layer of papers from his briefcase, exposing thirty thousand dollars in cash, money he was authorized to turn over to me as soon as I signed the papers. An additional thirty thousand was to be delivered to me in person after the election, which they confidently expected incumbent Katz to win. Hatcher and I would split the black and opposition votes. "You don't even have to campaign," he said. "We know you are in school and have to study. Just make a few appearances, tape a few radio interviews—they will all be arranged and paid for by party leaders. Nobody will know."

I was stunned. By this time, Lois had come into the room. In his agitation, John had been talking so loud that Lois had heard the part about me running for mayor. My surprise quickly turned to anger. How could this young man come to me with this kind of offer? I was trembling with rage. John knew me well enough to predict what my response would be. I got up, retrieved John's coat, and asked him to leave my house immediately. I told him that if he ever came to me again with this kind of offer, I would notify the appropriate authorities at once. John looked at me as tears began to trickle down his cheeks. Breathing heavily, he said, "I had to come, Bernard. I didn't have a choice."

Slowly, I began to understand, as I should have from the beginning. John's parents were in deep financial trouble with their business, and things were so bad that even their home was in jeopardy. John had been running the business for his father, and the problems were not only financial: certain dealings could possibly lead to criminal charges. Both John and his father were at risk—a situation which was common knowledge among some of his closest friends. Apparently, somebody had offered him a deal if he could pull this off, and he had to try.

John left my home in tears. My wife and I sat in the kitchen in a state of shock that he had come to this. For the first time, Lois understood the perils and costs of politics in my hometown, how money, significant amounts, could be used to corrupt. Hatcher, of course, won the election. John was able to resolve his problems, but he was never the same after that episode. Although we never spoke of it again, our relationship was strained and tarnished forever. How sad! Lois and I had moved to Philadelphia by the time Hatcher was elected to his first term as mayor of Gary; he served for twenty years. On a recent visit to Gary, Hatcher told me of a similar bribe attempt during his first run for mayor. Until that conversation, neither of us had known that we were both targets. The similarities suggest that the same people sent the messengers.

The year 1967 was a time of hope and promise—and increasing political activity in black communities across the country. The late Carl Stokes had won in Cleveland, Ohio. Kenneth Gibson had lost his first bid for mayor of Newark, New Jersey, but he and his supporters were already planning their next campaign. I met Ken in 1968 during one of his visits to Philadelphia. He asked how Gary's black community had successfully mobilized to insure Hatcher's victory. After a lengthy conversation, I arranged for Ken to get in touch with Dick Hatcher and his campaign manager and chief aide, Jesse E. Bell. That first meeting was the beginning of a long and continuing relationship.

Over the years of Gibson's terms as mayor, I worked with a number of white "movers and shakers" who were interested in supporting him and his programs and in bringing Newark back after the riots. Gibson's housing director was Thomas Massarro, a young Italian American whose father was a stone mason, who had grown up in the projects, and who had attended Harvard Law School. Massarro later became Philadelphia's housing director under Mayor Bill Green and, after he resigned, a developer and builder in the city and its suburbs. Massarro remains a good friend and is a continuing link in my relationship with Ken Gibson. He was the contractor who, with the young people, built the House of Umoja Urban Boystown, pioneered by Sister Falaka Fattah and her husband, David. It is among the most successful and long-lived programs for helping gang members and youthful offenders, many without families.

Philadelphia

When we arrived in Philadelphia in 1967, independent black politics was just beginning to develop. There were three African Americans on city council: Marshall Shepard, Jr., a member at large; Thomas McIntosh, from the fifth councilmanic district in North Philadelphia; and Charlie Durham, from the third district in West Philadelphia. After the November election, Charles Bowser, who had managed Mayor Jim Tate's campaign in North Philadelphia, was rewarded with the position of deputy mayor. Representative Robert N.C. Nix was serving in the U.S. House of Representatives. All the black elected officials were endorsed by the party they represented. It had been a long and tortured road, as the late Austin Norris noted in a brilliant series he wrote for the *Philadelphia Tribune*, to get to the point where the two major parties would endorse black candidates for public office. It was the same in other big cities.

The catalyst for changing this system was the Black Political Forum, a singular organization that was the brainchild of John F. White, Sr., and was co-founded in 1968 by White, Hardy Williams, and W. Wilson Goode. Williams, an attorney who was active in West Philadelphia politics, had been a star basketball player at Penn State and was a graduate of the University of Pennsylvania Law School. The Forum became the vehicle for bringing together and focusing black political power in Philadelphia. White was able to secure the cooperation of other prominent black politicians, both in and out of government, and he provided the leadership that held the organization together.

After months of planning, the Forum's inaugural dinner was held at the Holiday Inn on City Line Avenue. It was an absolutely stunning debut. Both of Pennsylvania's U.S. senators, Republican Hugh Scott and Democrat Joseph Clark, attended; the mayor and most of the politicians and power-brokers were there; every seat was taken. I had helped to get Mayor Richard Gordon Hatcher of Gary as the keynote speaker. His speech, and the event itself, put the city on notice that a new day was dawning, that the Forum intended to play a prominent role in politics from then on.

In 1969, W. Wilson Goode, then head of the Paschall Betterment League in Southwest Philadelphia, was elected to the position of political action chair of the Forum. Among his duties were interviewing potential candidates, identifying selected races, and analyzing them for possible endorsements or entering candidates. The next year, 1970, White asked Goode to run Hardy Williams' campaign for state representative against the longtime incumbent who had again been endorsed by the party. Paul Vance, a school principal and civil rights activist, became the co-chair of Williams' campaign. Although the opponent had more workers in every ward and division, and every poll showed that he was ahead, Williams won the election. It was the first time that an African American had won as an independent, without party endorsement. It was a harbinger of things to come.

Hardy Williams, now in the state legislature, was not satisfied. In 1971, he decided to run for mayor of Philadelphia, declared his candidacy, and asked Goode to serve as chief executive of his campaign. Others, from within the city and from the outside, came in to manage certain aspects of the campaign. In the Democratic primary, Williams ran against Frank Rizzo, the police commissioner, and Bill Green, Jr., son of the city's most powerful Democrat. When the results were in, Bill Green had lost to Frank Rizzo by about 50,000 votes—almost the same number as Williams had garnered. There is a continuing controversy over whether Williams was in the race to siphon off votes from Green and thus guarantee Rizzo's victory. I worked in that campaign, and I do not believe this charge. I have been told by credible sources, however, that Hardy was offered (among other things) an endorsement for a Common Pleas Court judgeship in return for withdrawing from the race. He refused. Other African Americans—the Rev. Leonard Smalls, Cecil B. Moore, and Lennert Roberts—had run for mayor earlier, but Hardy Williams' campaign was the first to be taken seriously by the party and the political establishment, both black and white.

The Black Political Forum became the vehicle through which aspirants for public office could get information about the political process. There were three major components of the Forum's program:

- recruiting candidates and teaching them how to organize and run campaigns;
- providing education and instructions for poll workers and poll watchers; and
- providing post-election analyses.

The Forum learned from every race, whether the results were positive or negative. The post-election analyses were, in my opinion, more important than the other activities because they became the basis for planning future campaigns. A case in point was the fall mayoralty campaign in 1971, when Frank Rizzo was opposed by Thacher Longstreth, the Republican candidate. Many pollsters and analysts predicted a Longstreth victory, but Rizzo said he would win because he knew he could energize his supporters and they would vote for him in overwhelming numbers. In his bastions of strength—South Philadelphia, the river wards, and the Northeast—that is exactly what happened. The turnout of voters in North and West Philadelphia, where Longstreth expected to prevail, never equalled the percentages in Rizzo's strongholds. Rizzo won, Longstreth lost. From that election, the Forum learned that you couldn't take anything for granted: it was important to develop a strategy for pre-election and election day activities.

After every election, the Forum held seminars at which voting patterns were analyzed and explained, along with voter registration and education strategies. Division and ward totals were dissected and discussed. I enjoyed these seminars, a number of which I led. Among current and former elected officials who participated in these seminars were state senator Hardy Williams (the first independent victor), the late Dave Richardson (the second), and John White, Jr. (the third).

The importance of the Forum's post-election seminars can be illustrated by two cases: John White, Jr., and Dwight Evans. White lost his first race for state representative to a longterm incumbent who had the party endorsement and a big, well-financed organization. Although his margin of defeat was small, White was discouraged and contemplated quitting politics. I happened to conduct the seminar in which his race was analyzed and, noting his disappointment, I talked to him, explaining that he had almost pulled off a victory with little organization and even less money. I encouraged him to try again and predicted that he would win the next election hands down, which he did. John went on to a distinguished career as a state representative, a Philadelphia city councilman, a state secretary of welfare, and now as head of the Philadelphia Housing Authority, where he is trying to improve a system that has defied previous reform efforts.

State Representative Dwight Evans was a careful and attentive student at the seminars; he even used to tape portions or all of them so he could study them later. He learned his lessons, patterned his first campaign on the three-part paradigm of the Forum—and won. Evans has run for lieutenant governor and governor, and made respectable showings in each of his statewide races. He served as chair of the appropriations committee of the Pennsylvania House of Representatives, and he is all but unbeatable in his own district. Both Evans and White have bright political futures, should they choose to continue in politics.

Charles Bowser played an important role in the development of independent politics in Philadelphia. My most intense political involvement was in Bowser's campaign for mayor in 1975. In fact, Dr. Wally Rich and I wrote the music and lyrics for his campaign theme song. (Wally was a friend and colleague at Temple, where he was a professor of mathematics education. He was also a fine jazz pianist, and he died suddenly and too early of meningitis.) Bowser ran as a third-party, independent candidate against Frank Rizzo (then a Democrat) and Tom Foglietta (then a Republican). Rizzo had been denied party endorsement in the primary, but by mobilizing and energizing his supporters he had defeated the party candidate, Louis Hill. In the general election, Frank Rizzo won overwhelmingly—but Bowser came in second, with 134,000 votes, although he had raised less than $200,000 for the campaign. Foglietta was unable to carry a single ward. This was the race that made it clear that an African American would some day, soon, become mayor of Philadelphia.

In the next election, Bowser again ran for mayor. His opponents were Bill Green, former city controller Bill Klenk, and Al Gaudiosi, a former

Rizzo press secretary and senior aide. Bowser ran a good campaign, and with three white candidates to split the white vote he had a real chance of winning. Strange things happen in elections, however, First, Gaudiosi dropped out of the race and, at the last minute, so did Klenk. Bowser found himself in a two-man race, facing Bill Green. Green won but, as Wilson Goode has said publicly many times, Bowser laid the groundwork which made it possible for Goode to become the first African American mayor of the city.

The Black Political Forum was the logical outgrowth of an earlier organization, the Citywide Community Council, which was co-chaired by Mattie Humphrey and Walter Palmer. The Council had been formed in the mid-sixties to bring together the leaders of all African American groups in order to plan ways to get some control over the lives of the black community. Communication and cooperation were stressed, not necessarily running for elective office.

Many people, some of whom were not candidates or elected officials, played important roles in the development of the independent black political movement. (See Appendix III for some of the names.) One of the most important was Father Paul Washington, rector of the Church of the Advocate in North Philadelphia. In 1968, he hosted a Black Power Conference at his church; thousands of people attended. Security was provided by off-duty black police officers and by Maulana (Ron) Karenga's "US" organization from southern California. (Karenga has an earned doctorate, is multi-lingual, and originated the Kwanzaa celebration.) Father Paul's courage and wisdom, and the respect in which he was held by everyone, including Police Commissioner Frank Rizzo, probably prevented a race riot when several white policemen, disobeying orders, drove through the neighborhood during the Black Power Conference and shouted insults at delegates. (They were promptly reprimanded.) I released all the senior staff members from the School District's planning office so that they could attend this conference, if they wanted to go. Those who did were petrified: they had never been in a situation where blacks were in charge and not terribly friendly to white outsiders.

This city will likely never know the debt it owes Father Paul and some of the others. Without them, Philadelphia could have exploded at any time. When Dr. King was assassinated in 1968, Charlie Bowser, the deputy mayor, asked me and several others to go to city hall. He had come up with an idea—to shut down city hall, ask downtown businesses to close, and request drivers to turn on their automobile lights as a message of respect—and he wanted us to help him get Mayor Tate's approval. The mayor agreed, and I am convinced that because of these symbolic gestures, along with courageous leadership in both the black and white communities, Philadelphia was the only major city that did not experience major unrest or rioting in the wake of Dr. King's murder.

It was my privilege to meet some of the black elder statesmen, like Austin Norris and Raymond Pace Alexander. Norris was a Yale Law School graduate (1917) who came to Philadelphia to find only six other black lawyers in town. After a brief stint on City Council, he was appointed to the Board of Revision of Taxes in 1937, a post he retained for 30 years. But his most notable contribution was his encouragement of young African Americans, particularly the junior partners in his law firm like Harvey Schmidt, Bill Brown, Clifford Scott Green, and A. Leon Higginbotham, Jr., all of whom went on to notable positions. Long before the term was well known, Norris held "rap sessions" with people like Thurgood Marshall and Paul Robeson. In those days, no black lawyer, regardless of credentials, could get a job with a major white firm. William T. Coleman, Jr., became the first black attorney to do so, when he was hired by Richardson Dilworth's firm in 1956. (Coleman served as secretary of the Department of Transportation from 1975 to 1977.)

Alexander earned his law degree at Harvard (1923), but when he arrived in Philadelphia with a recommendation from the dean, he was rejected as soon as they saw the color of his skin! He also served on City Council and then became the first black judge on the Court of Common Pleas in 1959. A distinguished and courtly gentleman, Judge Alexander began the fight (which continued until 1968) to force Girard College to admit black students.

The political activities were affected by other events: the civil rights movement, the community action programs, demands for involvement by the poor in the distribution of federal grants to states and localities. Fortunately, there were several African American radio personalities who could and did help publicize the flow of events. For instance, Georgie Woods, a famous disc jockey and promoter, had a large following among black Philadelphians, and he used his program to inform and educate young people. Mary Mason was a radio talk show host who had a direct line to the black community, although thousands of whites also listened to her daily program. Mason's opinions were very, very influential. Hers was a powerful voice, and she could literally command the appearance of celebrities, local and national, on her show when they were in the vicinity. Through the various organizations she founded and led, she extended her influence while also meeting the needs of her followers and listeners. Politicians, white or black, ignored her at their peril. Although WHAT-AM was then a white-owned station, Mason turned an hour of her Sunday program over to the Black Political Forum to educate citizens about the electoral process and inform them about the issues—a gutsy and intelligent thing to do in those days. She remains a powerful, independent figure today. She continues to broadcast, and her program is probably the most influential in the black community.

Cody Anderson, once general manager of WDAS and now owner of WHAT-AM, was and is a significant molder of opinion in the African American community. His station provides an independent voice for thousands of black Philadelphians. Cody, unlike any other person I have met in my years in this city, is reasonable and tolerant, whatever his own fiercely held opinions. He is unfailingly courteous and open to ideas other than his own, even though he may strongly disagree with them. Access to the airwaves, made possible by people like Anderson and Mason, played a major, but under-recognized, role in the growth of independent black politics in Philadelphia.

At the beginning of the independent black political movement, it was crucial to designate a single black candidate for an office and then unite the community behind him or her. As the movement matured and more individuals presented themselves as candidates, this was no longer necessary, and we began to see African Americans running against each other. For instance, Robert N.C. Nix, Sr., a U.S. Congressman from Philadelphia for many years, was defeated in 1978 by William H. Gray, III, pastor of the Bright Hope Baptist Church. (When Bill Gray challenged Congressman Nix for the first time, he lost by 339 votes, and his supporters, including my wife and me, pledged $339 for his next campaign. We became members of the "339 Club" and were given pins to wear. Three of the people working for Gray were elected to city council, and one also became a deputy mayor and mayoral candidate.)

Gray resigned in 1991 to become president of the United Negro College Fund, and he was replaced by Lucien Blackwell, a union leader and former member of both city council and the state legislature. Blackwell, in turn, was defeated in 1994 by Chaka Fattah, a former state representative and state senator. Vincent Hughes, a state representative, took Fattah's place as state senator when Fattah went to Washington. The new group of black politicians includes state representatives Anthony Hardy Williams (the state senator's son) and Gordon Linton, who resigned to become head of urban mass transit operations in the U.S. Department of Transportation under President Bill Clinton. Not all elected black officials were

Democrats: the late Dr. Ethel Allen, a lifelong Republican, became a member of city council.

Milton and John Street came to power through other means, although they were obviously beneficiaries of the movement I have been describing. Milton, the older of the two brothers, was a tireless housing activist and a loud, persistent voice for street vendors. The vendors, many of them black, sold all kinds of merchandise downtown, in the neighborhoods, and on university campuses. Milton owned and operated several street vending enterprises himself, but it was as an advocate for housing for the poor and homeless that he became best known. Prodigiously intelligent, he seemed always to have the facts on housing: what was available, how funds were allocated, what the rules were. In this he was ably assisted by graduate students (including one of mine, Dr. Rosa Lewis) and others who used their own time to provide him with the necessary data. Milton was popular with many people in Philadelphia who admired his courage and audacity: he organized demonstrations, marches, and sit-ins at city council and in court hallways. He was elected a state representative and then a state senator as a Democrat, but when he switched to the Republican party he was rewarded with a powerful committee chairmanship. He was later defeated by Roxanne Jones, the former head of the Welfare Rights Organization.

John Street was less vocal, but no less militant and committed to the cause. A lawyer, John provided counsel and representation for his brother Milton. John was elected to the seat in city council formerly held by Cecil B. Moore. Through a series of adroit, even brilliant, moves, John kept the spotlight on the Abscam corruption cases which had resulted in the forced resignation of several powerful members of council, including president George Schwartz. (The Abscam scandal was partially responsible for accelerating the rise of independent black officials.) Joseph Coleman became the first black president of council and served in that position during W. Wilson Goode's first term as mayor.

When John Street assumed that position after Coleman retired, he became the most influential local black politician. Under his presidency, council became an orderly and productive body. Bills moved to a vote through the proper channels and on time. Council hired its own competent staff (despite howls from citizens and media criticism) and thus obtained the necessary expertise and analyses to make wise, or at least informed, decisions. The staff enabled council members and the president to differ intelligently from the mayor and his administration, or to agree and cooperate. In the process, John Street became a force to be reckoned with. He was astute and energetic, he was willing to work long hours and do his homework: these qualities made him a major participant in most of the important decisions affecting Philadelphia.

Literally thousands of Philadelphians were active participants in the movement to black political empowerment. Their names may never be known, but it could not have succeeded without their contribution of energy, time, and financial resources, no matter how limited. The five dollar bills, the small change, and the fundraisers that barely broke even were crucial to the development of a sense of possibility, a belief that anything could happen if we could stay united. These campaigns were among the most exhilarating and hopeful experiences of my life. I saw a people come together for a single purpose: to inject the African American community into the decision-making process in the city's political life; to make sure that we were represented at the bargaining table by persons of our own selection, not those chosen for us by others.

Many largely white organizations were also involved in changing the political climate in Philadelphia. Americans for Democratic Action, whose executive director was Shelley Yanoff, was very active. The Lawyers Committee for Civil Rights, whose Philadelphia chapter existed primarily because of the efforts of the late Edwin "Ned" Wolf and some other young lawyers, played an important role. As a matter of fact, it was Ned Wolf who saw the future of black mayoral politics before many. One night during a party at his home, while Ned and I were engaged in one of our interminable conversations about how to change Philadelphia, he said to me, "Bernie, W. Wilson Goode will be the first black mayor of Philadelphia." I thought Ned had lost it, had gone over the edge. I knew that he and Wilson were good friends and that they had worked on a number of projects together—but Wilson Goode as mayor? After all, Hardy Williams, Charlie Bowser, Cecil B. Moore, Joe Coleman, A. Leon Higginbotham, Leon Sullivan—to name a few—were much more logical candidates in my opinion. I believe the year was 1971.

Ned apparently knew something about Philadelphia that many of us did not know at the time, but he was not the only one. My friend Richard Gilmore and I had worked together in numerous campaigns, and we had also shared the disappointment of many losses. Dick had been the finance chairman and chief fundraiser in Bowser's first campaign. One evening, at a dinner meeting at the Chestnut Hill Hotel, Dick said to those of us at the table, "That could very well be the first black mayor of Philadelphia. He has the best chance of anyone I know." He was pointing at W. Wilson Goode, who had just been appointed Philadelphia's managing director by mayor-elect Bill Green. To this day, I do not know how first Ned, and then Dick, saw this coming. At the time, Wilson had indicated no interest in elective office; he saw himself as the ultimate competent administrator. All of his political activity had been in support of other candidates, such as Hardy Williams, Charles Bowser, Bill Gray, and Dave Richardson.

Unfortunately, Ned Wolf died of cancer before his prediction came true. Even more tragic, he died before many of the things he had fought for through the years were achieved in Philadelphia and the country. I became active in a number of organizations because of Ned's interest and energy: Lawyers Committee, Rutgers Center for Law and Education, Philadelphia Public Interest Law Center, and Americans for Democratic Action. It was in these organizations that I found, for the first time, genuinely committed white people who fought for things because they believed in them, not because they could gain some advantage by belonging and being active. If they held paid positions in these organizations, it was not because they lacked better-paying, more prestigious opportunities. Yes, some of them were financially independent, but others were no better off than the average citizen. Ned Wolf's parents, Robert Wolf and Elly Newbold, are still special friends. Shelley Yanoff, Graham Finney, Thacher Longstreth, Eunice Clark, Jerry and Marciarose Shestack come to mind, as do others no longer with us—Bill and Sylvia Meek, Richard deLone, Miriam Gafni. We fought many battles side by side; we shared the defeats and the victories.

It was through my involvement in politics that Lois and I met and came to know a number of our white friends. Like most African Americans of our generation, particularly those who lived in smaller cities, we had grown up in our own separate world. As young adults, except for business or professional interactions, our lives were essentially separate, politically, racially, and socially. Neighborhoods, schools, and churches were segregated. It was as if we inhabited parallel universes—invisible to each other, barely understood, rarely touching. As I noted earlier, even when you grew up in a multi-racial neighborhood, as I did, the public schools separated blacks and whites from kindergarten on. Later, we may have been on the same campuses when we attended colleges and universities, but our lives rarely intersected. Although few would admit it, most white people knew very little about black people. And although black Americans knew more about white people, it was because they had to know more in order to survive. It is still fair to say, however, that there was very little real knowledge about the other race at a level of understanding where individuals are viewed as human beings with more similarities than differences. Many simply used the old dichotomies to place themselves and others as members of groups which were superior or inferior, advantaged or disadvantaged, privileged or underprivileged.

Until the 1970s, neighborhoods like Mt. Airy were the exceptions. So were schools like Central and Girls High in Philadelphia, the Bronx High School of Science and the High School of the Performing Arts in New York, and Hyde Park High School in Chicago. Banks, factories, industries, businesses, airlines, railroads, shipping companies, medical practices, colleges and universities, law firms, craft unions, orchestras, post offices, hotels, nightclubs, restaurants—you name it—almost none had an integrated staff above the menial level or more than token integration among their clientele. The major universities had only recently begun to admit non-whites, and the number of minority graduates was still small. My wife and I, on our wedding day, were among the first to have dinner and stay overnight in the restaurants and hotels of St. Louis, Missouri. They had been desegregated that very day, July 1, 1961. When a famous report said that we were moving toward two societies, one black and one white, separate and unequal, I thought that we were already there.

I have watched and participated in political developments in Philadelphia over a period of more than a quarter-century. During this time, I have seen independent candidates challenge and, in many cases, defeat party-endorsed incumbents. In most instances, these were black candidates confronting white incumbents. In others, younger blacks faced older, more entrenched blacks. Throughout, the independent political movement was fueled by an intense desire to obtain a seat at the table when decisions were made, to be a participant in determining the issues which affected the black community. That movement culminated in the election of W. Wilson Goode as Philadelphia's first African American mayor in 1983. Goode resigned as Mayor Bill Green's managing director to seek this position.

Wilson Goode had the almost unanimous support of the city's black community. He obtained the endorsement of every black elected official, the backing of a significant percentage of the business community, and the enthusiasm of people who had rarely been involved in politics. Voter registration and education efforts during the primary and general election campaigns were something to behold: they reached into every neighborhood and community. Along with Richard Gilmore, Maurice Clifford, Shirley Hamilton, and others, I served in Goode's "kitchen cabinet" of advisors during both campaigns. The outpouring of support was amazing. Money and volunteers came from across the country as people began to sense the possibility of victory. Registration in the predominantly black wards was higher than it had ever been before, and on election night so many people wanted to vote that hours had to be extended at several polling places. Goode won. I introduced him to the screaming throng at the Civic Center, a crowd that included local and national politicians as well as citizen supporters. Four years later, after a tough and divisive campaign, Goode was re-elected.

The number and variety of individuals who worked in both those campaigns defy imagination. All of the work of the previous two decades had its culmination in the 1983 and 1987 elections. The electricity was everywhere—on the streets and in the churches, schools, community centers, lounges, bars, and malls. Here was a visible symbol of what could be accomplished despite the odds. Finally, black people were not only at the table but calling some of the shots. It was a heady time, one that gave hope for the future as well as a sense of accomplishment, of fulfillment.

A different reality has set in at this writing. The African American community is now well represented in positions of power and responsibility, yet problems remain: homelessness, unemployment, inadequate schools, a welfare system that too often promotes dependency rather than leading people toward independence. Drugs devastate many of our communities; too many children never have the luxury of a childhood. Simultaneously, the country appears to be tired of confronting problems, and many political leaders seem eager to return to the good old days of intact families, quiet small towns, good education, jobs for everyone, and perfect harmony. Those good old days never existed; that dimly remembered past is only a fantasy.

African American elected officials, and indeed the African American community, are faced with new questions today. How do we move forward, now that we have gained the position and the voice for which we fought so long? Which major political party should we support if they are both promoting unacceptable platforms? How do we form coalitions and develop strategies to address important issues, such as education (which is inadequate and often truly awful for students whether they are white, black, Latino, or newly arrived immigrants)? If black elected officials are not accountable to the communities they represent, should they be challenged by independent candidates, even if the incumbent is in a powerful position? Black people have always voted for white candidates, although whites rarely vote for blacks. If a black candidate is opposed by a white or Latino or any other non-African American, do we vote for the black candidate or for the individual who offers the best program? These and other questions have recently been confronted in Baltimore, where Mayor Kurt Schmoke defeated a white woman, and in Gary, where the black incumbent mayor decided not to seek re-election and was succeeded by a white male. After serving for eight years, Philadelphia's first black mayor, Wilson Goode, who was legally prohibited from a third term, was replaced by Edward Rendell, who is white. In New York City, Chicago, and Los Angeles, the same thing has happened.

Perhaps the Black Forum's three-part agenda—recruiting and instructing candidates, educating voters, and analyzing election returns—needs to be resurrected. Voter turnout in Philadelphia and across the country is so low that it is a national disgrace. When fewer than half of those eligible bother to register or vote, what hope is there that minority voices will be heard? When a president, governor, mayor, judges, and other significant officials can be elected by so few citizens, what hope is there for change, for improvement? It just may be time to come together to deal with these and other issues of equal importance.

CHAPTER VII
FAMILY LIFE IN PHILADELPHIA

Finding a House

When we left Gary and Chicago to move to Philadelphia, I promised Lois that she would never live in accommodations any less attractive than those we were leaving. Since looking for a house was out of the question at this stage, we deposited the money from the sale of our Gary home and rented an apartment at Park Towne Place, a complex across the street from the board of education building. David Horowitz, the deputy superintendent for instruction in the school district, lived there and he had suggested it to us. He was very helpful in many ways before and after our move. Park Towne was perfect. Our apartment was on the twelfth floor, facing the Philadelphia Museum of Art, and at night the view was spectacular. I walked to work, first downstairs to offices the school district had rented, and later across 21st Street to the administration building on the Parkway. We had four bedrooms, because we needed space for all our furniture—and also because Lois was pregnant and we were expecting our first child in January 1968. We were both delirious with joy.

We loved living downtown, the hustle and bustle, all kinds of people, being able to walk almost everywhere. We owned only one car, having sold Lois's car prior to the move. And what a car it was! A red, two-door 1966 Mustang with wire wheels, sprint stripe, and black leather upholstery. It was our toy and we loved it, but I rarely needed it in my job. We used it primarily to drive to social events on the weekends, to visit our families in the midwest, to drive to Cambridge during the summer I spent at Harvard, or to go to Martha's Vineyard, our favorite place in the United States. We were introduced to the Vineyard by Charlie Bowser, and we have visited there almost every year for the past twenty-six years.

The first six months in Philadelphia were very lonely for Lois. She was pregnant, in a strange city far away from family members, and in an environment unlike any we had encountered in the first six years of our married life. I worked long hours, six days a week, and we often had meetings on Sunday. The school system was undergoing dramatic change under Dilworth and Shedd, and the televised school board meetings were sometimes the most entertaining programs on the tube. Racial tensions were high, and students were expressing themselves in ways that bore little resemblance to the "olden days" when teachers and principals were in charge. The times were exciting, but they were also dangerous. Four months after our arrival, on November 17, 1967, a large student demonstration at the board of education was broken up by police and threw the city into turmoil, as I described in Chapter V. I was in the middle of all this activity and was often away at night in various parts of the city which Lois knew only by name. It was a really tough time for her, but she handled it better than I had any right to expect.

The date when we expected the baby to be born came and went—several times. Finally, Lois's physician, a really wonderful practitioner, advised us to forget about it and have an evening out. We did. We went to Pagano's in the University of Pennsylvania area and had a great dinner with a glass of wine. We returned home relaxed and retired early. At approximately five o'clock in the morning, Lois woke me and said it was time; she was calm although in some pain. We drove to Thomas Jefferson University Hospital, she checked in, and I was sent to wait in a room apparently reserved for expectant fathers.

In a couple of hours, a nurse came to tell me that I could see my new daughter. I went into the delivery room and there was Lois with a beautiful little baby. "Look at her, isn't she wonderful? Aren't you happy?" asked Lois, with tears of joy in her eyes. Barbra was lying on her back, looking straight at me, and when I moved, her eyes followed me. I knew that babies are not supposed to be able to focus their eyes and follow movement so early, but she did. I cannot tell you how proud we were at that moment. Dr. Wellenbach was beaming as he told us we had a happy, healthy infant. It was the beginning of another phase of our family life, one that would change us forever.

Before long, relatives came to visit: Lois's mother and aunt, and my mother and nephew. Dave Horowitz's wife, Sylvia, was a great support, not only because she lived nearby but because her husband was also involved in the school district turmoil. And it was during this first year that we met the Gilmores, Richard and Jackie, who were to become lifelong friends.

Lois wanted to continue her career, so in September 1968, when Barbra was seven months old, Lois accepted a position as the librarian at Duckrey, a new elementary school in North Philadelphia. The school district was happy to hire her, as there was a shortage of librarians, and many elementary school libraries were staffed by assistants who did not have degrees or training. Fortunately, we had found a person to take care of Barbra during the day. Gladys had been referred to us by a neighbor for whom she had worked for years, and she was a gem. Honest, hard-working, intelligent, and a mother herself, she truly loved Barbra, and we loved and trusted her, knowing she was taking excellent care of our daughter. Gladys remained with the family when we moved to Chestnut Hill and until after the birth of our second child, when Lois decided to take a leave of absence. For several years, Gladys would make the trip from South Philadelphia just to see Barbra and Chuck. She was a remarkable person.

Lois learned she was pregnant again in 1970, and she quietly informed me that she did not want to raise her children in an apartment, where they would have to play on the concrete playgrounds which Park Towne provided or go to a park to see grass and trees. Both of us had grown up in the midwest, where land is plentiful and even the smallest houses have lawns and yards. She wanted that for our children, and although I loved living downtown, I knew we had to start looking for a house. When Lois makes up her mind about anything related to home, it is fruitless to argue; she will eventually prevail. We were going to move; the only question was where.

We elected to look in West Mt. Airy because it was a successfully racially integrated area and we knew people who lived there, people who were involved in independent and liberal politics, education, and other civic activities. We liked its proximity to Fairmount Park, the large old houses and trees, as well as its racial and economic diversity. Our friends, Dick and Jackie Gilmore, were also looking, but they wanted a new house, one they could design and build to their liking. We, on the other hand, had just gone through that process in Gary, and we wanted an existing home. In the midwest, there are few if any homes like those in Philadelphia: made of stone, gorgeous, stately, and old.

We looked and looked, at dozens of houses. They were either too large or too small, too expensive or in need of too much renovation, in the wrong block or too isolated. Lois was very discouraged. She was three months pregnant, and she wanted to be settled in her home before the baby was born. We looked every weekend. We scanned the newspaper real estate advertisements every day. We asked friends if they knew of prospects.

One evening when I came home—very late, as usual— Lois said we should look at a house in Chestnut Hill that had been listed: a three-story stone, Normandy-style, with five bedrooms and three baths. It was on a quiet street, across from the University of Pennsylvania's Morris Arboretum. I was surprised, because we had never considered this part of the city, a neighborhood north of Mt. Airy which was known as an enclave of rich and powerful WASPs. There were no black people living there, and the only Jewish family we knew (the first to move to Chestnut Hill, we had heard) were Robert and Elly Wolf. We had become friends with them and their son, Edwin, an activist liberal lawyer. By this time, however, Lois was ready to consider anything which met her basic specifications: space, safety, and quiet; grass, trees, and shrubbery.

We were not very optimistic, because we had been disappointed so many times before, but I called my realtor, George Scott, who was the highest-ranking black in the real estate department of the school district. He was a licensed appraiser, held certifications in most things realtors strive for in their field, and with his wife ran a real estate business. He had contacts all over the city. George called one of his colleagues in Chestnut Hill and arranged for us to see the house the next evening. Lois and I met George and the local real estate agent, and we all went to visit the home, which was owned by a widow who lived there with her dog, an elderly Dalmatian. When we went in, the local realtor introduced us to the owner, who simply nodded and remained seated in the enclosed porch with the dog beside her.

We looked at the first floor: kitchen, living and dining rooms, entrance hall and enclosed porch. By the time we got to the first floor landing, Lois whispered to me, "I want this house. It is just what I wanted." She didn't change her mind after we saw the rest of it. She already saw possibilities, although the kitchen clearly needed to be replaced. It was one of the first all-electric models and had not been used for months. Apparently, the owner did not cook anymore: the oven, range, and everything else showed it. In the basement, there was an old oil burner and tank which also needed replacement, but the house was exactly what Lois had had in mind.

I must admit I liked it too—although I was not thrilled about the prospect of living in Chestnut Hill, the bastion of upper-class, wealthy WASPs. We preferred West Mt. Airy, but we had been unable to find what we wanted there. It was far from clear that black people would be welcome in this neighborhood, but at this point it didn't matter. We were not about to be denied—as we had been in Gary—a home we wanted and could afford. Although this was not our first choice, time was running out. If my wife liked this house, she was going to have it, come hell or high water.

As we rode to the real estate office, George and the other realtor, who apparently had known each other for years, were deep in conversation. When we got to the office, they said that they did not like the way the owner had responded to us and suggested that, if we were interested in the house, we should sign a proposal immediately and include a five-hundred-dollar binder. They thought the owner might try to find some way to avoid selling to us, black people. Lois and I agreed. We made the deposit, signed the offer, and went home happy. The realtors contacted the widow at once and clinched the deal. I am glad we did that because from that day on the owner refused to speak with us. She would let us visit the house for further inspection only when she was not there, and she did not attend the closing. We never saw her again.

It wasn't over, however. After we took possession of the house on April 1, 1970, we had workmen begin to make improvements. They redid the walls in the basement, sealed the floor, built a laundry room, and replaced the kitchen. Other work was also being done in preparation for our move in June. One day we received a notice in the mail telling us that our insurance had been canceled because the house was not occupied—and was therefore considered abandoned. No matter how many times I called the insurance company to explain the situation, I could not get a reason for the cancellation and I concluded we were getting the runaround. I wrote Senator Scott a letter about the matter, and our friend Elly Wolf called him. Within a matter of days, it was cleared up. We had no more trouble, but as soon as we moved into the house, I changed insurance companies. I used a black insurance broker (Watlington and Cooper), a black bank (Berean Savings), and a black realtor (George Scott). The people who did the work on the house from then on were black contractors, Ken Dixon and Sons. It was a time of pride and mutual support among black Americans.

We completed the purchase on April 1, 1970—April Fool's Day—and moved in in July. I must say that our neighbors could not have been nicer, and our relationships with them were excellent throughout the twenty years we lived there. One of the traditions on our block was a welcoming party for anyone who moved into the neighborhood, to give the newcomers and the neighbors an opportunity to meet and become acquainted. The tradition was continued for us. Almost everyone came to the party, hosted by the Pearsons. Senator Hugh Scott came up from Washington, and the Wetherills, our next-door neighbors, were there. We had a lovely evening and felt very comfortable in our new surroundings. We were surprised because we never expected to be received with this degree of warmth and openness. We had already met a number of Chestnut Hill residents through political and civic activities—among them were Walter Phillips, Thacher Longstreth, Senator Clark—but actually living in this neighborhood was something else again.

We settled into our new home and awaited the birth of our second child. On October 22, I had an important meeting in Washington but I debated about going because Lois's delivery date was imminent. However, she had no pains, so we decided that I should go. That evening, we talked on the telephone, and everything was okay. I had arranged with Bruce McPherson, a friend from Chicago whom I had recruited to the school district, to stand by, just in case. Bruce, who was an associate superintendent, had stayed with us when he first came to Philadelphia, and he had found a house in nearby West Mt. Airy.

Around three a.m., Lois started having labor pains, and at five, she called her doctor, who told her to go to the hospital as soon as possible. Bruce came immediately, and after dropping Barbra off at the Gilmores' home, they went to Jefferson Hospital, where Barbra had been born. This time things were different. Bruce went to park the car, and Lois had to walk in alone, not on the arm of a loving husband. She sensed the stigma attached to a single mother, and the receptionist appeared to be interested only in whether Lois had medical insurance. She was taken upstairs and casually told to sit down and wait. When Dr. Wellenbach, her physician, arrived, he was furious that she had not been prepped—and he let the staff know it. By this time, Lois was in tears. But at nine a.m., Bernard Charles Watson, Jr., made his appearance, and Bruce called me in Washington. I caught the next train to Philadelphia and went straight to the hospital. Chuck was a handsome and energetic baby. Fortunately, he got his looks from his mother.

We were blessed to have two happy and healthy children. Lois and I both believed that children were a gift, to be cherished, nurtured, loved, supported, guided, and, above all, accepted fully as important members of the family. We shared everything: we both fed and bathed them, took them to the pediatrician and dentist, got up at night with them, pushed the stroller to the playground or park, and took them to the mall, downtown, and for visits with friends and family. Later, we attended their piano recitals, Barbra's dance recitals, their plays, sports events: tennis, gymnastics, basketball, soccer, track and field, hockey games. We dutifully drove them to their first overnight camps.

We installed a playground in the back yard. During the winter, we built snowmen, had snowball fights, chased each other. In the spring and summer, Chuck followed our gardener around and learned to do just about everything. Mr. Waterford was like a second father to Chuck, teaching him about grass, flowers, and shrubbery, allowing him to help and making him do the job right, eventually paying him for his assistance. Whenever Chuck heard Mr. Waterford's car in the driveway or the lawnmower start early in the morning, he immediately jumped out of bed and went to join him. They forged a friendship which lasted until Chuck went away to college and we moved to another home.

When we built an addition to the house, Chuck got up early every day to watch and bother the contractor. He worked as a laborer so diligently that Mr. Dixon put him on the payroll, saying he did as much work as his regular laborers although Chuck was much younger and didn't have to do it. I can assure you that Chuck earned every dime. At the end of the day, he was so tired and dirty that we sometimes felt sorry for him. But Chuck liked the work, enjoyed the camaraderie with Mr. Dixon's sons, and was delighted to earn his own money. He was eleven years of age.

We have many fond memories of the place where we lived for twenty years: seeing the first signs of spring, smelling the freshly cut grass, hearing the sound of Mr. Waterford's clippers and lawn mower. Sometimes, a family of ducks would mysteriously appear in the stream in our back yard. In the winter, when the snow outside was picturesque, we loved the crackle of logs burning in the fireplace. For fifteen years, we gave a Christmas Eve party, attended by about 100 people of all sizes, shapes, ages, races, and incomes. It was diversity at its best, and it became an annual tradition. When people who expected an invitation had not received one by the usual date, we would get discreet (and sometimes not so discreet) inquiries. The children enjoyed the parties as much as we did, and we never had a problem with their behavior.

We also remember the expressions on the faces of people going to the arboretum, when they saw Barbra and Chuck playing in the front yard or next to our driveway. When the children were older, they made a game of it—deliberately playing where they would be in full view of passersby. (When Chuck was working with Mr. Waterford, however, there were no stares.) For the first few years, delivery people would come to the door and ask if they could speak to Mrs. Watson: they automatically assumed that Lois was the maid.

Barbra was two years old when we bought that house, and we were already living in it when Chuck was born. Our family literally came together there. Ironically, we never intended to live in that community. It was almost an accident.

The Break-in on Hillcrest Avenue

When I was named Vice President for Academic Administration at Temple University in 1976, I became the first African American to hold that position. A fair amount of publicity was generated: Nels Nelson of the *Daily News* did a feature story with a photograph, while the other local dailies and the *Philadelphia Tribune* published articles as well. They all mentioned the fact that my residence was in Chestnut Hill, a section where black people did not live. (An earlier article in the now defunct *Philadelphia Bulletin* had compared my real estate taxes with those of my next-door neighbor, Senator Hugh Scott. My taxes were higher, although Senator Scott's home was larger and he had more land.) The point is, people knew where we lived.

One Sunday, we left for a week-long vacation. That Tuesday evening, someone cut a small opening in one of the rear windows in the living room. The opening was large enough for a child to crawl through. The child entered and opened the rear door through which the adult burglars entered. They systematically took things of value: expensive Sony video equipment worth thousands of dollars; my wife's good jewelry which we had purchased in Mexico the summer before; television sets and cameras; and a number of personal items that could never be replaced, such as the gold cufflinks and studs my father gave me, the gold engraved pocket watch which was my wife's 15th wedding anniversary present, and my high school graduation ring. When they reached the third floor where my study and library were located, they entered the bathroom, plugged the wash basin, and turned on the water. The water ran for the rest of the week, destroying the walls, floors, and carpeting. In the basement there were two feet of water. The burglars left through the front door after locking the rear door.

In those days, I always traveled "prepared." Whenever we returned from a vacation, I left my family in the car and went into the house alone to make sure that everything was all right. On this occasion, everything seemed to be fine—until I got to the landing leading to the second floor bedrooms, where I encountered a drawer from my wife's dresser with the contents spilled on the floor. I immediately went back to the car, called the police, and waited until they responded (which was almost immediately).

The house was a mess, a disaster, $50,000 worth of damage. We called our close friends, the Gilmores, and we stayed with them that night. The next day, I contacted my insurance company and we went to the Marriott Hotel on City Line Avenue. To make a long story short, we had to move out of the house and live in an apartment for several months while it was being repaired. The disruption was more than physical: my family felt violated. My children were devastated, asking why someone would do this to us. My daughter lost a collection of dolls from around the world. Since she was an infant, we had collected dolls from every country we visited, and other people had given her dolls from exotic places. They were all over her bedroom, on shelves, in cabinets, on dressers, on her bed.

When we finally returned to Hillcrest Avenue, the children, for the first time in their lives, began closing and locking the back door when they came in from the yard. (We had more than an acre there, with a complete playground, a large patio, a stream running through our property, and ducks from the Morris Arboretum across the street who came to swim. Frogs, squirrels, raccoons, birds, pheasants, and other wildlife were familiar.) They seemed unsure. They had never bothered to lock the door before, but now, no matter how many times they went in and out, they always did.

One day, we had an unexpected visit from Dr. Katherine Goddard, a child psychiatrist who was the wife of the provost of the University of Pennsylvania. She introduced herself as a neighbor, expressed her dismay and concern about the break-in, and said she had come to offer her assistance. Children are often traumatized and become apprehensive about their environment after a robbery like this, she told me. She had seen our children playing and she thought they would be all right, but she felt we should be aware of this possibility and provide as much reassurance and support as possible over the next few weeks. She offered her services if they were needed and she again expressed her sympathy for our losses before leaving to walk home. We were moved by this act of compassion, especially for our children. I shall remember it as long as I live.

Within days the news had spread all over Chestnut Hill and throughout Temple University. Jim Logan, Vice President for Finance, tried to find us a place to live temporarily in one of the many houses owned by the University. He was unsuccessful, but his efforts were appreciated. Our good friends, the Gilmores, were always there for us. But the question that always came up was whether the vandalism was racially motivated. The destruction was intentional: it had begun on the third floor, where my photographs, citations, and African American art were clustered. Although we never let it become a public issue, we are convinced that the vandalism occurred after the intruders saw photographs of prominent African Americans and civil rights leaders, black militant posters and paintings in the halls and on the walls of the study and library.

When we moved back into the house, we installed a state-of-the-art burglar alarm system and outdoor floodlights which worked on a timer. We had never felt the need for them before, although the houses were so far apart and hidden by trees and other foliage that you could not see your next door neighbors' home except during the winter. Why anyone would choose our house to burglarize when there were much more lucrative targets is a mystery—unless there was indeed a racial motive.

Schooldays

In Chestnut Hill, the old established families sent their children to private day schools (there were five in the area) or to boarding schools. Our children attended Jenks, the local public elementary school, which had a history of providing a fine education. It had been built for the children of the Irish and Italian workers who lived in the lower end of Chestnut Hill, but as early as the 1950s, black children had come to Jenks from other parts of the city on the "23" trolley. Later they came by bus, and when Barbra enrolled the student body was 40 percent black. There was a strong parent organization, although there were battles between those who lived in Chestnut Hill and those who lived elsewhere.

Barbra started kindergarten in the fall of 1972, very excited about going to a "real" school, not a nursery school like the one she had attended at the local Presbyterian church. Although she was only four and a half, she had no trouble adjusting. She was eager to learn, but her kindergarten experience was interrupted by a major teachers' strike. The following year, Barbra (and later her brother) had the good fortune to have one of the finest teachers I have ever met: Mrs. Marshall, who taught first and second grades, sometimes in the same room. She loved children, respected learning, and was active in drama and other student activities. Everyone thought she was wonderful, and it was not unusual for parents to employ any subterfuge to get their children assigned to her classes. Both our children thrived under her care.

Each year, at the end of May, Mrs. Marshall presented a play for the parents and the community. It was almost like a Broadway production: parents painted scenery, made costumes, and practiced their children's lines, songs, and dances. It was a great learning experience for the children—each one of whom was included—as they read, memorized, and acted out their parts. It also gave them great confidence.

The play for Barbra's class was *The Wizard of Oz*. Sharing the role of

Dorothy with a white friend, she performed in the first act and her friend in the second. Make no mistake about it: this was true integration. Mrs. Marshall made a point of being fair and giving each child public exposure. The auditorium was packed for each performance, day and evening. Photographs were displayed all over the school. Things were going splendidly until *The Chestnut Hill Local* spoiled a beautiful experience.

The one photograph which appeared in the paper showed the white Dorothy in front of the rest of the cast, which was mostly black. There was no picture or mention in the story of the two Dorothys who shared the lead role. When the paper came out, Lois was livid, I mean really livid. She called me at my office and told me about it. Lois had spent many hours working on the play with the students and their teacher. Mrs. Marshall, who had provided the paper with photographs and explained how it worked, was also upset. Barbra was almost in tears.

When I got home, read the article, and saw the photograph, I decided it was time for me to speak out on behalf of my children. Because I was an educator, I had tried to keep a low profile and leave school matters to my wife, but this was different. I sat down at my typewriter and wrote a blistering letter to the *Local*, chastising them for their insensitivity. I said, among other things, that I was sure that if Jenks had been a predominantly white school in a black neighborhood they would not have published a picture showing a black child, alone, in the lead. I still have a copy of that letter which I hand-delivered to the office of the *Local*.

Within an hour, the editor's office called to say my letter would be printed in the paper's next issue. I was even angrier at that offer; that was not my purpose. I wanted them to understand what they had done, intentionally or not, to sabotage a wonderful effort to help children in a changing school. I told them that publishing the letter was irrelevant, that I wanted to bring to their attention their insensitivity and arrogance. The following week, another, longer article appeared, with photographs. My anger was mollified.

My daughter had done a fantastic job: she was a natural "ham" and loved performing. In second grade, she played the role of Cinderella, and my wife was convinced that she was going to be a star of stage and screen. This little incident made me realize that, much as you might want to avoid conflict with other educators, you had an affirmative duty to protect your children and speak out when necessary. I continued to do so over the years, and I had more than one confrontation with teachers and administrators in the schools Barbra and Chuck attended, over injustice or failure to recognize individual differences.

Jenks was not a bad school; the children enjoyed their years there, in part because there was real diversity in the student body. Lois and I remember many of their activities: staying up all night with Chuck to finish a model of an aircraft carrier; helping him to build and paint a model of a flying machine designed by Michelangelo; Lois designing and sewing a costume for one of Mrs. Marshall's plays; helping Barbra learn her lines or write an essay. Lois was active in the parents' group and worked closely with people at Jenks, after putting in a full day at her own school. Our children were like most others their age, alternately loving and hating school, liking some teachers and not others, having "overnights" with friends at their house or ours.

After Jenks, Barbra attended Masterman Demonstration School, which drew students from all over the city. You had to qualify to get into Masterman. Barbra hated it—not because of the academic demands, with which she had no trouble. She felt that the school did not place enough emphasis on other things. Barbra and Chuck had studied piano at Combs College of Music and with private teachers. Barbra was also learning to play the guitar and she sang. She loved athletics, and in high school she participated in three sports as well as in the choir and chorus.

At the end of her second year, I had to go to the school to challenge a grade she had received. Barbra was furious because it did not represent the other grades she had received on tests and papers. After a long and fairly civil discussion with two teachers, it turned out that Barbra's grade had been based not on her actual performance, but on what her teachers believed she should have achieved, according to her "ability and test scores." One of the teachers went so far as to assert that they had the right to grade students this way under school district policies, an amazing and inaccurate statement. At about this time, the principal of the school joined us and informed us that he would handle the matter from his office— which he did by giving Barbra the grade she had earned. At this point, Barbra was thoroughly disgusted with Masterman, as were a number of her friends, and she transferred to Germantown Friends School.

After learning of Barbra's experiences at Masterman, Chuck had no interest in attending. To complicate matters, his last two years at Jenks left something to be desired. One year he had a total of six substitute teachers; then he experienced the disruption of a teacher strike. Lois had to work hard to make up for these deficiencies: her experience as an elementary school reading teacher came in handy. Poor Chuck had to go to school all day and then face working with his mother at night and on weekends.

We agonized over what to do, given our commitment to public education, but after much soul-searching, we reluctantly made the decision to enroll Chuck in a local private school. Unlike many parents, we always believed that our children should have something to say about the major decisions in their lives—and selecting a school is certainly one of them. Barbra had been deeply involved in the choice of Germantown Friends: it had not been easy, because some of her friends planned to enroll in other public schools both in and outside the city. Chuck was given the same opportunity. He applied to Germantown Friends and to the William Penn Charter School. He was admitted to both: to Penn Charter for his next regular grade; to GFS to repeat the grade he had completed at Jenks. After a good deal of discussion among the four of us, we left the decision up to Chuck, who settled on GFS. I did not think this was the best choice, but I did not share my feeling about this until he had been at GFS for several weeks. After five years at GFS, where he learned a lot and was successful in three sports (track and field, basketball, and soccer), he transferred to Penn Charter for his last two years and graduated in 1989.

Barbra's interest in gymnastics took her to gymnastics camp at Wells College in upstate New York for two summers. For her junior project at GFS, she attended Interlochen Music School in Michigan. There, for the first time, she saw serious music students from all over the world, studying jazz. She had lived in a home filled with jazz, but she had never shown an interest in studying it herself. When she returned from Interlochen, she asked if I would see whether Gerald Price, a well-known jazz artist and teacher, would give her lessons. I refused, but told her to call and get an appointment with Mr. Price, then ask him herself. She convinced him that she would be a conscientious student, and she studied piano with him throughout her senior year in high school.

Following her junior year at GFS, Barbra went to Nantes, a suburb of Paris, to spend the summer with a French family and polish her language skills. She continued studying French during her undergraduate years at Northwestern. Later, after her second year of law school, she had the opportunity to improve her Spanish, when she spent the summer in Mexico in a legal studies program sponsored by Loyola School of Law.

Chuck continued to participate in athletics throughout high school, and one summer he attended the LEAD program at the University of Virginia's Darden School of Business. During these years, both children had regular chores at home and paying jobs during the summers. Barbra worked at an ice cream parlor, waited tables in a Chestnut Hill restaurant, and was a sales clerk at a Gap store in a nearby mall. Chuck had jobs with our gardener, at the Morris Arboretum, and at the Franklin Institute, Philadelphia's science museum.

A special treat for me—and perhaps the defining moment of my relationship with my son—were the fifteen days we spent together visiting the People's Republic of China. I had been invited by the government to discuss various issues they were facing in higher education, and I agreed to go only if Chuck could accompany me to all the meetings and other activities.

The invitation had been extended through an intermediary, my friend and Temple University colleague, Dr. John Chen. Dr. Chen's father was a distinguished philosopher who had served as secretary of education for Shanghai under Chiang Kai-shek. After the revolution, the family moved to the United States, where the father taught philosophy at the University of Pittsburgh and Columbia University. John speaks all nine major Chinese dialects and has maintained an active interest in his native land. As chairman of the board of Huanghe University, the only English-speaking university in China (which he helped to found), John is familiar with that country's problems with expansion, diversity, and curriculum change.

That trip was one of the extraordinary experiences of my life. For fifteen days, my son and I traveled across China, mostly by train, and visited rural villages, collective farms, private factories, and large and small cities, including Beijing and Shanghai. We climbed the Great Wall together, and we saw the Forbidden City. We visited some of the nine universities open only to minorities, as well as other integrated institutions which were required to provide spaces for a certain number of minorities. In Xian, we saw a university president who is essentially responsible for an entire city, and we met the person who is in charge of the education of 1,200,000,000 people. (The latter and his wife earned their doctorates at U.S. universities, as did most of the leading officials we met.) Chuck got to meet the first Chinese to obtain a doctorate in mathematics.

After I gave a series of lectures to the graduate students at the English-speaking university, most of whom were in their twenties, I was asked if Chuck could speak to them about his life as an African American teenager. I agreed, and Chuck spent ninety minutes alone with them. He was a hit, and they presented him with a set of six porcelain horses which he still cherishes. Later, Chuck told me about the questions they asked and how fascinated they were with his relationship with his father. Our easy-going, kidding, openly affectionate style is apparently uncommon in China.

When the time came for them to apply to college, we saw that our children obtained enough information and then made their own choices. Having been raised in the east, both of them had succumbed to what I call

"The Disease": the belief that the only good schools are on the east coast. We insisted that they look at colleges in the south and midwest as well. We told them that we would send them to any school which accepted them, but only after they had visited schools in each of the three sections of the country. (We ruled out the west coast for undergraduate education unless there was some compelling reason to go there, such as a specialized curriculum they could not get anywhere else.)

Barbra was at first interested in Cornell, the University of Virginia, and Brown. She made the required visits to southern schools, including Duke, and she looked at Washington University in St. Louis, Missouri. But after two days on the campus of Northwestern University in Evanston, Barbra was so excited that she applied for early decision and was admitted. She loved every minute of her four years there, graduated in 1990 with a degree in political science—and has said if she were offered a job there, she would go back without a second thought. She stayed in the midwest for graduate school and was granted a law degree from Washington University in St. Louis in 1993.

Chuck had enjoyed his summer at the University of Virginia and decided that he would go there or to Northwestern. However, he had heard students talking about Emory University in Atlanta, and he added Emory to his list. On his second visit, he decided to apply for early decision and to major in history. He graduated from Emory in 1993. During his college years, he continued his interest in athletics and was a freshman member of the Emory University, Division III, Conference Championship basketball team.

Reflections on Parenthood

Both our children received good educations, good enough to prepare them for quality colleges and universities—but the schools did not do that alone. As parents, we tried to provide the important things for our children: love, support, understanding, discipline, and a set of values which included respect for others, integrity, and responsibility. Some people don't understand why we were relatively relaxed about grades. Both of our children had been tested by independent experts outside the school system, and we knew that they had the ability to achieve just about anything they made up their minds to achieve. But we also knew that these tests had limited predictive ability and that other qualities were more important to their success: focus, determination, confidence, high expectations, hard work.

Our own lives and the lives of most of our African American friends provided evidence of this and we tried to imbue our children with this understanding. We also tried very hard to teach them certain basic truths: life is not fair; competition does not take place on a level playing field; African Americans must still be better than whites to succeed at the same level; poor people do not have the same opportunities as people who are better off economically; you are the person most responsible for your success or failure.

At the same time, we insisted that they must accord to others the respect they demanded for themselves. Although African Americans have been oppressed, enslaved, segregated, discriminated against, and even brutalized, that does not mean that all white people are bigots or racists. Judge people not only by their words, we told them, but by their behavior as well. This country is not perfect and equality has not been achieved, but there has been progress. Still, that progress must be monitored, protected, and advanced; there are always those who want to turn back the clock. When you reach a position of power, we said, don't adopt the attitudes and behavior of the oppressors. That is not what our struggle is or has been about. Our struggle is about making this great country live up to its own ideals and pronouncements about equality and justice, about fairness and compassion, about honesty and responsibility.

You don't teach human relations in a vacuum. Our children were exposed to a wide variety of people, our friends and acquaintances. Their babysitters were black, white, Asian, Central and South American, Catholic, Protestant, and Jewish. When we entertained at our home, we never excluded the children from the party, so they became comfortable with adults and with the wide variety of people whom we knew. We took them with us across the country: California, Illinois, Indiana, Missouri, Massachusetts, New York, Connecticut, Ohio, Virginia, and Washington, D.C. And we took them abroad: Barbados, the Bahamas, the U.S. Virgin Islands, Aruba, Mexico, England, France, Switzerland, the Netherlands. Each trip was a learning experience.

Encounter with the Police

Unfortunately, African American parents also have to teach their children other things about the reality of their existence in the United States. This is particularly true if you have a son. Young black men seem to have difficulties with the police in this country, especially if their encounters are at night or in some isolated area or in a white neighborhood. Earlier,

I recounted my own traumatic experience of meeting an armed, racist policeman in Bloomington. More than forty years later, it was Chuck's turn.

He and two of his friends had been to a wedding and they were on their way to a party at someone's house on a quiet residential street in North Philadelphia near Temple University Hospital. Chuck was then a senior at Emory, one friend was a Morehouse graduate, and the other was a young executive with a major insurance company. They parked their car and went to the door—but it was the wrong number. Suddenly, as they were walking to the right house, squad cars with sirens screaming and lights flashing came roaring down the one-way street in the wrong direction. Additional cars came up the other way.

Before they knew what was happening, the policemen, hands on their holsters, ordered the three young men up against the squad cars, placed their hands behind their backs, searched them, and handcuffed them. Petrified and angry, Chuck and his friends asked what they had done and why they were being treated this way. The reply: "Shut up; keep your f...... mouth shut, and don't move." Soon, a policeman opened the door of his car and a diminutive white woman got out. When the cop asked her if these were the men, she shook her head and answered "No." Chuck and one of his friends recognized her immediately: she was a well-known local character, a prostitute who had worked the corner of Broad and Belfield regularly, day and night, for years. They were livid! When the policemen told them they "were lucky" and could go, they protested their treatment. But although they were careful not to become belligerent—they had been taught how to act with police—one cop, a young black man himself, became enraged. "OK, you smart asses," he said, "you're going to jail. I don't give a shit who you are. Out here, I am the law and your asses will respect that."

They were taken to the precinct station on Broad Street and locked up. This was about 9:00 p.m. At 3:00 a.m., Lois and I received a telephone call from Chuck, saying "Dad, please come and get us, we are in jail." He gave us the address, and we dressed and drove to the precinct house as fast as we could. When we arrived, the three young men were waiting on the sidewalk. They had been released and put out on the street many blocks from their automobile.

We took them to their car and they followed us to our house, where the two friends called their parents. I was furious, and my wife was distraught. I sat the young men in my living room, got my video camera and a tape recorder, and asked them to tell me exactly what had happened.

They were still dressed for the wedding, they had not been drinking, not even a beer, and I wanted this on tape. It turned out that they had been denied a phone call, kept in cells, and then charged with disorderly conduct or disrespect for an officer. They were told to report for a hearing at a later date and then released.

Naturally, we engaged a lawyer and prepared to fight the charges all the way to the Supreme Court. I turned the tapes over to my lawyer and asked him to consider a suit against the city and the police department. It looked as if we had a good civil rights case, but we decided to await the outcome of the hearing. The day of the hearing, the black cop who had been the most aggressive met with our lawyer and the three young men. The cop dropped the charges and told the men he was not trying to "jam them" but that they had to understand that "College boys or not, I am the law. On the streets, I am in charge." We did not sue because the oldest of the three (the insurance executive) did not want to.

Responsibility

Raising two children has been a joy. We relished every stage of their development from infancy to young adulthood, and we like the kind of people they have become, although—as is inevitable—we don't agree on everything. Lois and I were right when we decided to wait until we could afford the time and had the resources to be the kind of parents we wanted to be. It was, however, a decision that was fraught with risk.

I rarely discussed my feelings about the difference in our ages, but the fact is that I am ten years older than my wife. I was thirty-nine when Barbra was born and there was no guarantee that I would be around to see her grow up. My mother and her family were long-lived. She was 80 when she died, but my grandmother lived until she was 96. One of my aunts was a few weeks short of her 100th birthday, and the others were into their 80s or 90s before they died. My father's side of the family was not so fortunate; he himself died at 56 and, as I've already mentioned, my two brothers died young—one at age seven and the other when he was 26.

I was well aware of the risk to my own family, and I decided to reduce it. Early on, I began a savings program. I bought annuities and insurance policies so that if I died prematurely, my wife would never have to make compromises in her personal life for economic reasons and my children would be assured of a college education. In addition to my full-time employment, I engaged in a variety of consultancies: Rockefeller, Ford, Charles Stewart Mott, Standard Oil, Danforth, and Kettering

Foundations; a number of state education departments and local school boards; a variety of speaking engagements and several program consultancies. There was never a shortage of opportunities, and because I was conscientious and delivered what I promised, they almost always came to me unsolicited. After twenty years, I no longer had to be concerned about my children's education or my wife's independence if something happened to me.

These considerations were especially important to me because I had seen the devastation caused by the premature death of the major breadwinner. After my father died, I had to assume the role of head of the household. I moved my mother into a new home in Tolleston and lived with her until I married. I sent my youngest sister, Dolores, to college at Indiana University. I did not consider it an undue burden; it was my responsibility. It was the way we were raised by our parents. When we were teenagers, we worked and shared some of our earnings with the family. These voluntary contributions enabled us to have things beyond the necessities that my father and mother always provided. It is something Watsons do.

Many years later, in 1967, my niece was involved in an automobile accident in which her husband and two others were killed. The car in which they were driving was struck from behind by a semi-truck loaded with gravel, and the gas tank exploded. My niece survived because she was pulled from the burning vehicle by the truckdriver, but after weeks in a coma, months in intensive care, and several operations, she remained paralyzed from the waist down. I hired lawyers to pursue her case against the trucking company, and she was awarded an amount which made her independent for life. She lived alone in her own home until her death in 1993. Her mother (my sister) was in no position to help her; her father was dead. It was my responsibility to do what I could do.

I am gratified that my two children have also acquired the Watson sense of responsibility. It was not something that Lois and I crammed down their throats: they just seemed to absorb the idea of contributing toward their own educational expenses and of sharing their time with others. As I noted earlier, both of them worked throughout high school, and that pattern continued while they were in college. Barbra had jobs with a hotel, Smith Barney (stockbrokers), and Washington Life Insurance, while Chuck returned to the Franklin Institute and then went to the Penn Mutual Life Insurance Company. But I am even more proud of their volunteer activities. At Northwestern, Barbra served as a recruiter and counselor for potential students and also participated in her sorority's social action program. (In fact, she has received two national awards for social service from Alpha Kappa Alpha: one was presented at a convocation which Lois, also a member of the sorority, attended—quite a thrill for any mother.) After Barbra moved to Washington to begin the practice of law, she found time for tutoring some public school children. She has since married a fellow attorney and gone to St. Louis, but I am sure she will soon find a way to be involved in that community. Chuck helped out at an Atlanta food bank and worked with high schoolers during his time at Emory— and received the Ducemus Campus Life Award. After obtaining some experience in both newspaper and television journalism (at the *Atlanta Constitution/Journal* and CNN), Chuck is now a student at Northwestern's Medill graduate school of journalism.

Like all parents, we wonder how the years went by so quickly, but we feel exceptionally fortunate that our children are also our friends.

CHAPTER VIII
AN URBAN UNIVERSITY

By the summer of 1969, it was apparent to me that the Shedd administration's days were numbered. Rizzo's star was continuing to rise as the
Philadelphia Inquirer, then owned by Walter Annenberg, and *Philadelphia
Magazine* profiled the exploits of the colorful police commissioner. Many
erroneously attributed the absence of rioting in Philadelphia to the strong
law-and-order tactics of Frank Rizzo. I was told by a number of people,
Richardson Dilworth among them, that Rizzo was driving Annenberg
around at night in his police cruiser, cultivating support for his tactics in
keeping "militants" and "revolutionaries" (that is, the black community)
under control. In fact, the city's relative peace was due to organizations like
the Fellowship Commission, CORE, Fellowship House, OIC, the black
churches, and individuals like Dr. Leon Sullivan, Raymond Pace Alexander,
Charles Bowser, and Cecil B. Moore. The best description of the events of
that period, and the range of people involved in them, can be found in Father
Paul Washington's 1994 autobiography, "*Other Sheep I Have.*"

The Board of Education came under increasing scrutiny and attack.
People were beginning to leave the school system: those no longer faced
with the threat of being drafted and sent to Vietnam; those who had tired
of their liberal experiment in helping poor, disadvantaged ghetto dwellers;
those who had decided it was time to resume their planned careers in
the real world. African American school administrators also resigned,
wanting to go where they felt they could have a greater impact and exercise real authority. In 1970, Marcus Foster departed for Oakland,
California, to become the superintendent of schools. Samuel Woodard
went to Southern Illinois University (later to Howard), and I left to join
the faculty of Temple University.

Beginning in 1968, I received a number of offers of positions in other
school systems, and I had been approached by the University of Chicago,

Ohio State, Stanford, the University of California at Berkeley, Indiana, Howard, Atlanta, and the University of Massachusetts at Amherst. During my three years with the Philadelphia public schools, I had been a visiting professor at the University of Pennsylvania's Graduate School of Education and had lectured in Penn's Planning Department and School of Social Work. At Temple University, I had worked with four deans— liberal arts, social work, education, and communications—as we planned the curricula for new schools.

I was particularly interested in Temple, in part because Paul Eberman, dean of the College of Education and a nationally respected scholar, was really trying to improve the way future school teachers and administrators were trained. Among other things, he had appointed Dr. Roderick Hilsinger, who had been an official in the U.S. Office of Education, as head of the division of curriculum and instruction in the College of Education. Rod was outspoken, intelligent, humorous, and fearless, and he was the one who convinced me to join the Temple faculty. Rod was a unique individual who had amazing courage for undertaking innovative projects and, when necessary, taking the initiative. The most dramatic example occurred during a flight back from Ethiopia—accompanied, as it turned out, by a gang of terrorists. Rod saved the plane and its passengers by grabbing a grenade and lobbing it into the bulkhead where its explosion was contained. He was hospitalized for weeks because of shrapnel damage—but his motto remained, "Do the right thing."

An additional plus for me was that a university position would offer more freedom to become more actively involved in the independent black political movement which was then beginning to pick up steam. I was convinced it was the best vehicle not only for empowering the poor but for improving education and other opportunities for African Americans in this city, and I wanted to continue to help in whatever way I could. Finally, Lois and I had begun to feel at home in Philadelphia, and we didn't want to move and start again somewhere else. When I was offered a position at Temple, I accepted, and in September 1970 I became a full professor in the College of Education and chairman of the new Department of Urban Education.

The department enrolled only graduate students, some with bachelor's degrees in teaching and some with other majors. There were no required courses, but each student had to demonstrate knowledge in four areas: Urbanism and Education; The Urban School; Urban Minorities; and Analysis of Social Systems. Each student's program was planned and supervised by an advisory committee of faculty members who followed him or her from matriculation through completion of the dissertation (although there might be a different committee for the dissertation, depending on the topic). Most courses were taken in other departments, and even in other colleges, thus exposing students to experts in their field of study. Independent research and an individually designed field experience were required of doctoral candidates and were optional for master's candidates. Fundamental to the urban education department was my belief that graduate education should be demanding and rigorous, but not rigid.

I was helped enormously by the outside funding I had from both the Office of Education and the Rockefeller Foundation. Along with university support, I was able to employ the research assistant with whom I had worked at the school district and to hire an additional secretary to support the work of the department. The freedom afforded by these grants was important, because the new department was not greeted with open arms by members of the Department of Educational Administration. In fact, it was viewed as a potential threat to their hegemony over the certification of school principals and superintendents. Eventually, however, they accepted it for what is was: an attempt to improve the preparation for work in schools in big cities and complex urban areas.

We were able to attract excellent students from a variety of backgrounds: rich and poor; white, Asian, Latino, and black; majors in the liberal arts and business, as well as education. Their field placements ranged from the office of the director of Philadelphia's Model Cities program to WHYY (the local public television station), to the Rutgers Center for Law and Education, and our graduates easily moved into positions as teachers, principals, superintendents, and deans. Occasionally, we also had students, some of them undergraduates, who just took a course or two because of their interest. Paul Taylor, who was studying at Yale, was one of them; he became a well-known journalist, an associate editor of the *Philadelphia Inquirer* and later the *Washington Post*.

Soon after arriving at Temple, I entered into discussions with George Johnson, a professor of English and dean of the College of Liberal Arts. I wanted to start an interdisciplinary urban studies program, modeled on the University of Chicago's Committee on Social Thought, for which faculty would be drawn from such areas as sociology, political science, and history, while retaining their appointments in their home departments. A number of individuals at Temple who had studied or taught at Chicago were familiar with the concept, and after some negotiation Dean Johnson agreed to present it to the Graduate Board for approval. A master's degree program was finally approved and continues to this day. (I taught the undergraduate honors course in urban studies in the College of Liberal Arts.) I had hoped to initiate a doctoral program as well and had even convinced a vice president of the Ford Foundation to consider a non-elite, non-Ivy League university as a site for one of their grant programs. Temple President Marvin Wachman had joined me in seeking foundation funding, but our efforts were ultimately unsuccessful because of problems in some Temple academic departments, including an unwillingness to revise their student requirements.

In 1970, when I joined the Temple faculty, the university was in the throes of the changes and conflicts that were gripping institutions of higher education across the country, particularly those located in major cities. I had seen the same tensions at the University of Chicago, at Wayne State University in Detroit, and at the State University of New York at Buffalo. Residents of urban areas, newly empowered by the civil rights movement and the government's community action program, were rising up to protest university expansion without any consultation with them, and many were demanding that the university admit more poor and minority students. The University of Pennsylvania and Drexel University, both in West Philadelphia, were experiencing similar tensions in their neighborhood, but Temple's situation was unique. It was located in the heart of North Philadelphia, the poorest area of the city but one which had an unusual number of active community organizations and was the headquarters of the Area Wide Council, the umbrella group for the Model Cities program.

Temple was not prepared. The president of the university was Paul Anderson, a philosopher who had come from outside Philadelphia and who, it was widely believed and asserted, knew little about urban problems and was not comfortable with issues involving African Americans and other minority groups. The faculty and administration were over-whelmingly white, and many of them had become increasingly concerned about the number of people on campus who were not students. Proposals ranged from closing off the campus and prohibiting neighborhood residents from walking through on their way to school or work, to leaving North Philadelphia altogether and moving the university to the suburbs. Attempts to discuss these issues with community organizations had proved notably unsuccessful.

One glaring example was the highly publicized "charrette," an elaborate planning exercise popular during the sixties and seventies. This technique purported to bring together individuals and organizations to discuss differences, engage in joint planning, and arrive at a consensus which all parties would implement. The Temple/North Philadelphia charrette was, to describe it charitably, a dismal failure. Some called it an attempt to co-opt the community. Others called it a disaster that inflamed already bitter feelings and increased the mutual suspicions.

Meantime, Temple was embroiled in numerous internal controversies. Student groups were making previously unheard-of demands, and the faculty had begun speaking out forcefully. Women were beginning to organize around issues of equal pay, promotion, and tenure, while several deans had started to assert themselves about hiring and modernizing the curriculum. The campus was divided: the president had received votes of no confidence from the faculty, student government, and other groups, although he retained the support of the Temple trustees.

The situation would have been far more contentious had it not been for the fact that Marvin Wachman, Temple's vice president for academic affairs, was popular with faculty, students, and staff. Wachman was also infinitely more acceptable to the community. He had previously served as president of Lincoln University, an HBCU located about an hour from Philadelphia, and was there during the period when Stokely Carmichael and Charles Hamilton, then a professor at Lincoln, had co-written the book *Black Power*. Wachman was a healer, a consensus builder, a person who encouraged tolerance and agreement. In my opinion, had it not been for Wachman's presence at Temple in those volatile times, chaos might very well have been the result.

Wachman was available to consult with almost any organization or individual, and even when the problem was not resolved to the satisfaction of the participants, they left with a feeling that they had been heard. Equity for women in hiring, pay, and promotion was an issue of enormous importance, and even before Wachman became president, he was the point man. I was familiar with the inequities because members of the faculty in my own department were victims. Eunice Clark had been an associate professor for many years, while her male colleagues with similar credentials and experience had long since been promoted to full professor. The disparity in compensation was even more pronounced. Another female in my department, although she had been teaching a very popular undergraduate course in the College of Liberal Arts for nine years, had no status, no benefits, and no career ladder. She was simply a salaried worker, hired on a year-to-year basis.

Because of my personal intervention, Eunice Clark was recommended for and promoted to full professor, and her salary was increased to bring it into line with those of her male colleagues. Elaine Blake, the other female faculty member, was given the status of instructor, along with all the benefits awarded other faculty and staff members. Eunice Clark was white and had earned her doctorate from the University of Pennsylvania. Elaine Blake was black, had been hired during the sixties, and had not formalized her bachelor's degree. She quickly did so after my arrival, then earned a master's degree and enrolled in a doctoral program. Both women were bright, articulate, knowledgeable, and popular with their students. Within three years, a comprehensive study of women's equity was followed by the announcement of new policies and practices. Implementation took place over several years, but the university was firmly committed to equity for women. As in most issues of this kind, eternal vigilance and consistent monitoring determine how effective such policies remain through the years.

The matter of minority admissions was more complicated. Although African Americans had attended Temple University for years, it had the reputation in the black community of not being particularly hospitable. Temple may have been no less tolerant of minority students than Penn State or Drexel or Penn, but its location in the heart of North Philadelphia placed it under a microscope. In attempts to remedy the underenrollment of minorities, Temple had created a number of programs to recruit minority and disadvantaged high school graduates who, in the absence of these special efforts, would not likely have been admitted to Temple. The Special Recruitment and Admissions Program, known as SRAP, provided high school graduates, who had either a GED or regular diploma, with remedial and developmental courses, counseling, tutoring, and financial aid—and eventually a transfer out of SRAP into one of the many colleges in the university. There were several other programs as well, and when I became a vice president, one of my first priorities was to see that they were properly coordinated and made more efficient. It should be noted that there was constant pressure from students, faculty, trustees, community leaders, and the School District of Philadelphia (which wanted more of its graduates admitted to Temple).

There was also a push to hire more minority, particularly black, faculty. It was ridiculous in the extreme to argue that there were not enough qualified candidates. Predominantly white universities had only recently begun to hire minority and black faculty, and the pool was larger than the number of jobs available. The same could be said for administrative positions. Until Clifton Wharton became President of Michigan State University, not one majority university was headed by an African American. There were few, if any, in the senior ranks of administration: deans, vice presidents, provosts. When black individuals were hired, they were given "special" positions and titles: special assistant for..., assistant to the..., director of community relations, coordinator of minority affairs, director of special programs or special projects, to name a few. Temple was not different.

All of these positions shared certain characteristics: they carried little authority, there was no staff other than a secretary or two, the budget was small, and they were viewed as irrelevant and/or unimportant by the general faculty and administration. The persons in those positions may have been respected, but their responsibilities were not. On any number of occasions, I was asked to sign petitions for the hiring of black administrators. I did so, but in almost every instance, the position was peripheral and had little influence. I argued in vain with my black colleagues to fight for positions of substance, with real authority, responsibility, budget, and staff. I was always told that this job would be only a first step, but it never worked out that way. One individual resigned out of frustration and left the university to become a vice president of one college and later the president of another. Another individual had to fight, over several years, to retain his powerless position until he could retire. Another, despite impeccable credentials, accepted his lot and refused to stage an open fight for the position and title he deserved.

After Marvin Wachman became president, he asked me on more than one occasion about accepting an administrative position. I was not interested. I enjoyed teaching and leading an exciting new department which attracted very good and enthusiastic students, black, white, and Hispanic. I enjoyed having the time to write and to pursue my outside activities. It was a rewarding time for me and I had no interest in having my freedom restricted by the demands of a significant administrative position. During my first five years at the university I was able to write and publish a book, 100 career folios for use in junior and senior high schools, six monographs, six chapters in books, and ten journal articles. In addition, I founded and edited a national journal, *Cross Reference: A Journal of Public Policy and Multicultural Education*, that was completely funded by the J.B. Lippincott company, then one of Philadelphia's leading publishers. (I was the first outside member of its board of directors.) Throughout this period, I was also deeply involved in the issues on campus and active in faculty organizations.

One of the most important programs Temple offered during my tenure there was the VIPS program: Veterans in Public Service. This program was the brainchild of the late George Hutt, an African American engineer who was not satisfied with the education his daughter was receiving and who later served on the Philadelphia school board. Recognizing how many young blacks were fighting in Vietnam, and how many had come from Philadelphia, George had asked Temple to establish a program for them in the College of Education, where they could be trained as teachers while receiving special assistance, including counseling from sympathetic advisors who wanted them to succeed. George and I discussed his idea while I was still with the School District, and we convinced the college dean, Paul Eberman, to support it and also helped to get federal funding.

VIPS was a transforming experience for me. I had read about the war and had my own feelings about it, but those feelings did not extend to damning the young men and women who fought in it. Most of them came from the kind of background I was from and from neighborhoods like the one I grew up in in Gary, Indiana. Military service was a routine experience for the people I knew, and I was a veteran of the Korean War. But when I got to know some of the young men in the VIPS program—all of whom had been in combat—I soon learned that Vietnam was something else entirely. One became a good friend, a friendship which continues to this day.

Jesse Merrill was always, it seemed to me, angrier than the rest of the students. He was more thoughtful and ambitious, but there was an anger in him that I could never grasp, a wall I couldn't penetrate. He would say: "You don't understand, Doc. Vietnam was different. One of these days I will tell you about it. You wouldn't understand now." This went on for almost ten years until one day he called me at my office at the William Penn Foundation and said, "I'm ready to talk now, Doc. I can explain it so you will understand why you saw all of that anger in me." I quickly arranged to see him and his appointment, which lasted more than an hour, left me not only enlightened, but stunned and relieved.

Jesse had been the leader of a team of soldiers who slipped into Cambodia to rescue pilots and crew members whose planes had been shot down. At the time, the U.S. was not supposed to be in Cambodia or flying over their territory and bombing. Merrill had rescued a number of crew members, brought them out alive, and never lost a member of his team— a feat so unusual that he was extremely proud of his accomplishments. The problem was that he had never received the decorations he had earned, including the Silver and Bronze Stars. The Pentagon could not officially acknowledge his exploits because of the illegality of what the U.S. was doing at that time. Later, as a result of the Freedom of Information Act, the story had come out and the Pentagon was forced to admit what had happened. Receiving his medals, his public recognition, freed Jesse from his anger. He talked about the men who had been lost in battle, the friends from Edison High School who did not come back or who came back to scorn. Then, and in later sessions, I began to understand how badly wounded some Vietnam veterans were and how they had to confront the anger and rejection at home. It is a miracle that so many of these young men could put the horror behind them and get on with their lives. The VIPS did well. One became a lawyer and an assistant dean at a law school. One is completing his doctorate in engineering. One has a master's in engineering, another in vocational and industrial education. One was the only black project manager at the Philadelphia Navy Yard and his son is a graduate of the U.S. Naval Academy.

Another gratifying experience was teaching a summer course on gangs, along with Dr. Betty Schantz, a Temple professor who had worked with the well-known 12th and Oxford Street gang and others over several years. Students in the course, which was always oversubscribed, ranged from teachers, school administrators, and police officers to gang members and their parents. Betty and I tried to place gang activity in an historical context, and we, along with our guest lecturers, helped many people understand the conditions which led to gang membership and turf wars. The discussions in this very mixed group of people were at the heart of the course. They were exhilarating and exhausting. Most important, the course provided a place where people of all backgrounds could come together and learn from one another.

Although progress continued on minority enrollments at Temple, faculty recruitment and promotion moved much more slowly. The year (1970) that I joined Temple's faculty, Professor Lawrence Reddick, a distinguished and published African American historian, was appointed a full professor with tenure in the department of history. Several years later, as he approached the mandatory retirement age of 67, Dr. Reddick became the center of a controversy about minority faculty hiring, more specifically African American faculty. A very public disagreement took place between Reddick and Dr. Herbert Bass, who was the chairman of the history department. The controversy expanded to include two junior colleagues of Dr. Bass, both African Americans, President Wachman and, eventually, members of the Pennsylvania State Legislature.

Reddick had accused the department of racism and then broadened his attack to include the university and its policies. In response to these charges, President Wachman pointed out that Temple had made remarkable progress:

- During calendar year 1975, 26 new minority faculty were appointed, representing 12% of all new faculty appointments. Eleven were black, ten were Asian, and five were Hispanic.
- In the early sixties, there were only several hundred blacks attending Temple. By this time, it was estimated that there were 6,000 among all categories of students (full- and part-time, graduate and undergraduate).
- Of the full-time undergraduate enrollment of 15,000, approximately 2,800 were black.
- The medical and law schools had become the leaders among majority institutions in minority enrollment.

To be sure, the use of faculty figures was suspect. Included in that number were academic professionals who were not in the tenure line: they had received clinical appointments which would not lead to permanent academic appointments. The use and misuse of figures by all sides was common on campuses during this period. The debate became increasingly hostile and personal. Individuals, black and white, were insulted and aspersions were cast on their integrity and veracity. Student demonstrations in support of Dr. Reddick in the student activity center were covered by all the Philadelphia newspapers, as well as local radio and television. The Temple University trustees became involved, convening a special committee, and finally, a subcommittee of the Pennsylvania House of Representatives Education Committee held hearings in October 1976.

Most of this controversy took place while I was on sabbatical leave. During that time, I continued to write and, with my research assistant Linda Darling-Hammond, conducted the first national study of violence and vandalism in public schools, a topic which was then—as now—attracting a good deal of attention. Linda and I sent detailed questionnaires to a number of school systems, including San Francisco, St. Louis, Oakland (California), Gary (Indiana), Dade County (Florida), Washington, and Los Angeles. We then visited those districts to interview principals, central office administrators (including the superintendents), school board members and others. We conducted this research with funds provided by Congressman Augustus Hawkins, chair of the House Education Committee, and left over from the very successful conference I directed in 1972, the First National Policy Conference on Education for Blacks.

After I had made my report to Congress and had published it in the *Congressional Record* and as a monograph, the president of Temple again asked me about joining the university administration. Now that I had completed a sabbatical and written extensively, he thought I might be ready for a change. The vice president for academic affairs was resigning to return to teaching, and Marvin intended to divide that position because it had become too unwieldy for one person to handle. However, he wanted to include academic responsibilities in both of the two new job descriptions: there would be a vice president/dean of faculties and a vice president for academic administration. The president discussed with me the appropriate distribution of tasks over a period of several weeks, and then offered me the choice of either position. He had another person in mind for the position I didn't choose, but he was convinced that either of us could do either job. I decided I would become vice president for academic administration.

That portfolio included undergraduate and graduate admissions, registration, student records, financial aid, all educational opportunity and continuing education programs, Temple University Center City (TUCC), Research and Program Development, the Institute for Survey Research, Center for the Administration of Justice, Temple University Press, the Measurement and Research Center, and a number of others. These were the areas where I could exert the most influence and they were also the areas where my skills were strongest. I had no interest in presiding over the Council of Deans and dealing with the internal politics connected with that responsibility. I also knew that the deans were power centers in their colleges, and I did not wish to spend most of my time dealing with things that only the president could really influence in any meaningful way. With the portfolio I had chosen, I could really have an impact on some areas I considered of primary importance: hiring, admissions, data gathering and analysis, student aid, enrolling a diverse and fully qualified student body, and outside funding.

There was no hesitation on my part, but I was asked many, many times why I was not appointed to the other position which many saw as more powerful and one which would place the incumbent in line to become the next president. Both black and white faculty members, students, and others held this view, although not many ever raised this issue publicly. A few, however, immediately saw the power of the position I had chosen and were not surprised that I had selected this position. The only time I revealed in public that I had had the choice of either position was when the state legislative hearings were convened at Temple and Professor Reddick referred to my appointment as a public relations gesture on the part of the administration. Reddick knew better. He also knew that I could have been president of two institutions of higher education before I was appointed to this position at Temple.

The July 1976 announcement that John Rumpf, an engineering professor, and I were to become vice presidents took people by surprise. Engineers are not usually appointed to senior academic positions in a university like Temple, but Rumpf had a national reputation as an expert on bridges and had served as dean of Temple's fledgling college of engineering. My appointment was something else again: I became the first African American vice president in the 93-year history of Temple University. The appointment was well, even enthusiastically, received by the faculty and students. Naturally, it attracted considerable attention. The three daily newspapers and the twice-weekly black newspaper did feature articles and the news was picked up nationally. (As noted in the previous chapter, the publicity perhaps had an unfortunate consequence: the burglary of my home in Chestnut Hill.) Rumpf and I agreed to cooperate as much as possible. We both knew that there would be attempts to play us off against each other as faculty and staff, for their own reasons, tried to position themselves with the person they presumed to be the heir apparent to Marvin Wachman.

Rumpf and I did in fact work together reasonably well, attended meetings of the Council of Deans, served on the same committees. Our relationship was cordial, but within six months it became clear that he wanted to become president. I did not, and for several years, I had said so publicly and in print. I did not want to spend most of my time embroiled in the politics of education: dealing with rich donors, influential alumni, individual and small groups of powerful deans, members of the state legislature, the governor's office, and so on. I was reasonably good at that kind of thing, but I was much more interested in teaching and learning, student activities, and the intellectual work of faculty members. I had made continuing to teach one course per semester one of the conditions for my becoming a vice president, and President Wachman readily agreed, saying how much he missed teaching. One of my proudest contributions during my five years as vice president was not only that I taught every year but nagged and encouraged every other vice president to do the same. Even Marvin Wachman taught—and loved every minute of it.

There was only one fleeting moment when I thought about entering the fray as a possible successor to President Wachman. One day, after I had been vice president for more than a year, I was parking my car in the Temple lot used by many of the university trustees and administrators, when a prominent member of the Temple board pulled into an adjoining space. His automobile was the same year, color, and make as mine—but his sedan was the largest model available and it was driven by his chauffeur. As the man got out, he said, "Wow! We really pay our vice presidents very well here at Temple. Just look at the cars they drive!" He wasn't smiling and there was a hint of putting me in my place in his attitude. I didn't smile either. I walked a little closer to him, looked him in the eye, and said evenly, "You may pay some of them very well; I am not one of them. For your information, this is not my first Mercedes and it won't be my last, whether I am a vice president of Temple or not." The man turned crimson, smiled through gritted teeth, and tried to make light of his remark by saying, "I didn't mean anything by it, just that you have a nice automobile, the same make as mine." I was having none of that: I knew exactly what he meant.

Later, I heard from several reliable sources that this same trustee had said that Temple University would "have a black president over my dead body." That statement was a challenge to a "Race Man" (see Chapter I and Chapter III) and I would have gladly accepted it if I had truly wanted the position. I knew that I was fully qualified by experience and education to assume those duties. Moreover, I had developed and honed the skills necessary not only to survive, but to prosper in that environment. Moreover (although that trustee didn't know this), I had powerful advocates on the board of trustees and in the Philadelphia community who had approached me about the presidency as soon as Wachman had announced his retirement. The first dean who offered to help organize faculty support for me was Peter Liacouras, then dean of the law school and now president of the university. I reiterated my lack of interest and encouraged Peter to seek the position himself. I had been impressed with his work in the law school, his participation on the Council of Deans, and his belief, as strong as my own, in the importance of Temple's mission not just to Philadelphia but to higher education generally.

One of my first steps after assuming the vice presidency was to assess the activities designed to diversify the student body. An audit soon revealed that in many instances, the students enrolled in one program were also carried on the rolls of another. There was no clear differentiation of functions, allocation of resources, or means of accountability. There was no way of knowing how well the programs were serving their students or whether the university was getting the results expected after investing both financial and human resources.

With my special assistant, James Bolden, I began a series of consultations with the program directors, various university committees, and students from each of the programs. We also met with the Director of Undergraduate Admissions. Within six months, I had formulated a plan of reorganization which I thought would lead to a marked improvement in services and support for students. All the programs would be based in the new Russell Conwell Center, named after Temple's founder. The Center would have a director and a small staff to maintain administrative and budgetary control. The functions of the various merged programs would continue, and in no instance would their budgets be cut. In fact, some budgets would be increased because more students would be served. I had taken the precaution of hiring an outstanding accountant from the Philadelphia Federal Reserve Bank to be the finance chief and controller for all functions under my jurisdiction. I knew that I needed someone who was absolutely trustworthy, competent, and loyal. The day after I left Temple, this person was fired.

When the reorganization was announced, all hell broke loose. Although the people we had consulted had agreed in principle with the need for more efficiency, we had underestimated the strength of individual fiefdoms. The director of Continuing Education for Women, who had come from rural Pennsylvania and was unwilling or unable to understand urban problems, saw the plan as an attempt to roll back the clock on opportunities for women. In a memo which was widely circulated, she accused the administration of being "insensitive, if not inimical, to the needs and rights of women, while responding to those of minority groups who constitute a smaller proportion of the university population," and called for an aggressive campaign to regain support for women's programs. Hundreds of letters were written to the president and to me. Trustees were contacted, urging them to stop the reorganization. I met with scores of students and staff members, as did Wachman. The press covered the controversy on a regular basis and the picketing of my office was shown on television. But apparently nothing short of abolishing the plan could placate the angry director. Although her program was to be renamed Continuing Education for Women and Men, I assured her that the budget would be increased and I even offered to retain her as director. She refused the position.

Finally, a meeting of the student affairs committee of the Temple trustees was convened in the auditorium of Temple University Center City. The chairman convened the meeting, reviewed the history of the controversy, and listened to several speakers. When I was given the opportunity to respond, I did so in less than ten minutes, calmly listing the facts and saying that I was simply trying to improve and expand the programs. The chair then asked me if I would delay implementation of the reorganization.

My answer was no. Would I exclude this particular program? Again, my answer was no. Would I guarantee that it would not be scaled back nor the budget cut? Yes, I replied. Those in the audience, many of whom were supporters of the woman, were stunned when the chairman gave his verdict: I was within my rights to reorganize activities under my jurisdiction, I had consulted with the appropriate individuals, and there was no evidence that this particular program was being discriminated against.

The meeting adjourned and I went back to work, gratified by the verdict. I had done my homework, I had reached a decision, and I had adhered to it because I was convinced the students would be better served by the new arrangements. When I was appointed vice president, I knew that some individuals assumed that because I had good manners, I could not possibly be a militant. They were wrong. As one of the very few African Americans in a position of authority, I felt it was my obligation to keep tabs on how my fellow blacks were being treated and rectify injustices, wherever they occurred.

My concern led me into situations which were not part of my official list of responsibilities. For instance, I knew that hospital emergency wards often provided primary care in poor neighborhoods, and I wanted to know how North Philadelphians were treated at Temple Hospital. So I checked into the ER one night—practically in disguise, because nobody at the university ever saw me in anything but a suit and tie—and I was amazed at the results of my experiment. The Philadelphia policemen (who at that time, under Frank Rizzo, had a terrible reputation) were unfailingly polite, respectful, and sensitive to the people they were escorting into the hospital.

As a result, I talked to the president about instituting a human relations training program for our campus police, and he agreed, well aware that friction between them and black students or community residents only harmed the university. On another occasion, I had the opportunity to rectify an injustice in this department. My friend Dave Richardson told me about a capable young security officer who had been fired by Temple because he had been arrested. It turned out that it was a case of mistaken identity, but nothing the officer said or did resulted in a reversal of Temple's decision. I was furious and went straight to the vice president for finance, who was in charge of security. I'm happy to say that the young man was reinstated and, I believe, subsequently promoted.

My position made me something of a lightning rod for African Americans who were frustrated or angry. One young woman, a doctoral candidate at Temple and the wife of a prominent professor at Penn, came to discuss the problems she was having in obtaining approval for her dis-

With Roosevelt Principal, Mr Tatum (third from left)

Bernard and his bride, Lois Lathan,
July 1, 1961

With Roosevelt cross country team (Indiana State Champions)

Principal of Roosevelt Junior High School,
with staff members, 1960

With other staff associates of the University of Chicago's Midwest Administration Center, 1965

Our house in Chestnut Hill

Barbra and Chuck at home

Barbra and Chuck in winter with their mother

Barbra and Chuck with their father
at the Philadelphia Zoo

The four of us on vacation in Aruba

With Barbra and Chuck in a
Bahamas Hotel

Father and son with guide and
interpreter in China, 1988

Father and son on a
catamaran off the
shores of Aruba

With Charles Bowser and
Stewart Rauch at the opening
of the first high school academy,
Edison High School, 1968

With Rosa Parks and Virginia Governor Wilder at Lincoln University

With Robert Poindexter, Executive
Deputy Superintendent of the School
District of Philadelphia, in 1968

With the children and my
paraplegic niece

With Tom Massaro

Father and daughter at
graduation from
Germantown Friends School

With M. Carl Holman and the
Rev. Jesse Jackson

With John (left) and Otto (right) Haas at
the William Penn Foundation

With President George Bush

With Dr. Haron Battle,
Roosevelt mentor

With President Jimmy Carter

With President Bill Clinton

With (left to right) Mr. Jessie Owens,
Mrs. Benjamin Hooks, Mrs. Owens, Mr. Hooks

sertation topic. "There are still so few people to talk to," was her simple explanation. I became involved in a far more complex and serious situation when some faculty members appealed to me for help with a scandal brewing in their college. They reported that a department chairman had refused to recommend a young woman for promotion in retaliation for her refusal to accept his advances. She already had an international reputation, as did her husband (also a professor), and there were other factors which made this a particularly volatile and even dangerous situation. It was the most egregious case of sexual harassment I'd ever heard of. The chairman's recommendation had not been challenged by anyone in the hierarchy until I briefed the president, who overruled the chairman and dean. She received her promotion.

My next major "official" project was improving and expanding the activities of my other areas of responsibility, including admissions, financial aid, the Research and Program Development Office, and the Measurement and Research Center. One by one, all the units were examined and, where appropriate, changes were made. For instance, in both admissions and financial aid, we found ways to speed up decision-making. The Research and Program Development Office was good at obtaining grants—Temple ranked in the top twenty-five universities for doing so—but its staff had been acting like lone cowboys. Since I believed that the university administration had to know what funds were coming in and why, I insisted that applications, monitoring, and reporting had to go through my office.

The director of the Measurement and Research Center, Art Pappacostas, was an absolute gem. He had been a top psychology student, but he had not pursued a Ph.D. until I began nagging him to remedy this defect. Not only was he absolutely on top of current computer technology and future applications, he was a devoted workaholic. Art, more than any other single individual, helped to modernize the way the Center gathered and analyzed data, and because of him, we were able to provide accurate, up-to-date information about admissions, student records, and—very crucial—financial aid. Using the bully pulpit of my position, I could refute rumors and provide the facts on standards, the amount and distribution of financial aid, enrollment in special programs, and much more. At the start of my second year as vice president, I began providing the president with an annual report on all the functions and activities reporting to my office.

Temple University Center City was an exciting "campus" located in two downtown office buildings. (The university bought one and soon had to rent space in a second because TUCC was so successful.) Its programs attracted people from all over the area, including New Jersey and Delaware, because people could take courses before they went to work in the morning, immediately after work, and on weekends. Some were pursuing degrees, while others were simply improving specific skills. In addition, there were numerous non-credit workshops offered at all hours of the day and evening.

The programs at TUCC continued to expand, but unfortunately, the administration had not kept pace. The director was an idea man, full of energy, but not always on the same page as the rest of the university. His impetuosity led him into some unfortunate adventures which wound up being cited by the Pennsylvania Auditor General and embarrassing the university. Controlling this unit, while not breaking the director's spirit or dampening his enthusiasm, was one of the more difficult tasks of my tenure. It was exacerbated by the fact that the director was perceived as the president's friend who could bend the rules with impunity. Whether or not this was true, apparently nobody had tried to discipline the director until he had to report to me and have his budgets scrutinized by my financial officer and controller.

I had other battles. The Criminal Justice Program was in the process of being expanded from a two-year associate degree program to a full four-year program, and I had to chair the committee that was overseeing the change, a committee with representatives from the criminal justice program itself, the business school, the college of liberal arts, the law school, and the faculty senate. The problem was not about expansion, but about where the new program should be housed: both the college of liberal arts and the business school wanted it. The competition permeated every aspect of our deliberations, and the tension was further exacerbated by the rumor that John Rumpf and I disagreed about the appropriate location. The deliberations included an attempt by one faction to fire the only African American faculty member in the program; an effort to get rid of two excellent young teachers with impeccable credentials (so that they could not compete with the faculty of whatever college eventually became home for the program); and public accusations from a candidate for chairmanship of the new department that he had been offered the job in return for supporting the position of certain committee members.

The committee discussions were ludicrous: oh-so-polite and courteous in public, but fierce and vicious behind the scenes. An attempt was made to blackmail me into championing one faction over the other, and to combat the lies and innuendoes, I wrote an open letter to the committee and circulated it to the president and others. With that much duplicity and infighting, it was essential to document the facts. Eventually, however, a very good program was designed and approved, and the new department, which was assigned to the college of liberal arts, quickly earned a reputation for its quality. One of the real pluses of this period was the opportunity to meet and work with some very bright, committed people, even as the petty politics proceeded and the multiple agendas were played out. Carolyn Adams, for instance, was then a professor in the college of liberal arts and an articulate member of the committee, always impressive in the substantive deliberations. In my view, she was an "innocent" in the political wheeling and dealing. After she became acting dean of the college, I urged her to seek the permanent position, but she declined. I am delighted that she eventually was appointed and now is the dean. She has much to offer students and faculty.

When I moved to my new offices in Conwell Hall, where the senior administration was housed, I found only one African American secretary. Within eighteen months, my offices resembled the United Nations. My secretaries were white and black, Hispanic and Asian. The directors who reported to me knew that I expected a staff that was both competent and diverse. Quality was not to be sacrificed nor were standards, but I demanded a real effort to embrace diversity at every level. Before long you could tell which units reported to me because their operations reflected that diversity. Yet no one could argue that performance had suffered. Quite the contrary. All of my units were included in a performance appraisal system which based promotions and salary increases on written performance appraisals, a system which every staff member understood. Salary increases could range as high as fifteen percent, while those who did not measure up received nothing. Each employee had the right to respond to the appraisal in writing and to appeal the decision of a supervisor. In the five years I served as vice president, I never had a grievance filed.

Every secretary of mine has earned at least one degree. I arranged their schedules so that they had no excuse not to take advantage of Temple's liberal tuition policies, and I even made it a condition of their employment, although I am not sure this was completely legal. Those who already had degrees found it was easier to enroll in graduate school than to put up with my nagging about further education. Lonnie Moseley was already part way through college when she started working for me in the department of urban education. She completed her B.A. in English and joined a publishing firm before returning to Temple to become my administrative assistant. Of course I urged her to pursue a master's degree, and she earned one in psycho-educational processes (locally known as PEP), then left the university to start her own computer consulting firm. My research assistant, who had been with me at the School District, had an honors degree from Bryn Mawr, and she, too, soon found herself enrolled in graduate classes. By the time I was appointed vice president, she had received an M.A. and gone on to responsible positions elsewhere. Nearly two decades later, our paths crossed again, and we have worked together since 1991, first at the William Penn Foundation and currently at Temple. My advocacy of pursuing further education goes back a long way and continued through my tenure at the Foundation, as I note in the next chapter.

My special assistant, whom I had inherited from my predecessor, was James Bolden, a good-looking former college basketball player and an ex-marine officer. Until my appointment as vice president, he had been the highest ranking black person in the Temple administration. He had a doctorate in counseling psychology as well as a law degree (earned at night while working full-time), and he had a tenured position as an associate professor. He was considered arrogant by many, both black and white. I don't think he particularly liked or trusted me. Perhaps he felt that he deserved the position I held, but I can't be sure. At any rate, we had our disagreements until one day when Jim's views on a particular issue (which were opposite to mine) turned out to be wrong. My decision prevailed, but Jim learned that I had actually supported him and some things we both believed in. He was shocked, but he was man enough to write me a note saying "You have the responsibility to teach me also."

Jim was not fairly treated at Temple. His responsibilities were broader and more demanding than those of others who had better positions, and clearly he had superior credentials and experience. On more than one occasion I recommended that Jim be promoted to assistant or associate vice president, but nothing happened. I know that one of the president's assistants disliked Jim so much that he once tried to convince me to fire him, although his job performance was excellent and there was no reason even to consider such an action. Finally, in May 1979, I wrote a formal letter to the president, recommending that Jim (who was about to receive his J.D.) be made the associate vice president for academic administration. I never received a reply. But when I suggested to Jim that he had a good EEOC case, for which I would be a witness, he declined to take action—a decision I did not understand then or now. A similar incident occurred in the medical school with Dr. Daniel Hall, who was my personal physician. Danny refused to file a grievance, and soon after he left the university to become medical director of the Prudential Life Insurance Company.

James Logan, vice president for finance, and I became friends, although on the face of it we seemed to have little in common. He was from a poor background in Appalachia, had attended Kenyon College on scholarship and made Phi Beta Kappa, and even though he had become a big-time Republican politician, he was cool. We spent hours swapping stories and discussing current issues. Since we served on a number of committees together, I knew he was always interested in what was good for the university, although sometimes he had to do the political thing. I enjoyed working with Jim.

I had good relationships with most of the deans, both oldtimers and the many who were appointed during my term of office. George Johnson, the dean of liberal arts whom I mentioned earlier in connection with my proposal for an urban studies program, became president of George Mason University in Virginia. He had wanted a college presidency for years, but he always seemed to make the final cut yet never get the job. Under his leadership, George Mason developed a national reputation, in part because George was able to attract outstanding faculty, including the black conservative economist Walter Williams from Temple and Roger Wilkins, a liberal black historian, lawyer, and civil rights activist.

When I arrived at Temple in 1970, there were few black faculty members and administrators. The year before, in 1969, Dr. Ione Vargus and the late William Perry had been brought in to establish the School of Social Administration, but Harry Bailey of the political science department and I were the only African Americans who were full professors and department chairmen. Although precise figures were hard to come by, in spite of the various reporting requirements, less than ten percent of the undergraduate population was black; less than five percent Hispanic. Minority enrollment in the graduate and professional schools was even lower.

In 1970 the medical school, for instance, had only a handful of black and Hispanic students. Yet throughout the decade, as the percentage of minorities gradually increased, Temple ranked third—after Meharry at Fisk University and Howard University, two premier black institutions—in the production of black physicians. This was possible because of the Recruitment, Admissions, and Retention (RAR) program that the medical school established in 1970 in cooperation with a local community organization. Under the leadership of Charles Ireland, now an assistant dean, the program addressed the key problems faced by prospective minority applicants: information about opportunities, financial assistance, and academic support. The RAR program, funded by Temple and by $4.5 million in federal grants, has proven so effective that by 1994 minority students comprised 24 percent of the first-year class. In fact, Temple's medical school received 22 percent of all minority applications in the country.

The law school has its own interesting history. Only one African American had graduated during an eight-year period in the 1960s, and in 1969 the grand total of minority students was ten: nine blacks and one Hispanic. Nelson Diaz had already organized the university's Hispanic students, so he helped Carl Singley establish the Black Law Students Association (BLSA). Meantime, there was considerable turmoil over a report, "Racial Discrimination in the Administration of the Pennsylvania Bar Examination," prepared by a Bar Association committee chaired by law school professor Peter Liacouras and published in the *Temple Law Quarterly* over the dean's objections. Student demonstrations over various law school policies ultimately led to the dean's resignation and the appointment of Peter Liacouras as his successor in 1972.

The law school changed dramatically under Peter's leadership. The SpACE program (Special Awards, Special Admissions and Curriculum Experiments) led to the most diverse student body in the country, and Temple's SpACE program was cited as an example of excellence in briefs filed in the Bakke case. Patrick Swygert (now president of Howard) became the first African American tenured professor and later deputy dean. Masters' programs were established, as were programs in legal aid, the teaching of law in high schools, and courses in Rome, Athens, Tel Aviv, Tokyo, and Ghana. The law school faculty doubled, then tripled, in size, attracting top scholars.

The group of students who formed BLSA was unusual, all of them going on to distinguished careers. Nelson Diaz, the first Hispanic to pass the bar in Pennsylvania, was elected a judge of the Court of Common Pleas, became a White House Fellow, and currently serves as general counsel of the U.S. Department of Housing and Urban Development. Carl Singley earned a master's in law from Yale, joined the Temple law faculty, and became the first African American dean of the law school. Ernest Jones, who was vice president of the BLSA, is now president of the Greater Philadelphia Urban Affairs Coalition, while Dorothy Moore Duncan, BLSA secretary, is the regional attorney for the National Labor Relations Board.

Enrollment, both full- and part-time, continued to grow, from 34,950 in 1975 to 36,339 in 1977. More important, the number of minority students at all levels increased. There were the usual gripes about "lowering standards," but they could not stand up to scrutiny. Although some fought against change, wanting to cling to a world and a university that existed only in their imaginations, they were a distinct minority. Most of the faculty and staff, administration and trustees, were intent on confronting the challenges of the times, and on the whole Temple managed to live up to the promise described in Conwell's "Acres of Diamonds" speech.

I was pleasantly surprised at how good some of the Temple faculty and students were. In Philadelphia and elsewhere, it is the University of Pennsylvania, dating back to the 18th century and a member of the Ivy League, which has the reputation for academic excellence and a tradition of social prestige. By contrast, Temple is often disparaged as a "commuter school" or (in British terms) a "red brick university." Yet I met and worked with faculty members who were just as good as those I had known at Chicago, many of them with doctorates from first-class institutions and recognized nationally as experts in their field. What really impressed me, however, was the quality of so many students who could have been outstanding anywhere they chose to go. Some attended Temple because they could afford it, perhaps by living at home. Others selected Temple because of the reputation of its graduate programs. One of my students, Linda Darling-Hammond, was the brightest and best student I ever met, bar none. She could have become anything she wanted; fortunately, she was interested in teaching. An honors graduate of Yale with a double major, she came to Temple to pursue a master's in mathematics education and wound up taking a doctorate under my supervision. Linda now holds an endowed chair as a tenured professor at Teachers College, Columbia, is co-director of the National Center for Restructuring Education, Schools, and Teaching, and was recently elected president of the American Educational Research Association. At the age of 39, she was asked to become dean of Harvard's Graduate School of Education but had to decline the appointment because of family concerns.

During my five years as vice president of Temple, I became increasingly visible. My national activities exposed me to a wide variety of institutions, and I began to receive more and more attractive offers. Maybe, I thought, it was time to move on. Apparently some other people did, too. When the late Ernest L. Boyer (later president of the Carnegie Foundation) was at Temple to receive an honorary degree, he greeted me—in front of Marvin Wachman—with "Why are you still here? I thought that you'd be off running your own institution by now!" In the spring of 1980, Marvin's announcement that he planned to retire in 1982 rekindled speculation about his successor. That fall, the *Philadelphia Tribune* published an article entitled "Black in Line to Become Temple's Next President." The author quoted the influential Sam Evans, head of the Family of Leaders, as saying that his organization would give total support to my candidacy because "he is ably qualified for the position and he has had a long term service to Temple." The Reverend Henry Nichols, member of Temple's board of trustees, stated that he hoped a black would be given serious consideration by the search committee. The three daily newspapers ran articles about the impending vacancy. My phone rang constantly with expressions of support from trustees and others who wanted me to become a candidate. I appreciated their encouragement, but I was steadfast: my answer was no.

I had narrowed my choices to two positions, one in Washington, D.C., and one in the greater Philadelphia area. On September 2, 1980, I submitted my resignation to President Wachman, to be effective June 30, 1981. When word got out, the press had a field day. Speculation ran wild, because I did not disclose where I would be going. My future was a very, very well kept secret, and even the president and my closest friends did not know. There were those who were sorry to see me leave, and others (a small minority) who were delighted. Whatever their view, everybody knew that I loved Temple University, warts and all, and that I often said it was far ahead of almost any other majority university in the country. People who had heard me speak about Temple said I could give the modern version of the Conwell speech as well as anybody. That was because I truly believed—and still believe—that Temple is unique and much needed.

In the April 1981 issue of the *Temple Faculty Herald*, there was an editorial, simply titled "Farewell." (By then, my future plans had been revealed.) It said:

> Temple will soon lose one of the most forceful and dynamic men in Conwell Hall. Bernard C. Watson will leave us in July to become President of the William Penn Foundation. Temple will miss Dr. Watson. At times, his actions were controversial, his manner abrasive; nonetheless, he was widely respected for his quick and keen intellect, his admirable energy, and his straight talk—refreshing novelties in the waffling current academic world, a world pervaded by administrative buzz words and evasion. Here was no man to turn from a fight, no man to abdicate responsibility. And here was an administrator who, for once, could be honestly counted one of us, teaching regularly and participating in the scholarship of his field. Indeed, a number of faculty leaders looked upon him as a prime candidate for President of the University.
>
> In any case, we wish Bernard Watson success in his important new position. He was a worthy adversary—and a memorable colleague.

I loved Temple University because of the opportunities it offered to students who were the first in their family to go to college, who would not even have considered going if Temple had not been there, who could not afford to go elsewhere. I loved Temple because it provided a quality education in fifteen schools and colleges, including medical, dental, and law; it was in a poor neighborhood of a big city; and it scheduled classes throughout the year, day and night, for the convenience of working students. I loved Temple because it was enthusiastic about hiring and supporting people like John Chaney, a fiery and outspoken coach who was more committed to his players than to winning. And I loved Temple because, unlike many other colleges and universities, it was willing—sometimes reluctantly—to acknowledge its shortcomings and seek solutions. There were always people on the faculty and staff, in the student body and the community, who would take time to clarify issues and resolve problems. Temple was, and is, an institution that wanted to renew its founder's dream amid new and changing times.

CHAPTER IX
THE WORLD OF PHILANTHROPY

*One of the most astute observers of the great American foundations,
such as Carnegie, Ford, and Rockefeller, is Waldemar Nielsen, who
described them this way.*

> *As a group, they are institutions like no others, operating
> in their own unique degree of abstraction from external pres-
> sures and controls, according to their own largely self-
> imposed rules. They are private, and yet their activities cut
> across a broad spectrum of public concerns and public
> issues. They are the only important power centers in
> American life not controlled by market forces, electoral con-
> stituencies, bodies of members, or even formally established
> canons of conduct, all of which give them their extraordinary
> flexibility and potential influence.*
>
> *Yet they remain little known and even less understood,
> shrouded in mystery, inspiring in some the highest hopes and
> expectations and in others dark fears and resentments. By
> some they are seen as the Hope of the Future, our Secret
> Weapon for progress; by others as our Fifth Column; and by
> still others as our invisible Fourth Branch of Government.*

*Foundations differ from one another in many ways, and history pro-
vides little support for the sweeping generalizations made by either their
supporters or their detractors. Some foundations have great achievements
to their credit, some are mediocre, and some can only be characterized as
failures. Although philanthropy is practiced around the world, the private
foundations are a uniquely American phenomenon, emerging from an
intriguing combination of commercial success and enthusiasm for reform.*

*The William Penn Foundation was created in 1945 by Phoebe and Otto
Haas, a founder of Rohm and Haas, the international industrial chemical*

company. Over the years, the principal mission of the Foundation has been to help improve the quality of life in the Delaware Valley— Philadelphia, the four surrounding Pennsylvania counties, and Camden County, New Jersey. On the basis of grant payments made in 1994 (the latest year for which figures are available), William Penn was ranked as 27th largest of the 36,000 private foundations in the United States.

For ten years, the Foundation reflected the personal philanthropic interests of the Haas family; not until 1955 was Richard K. Bennett appointed as the first professional staff member. He eventually became the president, retiring at the end of 1981, when I succeeded him. The two children of the founders, the late F. Otto Haas and John C. Haas, and their wives were active in Foundation affairs for many years, and at an early age their children took their places on the board as well. The third generation of the Haas family assumed leadership in 1993, the year in which I retired.

❦

It had never occurred to me, even in my wildest dreams, that I would become the president of a foundation. Of course, like most executives in non-profit agencies, I had developed some familiarity with the world of philanthropy: schools and colleges always needed more money, and overseeing the preparation of grant requests had been for years a regular and critically important part of my job. I had also come to know several foundations closely, through serving as a consultant. I have already mentioned the Rockefeller Foundation, whose superintendents' training program under Chuck Smith I admired so much. There were several others, such as Ford, which commissioned an evaluation of the Rev. Jesse Jackson's "PUSH" program, and Standard Oil, which asked me to evaluate various grant requests that it had received. For the Charles Stewart Mott Foundation, I prepared position papers on grantmaking to community development corporations and worked with its national initiative on historically black colleges and universities (HBCUs). I was also involved in projects for Danforth, Kettering, and the 20th Century Fund. Still, these assignments were relatively brief, and none had prepared me for daily immersion in the internal operation of one of the country's foremost philanthropic organizations.

I was nominated for the presidency of William Penn Foundation without my knowledge or consent—a good thing, because I probably would not have applied for the position even if I had known it was available. As it happened, I had no idea that the Foundation's president, Richard K. Bennett, had reached retirement age and was planning to leave at the end of 1981.

I first met Dick Bennett when I was deputy superintendent of the Philadelphia public schools, but we had little contact in subsequent years. His work, however, was well known, and he had an excellent reputation as a courageous thinker and a bold activist. A Quaker, Dick was a conscientious objector in World War II and during his internment, he had been the subject of medical experiments, aimed at finding a cure for malaria, at Massachusetts General Hospital. (He later learned that a million lives had been saved, and many millions of disabilities avoided, because of these tests.)

When the war was over, he came to Philadelphia to work for the American Friends Service Committee. After planning and implementing extraordinarily successful efforts on behalf of European refugees, he became head of the community relations division and an outspoken advocate of civil rights. As regular supporters of the Service Committee, the Haas family came to know Dick and asked him to advise them on the management of the Foundation. As I noted earlier, he remained with the Foundation for over 25 years.

Dick invited me to lunch in the spring of 1981, saying that he just wanted to catch up and talk about a few things. Near the end of the lunch, Dick asked me what I was going to do after I left Temple University. (I had already publicly announced my resignation as vice president for academic administration, but had declared my complete lack of interest in seeking the presidency of the University.) I told Dick the truth: that I hadn't decided yet. I was a tenured full professor at Temple, with faculty appointments in three departments in two colleges. I had received numerous offers of positions in Atlanta, Chicago, New York, and Philadelphia, and there had been inquiries from several other places. Only then did Dick inform me that I had been nominated as his successor. I was surprised, even stunned. After we talked for another half-hour, he asked me if I would become a candidate and consent to an interview. I agreed and he said he would be in touch with me.

About a week or ten days later, Dick called me to arrange a time for the interview with the William Penn Foundation board search committee, which consisted of Haas family members and Federal Appeals Court Judge Arlin Adams. The meeting, over lunch in a private room at the Downtown Club, was pleasant. Both F. Otto's and John's families were represented, and they all, along with Judge Adams, participated in the interview. It was probing, but very informal, and lasted about two hours. I returned to Temple University feeling relaxed and, for the first time, really interested in the position. I knew that they were serious, that this was not a charade or a pro forma symbol of outreach and fairness, but there were other candidates to be seen and I would have to wait for further developments.

The next week, Arlin Adams asked me to attend a meeting in his office with a member of the search committee who had been unable to attend the lunch. This interview was different—not tense or strained, but lacking focus. Judge Adams tried unsuccessfully to guide the conversation, but finally we hit upon a topic in which the Haas family member and I shared an interest, and from there on it flowed. After about thirty minutes, I was asked about my ability to deal with the various organizations and individuals who would come to the Foundation. I thought the question was a little strange, but I told him that I regularly dealt with all sorts of situations. "But you are a Negro," he blurted out, "and these people are white. Won't you be nervous? Could you handle these powerful people?" Judge Adams turned red, then redder. I thought he was going to explode, but he was cool.

The person asking the question was serious, even if naive, and he had asked honestly, so I answered him with equanimity. He wasn't sure what to make of my answer, but he was clearly relieved that I had responded calmly, and soon after, the interview came to a close. We parted on a cordial note, and I went home that evening convinced that I had an excellent chance of being appointed. There were no further interviews. Dick Bennett told me that the board would decide after the search committee made its recommendation at the next meeting. They were down to two finalists.

I thought I knew what the outcome would be. I gave my wife a sealed envelope with my guess written on a piece of paper inside, telling her she could open it after the board had acted. She put the envelope in the safe. Two weeks later, I was notified by the chairman of the board that I had been selected to succeed Dick Bennett. I was ecstatic. When I got home that evening, the only thing I said to Lois was that the time had come to open the envelope. I was poker-faced. The note inside said, "Ah is de president." We laughed, had dinner, and drank a glass of wine in honor of the occasion. It was a good day.

I had based my prediction on the candor, honesty, and directness of the search committee. It had also helped to know the reputation for integrity and fairness of John Haas, whom I had already met, and of his brother Otto. My appointment was to remain confidential until the Foundation made a public announcement. I am pleased to say that absolutely nobody learned the truth, and Dick Bennett and I laughed at the rumors floating around; they were all wrong and way off base. Until the news was published in the *Inquirer*, it was the best-kept secret in Philadelphia.

I began my work at the Foundation during the summer of 1981 as "president designate." This gave me the advantage of a six-month period alongside the retiring president, Dick Bennett, and the opportunity to learn every aspect of the Foundation's activity. I attended all the staff meetings, interviewed and observed the work of every staff member. I had my own private office and access to all files and records. Dick was generous with his time and we made a variety of visits together, had lunch with potential grant recipients, and met colleagues from the Philadelphia Foundation which Dick had once run (concurrently with his duties at William Penn, I might add). We also spent a lot of time talking about our backgrounds and earlier experiences.

Although Dick had presided over the growth of the Foundation for twenty-five years, he had never been recognized for his formidable accomplishments. He had specifically forbidden a farewell dinner or any other tokens of appreciation by either the staff or the board. I thought this was ridiculous and did not feel bound by his prohibitions, so I called a few of Dick's friends who were not connected with the Foundation and secured their support for a surprise dinner in his honor. I agreed to be responsible for all of the arrangements.

We developed a guest list of Dick's friends and colleagues, and invited them to join us in the festivities. After arranging to fly in his daughter, a professor at the University of Arkansas, and to meet his wife, Louisa, at the local train station, we developed some subterfuge to get Dick to the party. It was a blast, a real blast. He was flabbergasted that we had managed to put the affair together without his knowledge but with the assistance of his own staff. I think he was also surprised that some of the leading people in Philadelphia attended and said nice things about him. He learned, maybe for the first time, just how highly he was esteemed by some of the city's movers and shakers. And of course he was delighted that his daughter was able to attend.

Early Changes at the Foundation

During my six months of orientation at the Foundation, I had learned a number of things about its administrative practices, some of which were rather out of date. For instance, every staff member reported directly to the president, job descriptions had not been revised for some time, and there was no salary schedule or system for performance evaluation.

Perhaps most astonishing was the fact that records were kept on the Royal MacBee system, with perforated cards and metal needles, a system I had used in the early 1960s when I was a junior high school principal. Although the Foundation had been run with unusual competence and efficiency, it was still a family enterprise. I believed that part of my mission was to transform it into a modern organization.

On my first day as president, I prepared to make changes in three major areas: personnel policies and practices, record-keeping, and office space. The first two were fairly straightforward, involving consultation with outside professionals and investigation of computer programs for investment management, payroll, grant payments, and so on.

The question of space was somewhat more complex. At the time, the Foundation offices were located in a downtown office building, but the facilities we leased were not adequate; there was little privacy and much of the space was wasted, as it could not be efficiently used by the staff. When we learned that a new owner was planning major improvements— and higher rent—we began to consider purchasing our own building.

My first step was to call on Harry Cerino (who became president of the William Penn Foundation soon after my retirement), a native Philadelphian and very well informed about housing in the city. For the next six months, we sneaked around the entire downtown area, from the Delaware to the Schuylkill, looking at properties for sale and alternative rental sites. When we found something interesting, we used a surrogate— usually a real estate professional who specialized in working with anonymous buyers—to get price quotations and an appraisal of the property's physical condition and value. We also relied on the expertise of Phil Herr, a Foundation board member who was both a lawyer and accountant. He is one of the smartest, most honest, and more clear-headed people I have ever met, and he was invaluable in helping us analyze the costs and benefits of renting vs. buying, as well as considerations of location.

Finally, we settled on a small building at the corner of 17th and Locust Streets, near Rittenhouse Square, soon to be designated an historic area. Designed as a private residence at the turn of the century by the well-known Philadelphia architects Cope and Stewardson, it had been converted to offices in 1941. We hired an outstanding local firm to design and oversee the interior changes and the restoration of the building to its original condition. Although the building was not historically certified, it seemed important to undertake this work, which was very much in keeping with Foundation priorities. The purchase was a good business deal and a sound investment, giving us our own quarters, with room to grow as the Foundation's assets, grant budget, and staff increased.

How were we able to do so much in such a short time? Primarily because I started out with a clear understanding of my relationship with the board of the Foundation. The chairman, John C. Haas, had told me that I was the president and, as such, would be expected to direct the Foundation. He told me that I could select my own staff without regard to who was already there (although he felt the existing staff was competent). He also assured me that there would be no interference from members of the board, especially Haas family members. Shortly afterwards, Dr. F. Otto Haas, his brother and the vice chairman of the board, invited me to meet with him at his office (the consulate for the Federal Republic of Germany, which he served as honorary consul). Over lunch at the nearby Bourse Building, Otto explained how he viewed our relationship. Although he would always be available to me for advice and counsel, I was expected to run the Foundation. I would report to John as the chairman, but since the brothers had always agreed on the operation of the Foundation, I could expect support from them both as I proceeded with my duties.

More important, he repeated what John had said: "You are the president, and you should do what you think best, without worrying about what John or I might want." In other words, they both made it very clear that I was not an experiment, not a token, not the black president—but simply the president of the Foundation. Race was not an issue in my appointment, as far as the Haas brothers were concerned. I would be judged on my performance. This turned out to be the truly exceptional experience I enjoyed during my twelve years as president of the William Penn Foundation, one which is unique for all but a few African Americans: I was evaluated on my performance and nothing else. It was an experience I never expected to have in my lifetime and one that I never expect to have again.

My predecessor, Dick Bennett, had been at the Foundation for twenty-five years, and much was understood between the family and the president. He had known the founders, Otto and Phoebe Haas, and he was well-acquainted with both the second and third generations of the Haas family. Since I did not have this history and experience, I had to proceed to establish my own professional relationship with the chairman of the board.

Following up on one of his comments, I suggested that we meet every week so that I could bring him up to date and he could report his concerns or provide information. We established that pattern early, and it continued for twelve years. When one of us was on vacation or traveling, we kept in touch by telephone and we always knew how to reach each other in an emergency. This system worked so well that we were able to conduct business twelve months a year regardless of where we were located. In fact, John authorized the purchase of the building at 1630 Locust Street by telephone: I had done my homework, involved the appropriate board member, Phil Herr, in the process, sent John materials, and kept him informed. We proceeded with the purchase, subject to executive committee and then full board approval.

Staffing the Foundation

One of my first actions was to hire an office manager who could oversee the administrative and support functions. I went after Mrs. Amy Pierce, then employed by the University of Pennsylvania. Her first employer, after her graduation from Dunbar High School in Washington, D.C., was Dr. Mary McLeod Bethune, and she went on to positions in the senior levels of the federal government. She had been executive secretary both to Secretary of Health, Education and Welfare Wilbur Cohen and to Elliott Richardson, who held three cabinet positions, including Attorney General and Secretary of State.

After Amy joined us at the Foundation, we established high standards for secretarial positions and hired a number of people of differing backgrounds. When I arrived at the Foundation, Roland Johnson, secretary of the board and program officer (and now president of the Grundy Foundation), was the only non-white. Over the years, the staff came to include individuals who were Asian, Latino, black; Jewish, Catholic and Protestant; people in their twenties, thirties, forties, and fifties; male and female. I am proud of that record. I try to let my behavior illustrate my ideals and values.

One of the Foundation's employee benefits was tuition reimbursement. It didn't matter whether it was a college-level class or a specialized training program, as long as it was approved by a supervisor and the employee completed the course with a passing grade. I thought this was an excellent opportunity, and I particularly encouraged the support staff to take advantage of it. I was especially gratified when one young woman received her degree from Temple University's School of Business and Management, with honors in human resources management. It took her nine years, but along the way, she also became an expert in computer technology. Two others graduated from Community College: one is now a senior at Temple University, and one was offered a full tuition scholarship to the Philadelphia College of Textiles and Science.

The program staff which I inherited had graduated from a broad range of colleges and universities; most had degrees in the liberal arts or social sciences. One program officer was an ordained minister and a social worker: he had been a settlement house administrator, and had lived and worked on a Native American reservation. Another had been a technical staff member at the Ford Foundation for a number of years. One had been a Peace Corps volunteer in Africa, while still another had been a planner in housing with the Pennsylvania Department of Community Affairs. Whatever their background, however, they were hired and assigned as generalists. They were expected to be especially conversant with one of the Foundation's grantmaking priorities while having general knowledge of all its areas of interest.

During my first few months, the program staff and I participated in a series of visits to each of the counties in the Foundation's geographic area. It was a venture which I proposed and it had many benefits: it gave me a first-hand glimpse of William Penn's activities; it supplied agency people with a unique opportunity to tell us about their problems and needs; and it provided all of us with new perspectives which we simply could not develop by sitting in a downtown office and dealing with isolated proposals. Of course, individual program officers routinely made visits to places where Foundation funds were at work (or for which they had been requested), but there was something different and special about going together as a group, without any agenda but listening. We repeated this process of finding out how things looked "from the field" a number of times, and always found it useful and invigorating.

One of the great dangers of working in a foundation is the tendency to lose perspective. People are so nice to you, so willing to agree with you, that you can become convinced of your own brilliance, your ability to know the answers, to understand everything. Slowly, you can slip into arrogance and begin, perhaps unwittingly, to treat individuals and organizations seeking grants with contempt. This is especially likely if the applicants lack prominence, social status, or education—and even more likely if they are non-white and poor. Such attitudes seem to go with access to influence over, or control of, significant resources. In my experience with a number of foundations, I sometimes saw staff members speak with great confidence although they knew little about the issue or had only second-hand knowledge: abstract, isolated, and piecemeal. This was particularly galling when the person requesting a grant was intimately familiar with the situation under discussion.

From the outset, I impressed this danger upon the Foundation staff, and I found it necessary to remind them periodically and in very direct ways. One way to level the playing field was to limit the "schmoozing"— accepting an invitation for a meal or cocktails "so we can chat about some things"—and staff members were told to pay for their own lunches or dinners if they had to meet with grant seekers. I personally avoided such occasions. Since I don't eat lunch, I had a convenient excuse. My instructions to the staff were to be professional, knowledgeable, and fair in their assessments of potential grantees. Under no circumstances were they to be concerned about an applicant's politics, social status, or connections. If anyone, whether on the board or on the staff or in the community, attempted to use influence or intimidation, they were to be referred to me. During the first several years, program officers had to do just that; later, they had few problems.

It was simple for organizations to get information about obtaining a grant. We had rewritten the application guidelines, clarified the priorities, and printed thousands of the resulting summaries; they were made available in response to a telephone or written request. We would talk to people on the telephone, visit their programs, and, when appropriate, provide technical assistance. I can still remember the stunned looks on some faces when staff members saw equal treatment accorded to individuals and organizations, whether they represented Philadelphia's elite or Philadelphia's poor. Courtesy, respect, an open hearing, and straight talk were the order of the day. It was terribly important to me that the less-sophisticated grant applicants be encouraged and given help in developing their programs. Some of them had wonderful ideas and lots of common sense—but little or no experience in articulating their vision of what they wanted to do. Perhaps my ability to relate to the "little people" was one of the best contributions I made to the Foundation.

It was easier for me because of my experience as a black person during a time when you knew exactly what people thought of you. When you are poor and relatively uneducated, the reactions are brutal, direct, and dismissive. When you are educated, relatively well known, and influential, the expressions are indirect, subtle, more guarded, surreptitious—but just as brutal. It is truly an amazing phenomenon to observe people, who dislike you and may even hate your guts, try to butter you up or act friendly merely because you may be in a position to help them. The dumbest, most inane ideas take on a credibility totally undeserved. It can confuse you if you are not grounded and clear. I always respected the people who were honest, straightforward, even aggressive in their pursuit of support for programs they thought were worthy of consideration. Nevertheless, a number of programs were funded on their merits, even when animosity, distrust, or contempt tainted the negotiations. Conversely, board members of various organizations sometimes tried to use their personal friendships to get an inside advantage. That didn't work under my predecessor, and it didn't work on my watch—but it took three years for the most blatant attempts to stop. They learned that the rules applied to everyone alike.

Some people were apparently amazed or shocked that a black individual could possibly be the head of a prestigious Philadelphia institution like the William Penn Foundation—they would probably have been surprised to find a black person in charge of anything—so their strategy was denial. For instance, one of our major grant recipients refused to speak to me except when he visited the Foundation seeking support. He would pass me on the street regularly, look right through me, and proceed on his way. He was a pompous idiot, but it never affected his grant requests: the Foundation was one of his major supporters over the years, often the largest. Another organization's CEO regularly talked about the shortcomings of the Foundation, and the defects of the new president (me) in particular—although our grants literally saved the organization on two occasions. During my first two or three years, another agency directed all requests to one of the two white male members of the program staff, arranged all meetings with them, and invited only those two to visit its programs. I often wondered whether one of these colleagues, who routinely received mail addressed to him as "president and CEO" until 1985, might have encouraged that behavior. Amy Pierce and I laughed a lot about this sort of thing.

Every other year, with the help of consultants, we reviewed staff salaries and benefits and compared them to those of similar non-profit organizations. When necessary, we recommended changes so that we could keep our organization competitive. I expected excellence from the staff, as the board and my chairman expected it from me, but I recognized that a high level of expectations demands appropriate compensation and fair treatment.

My own performance appraisal was somewhat different. Each January, I submitted a written statement of measurable goals and objectives to the chairman of the board, who either accepted or modified them. At the end of the year, I prepared a report of what progress had been made toward meeting those goals. The chairman and a small committee of the board decided on my compensation. I never had a contract, never consulted a lawyer, and relied on my performance as the determinant of my future employment. I can't imagine entering into that kind of arrangement with anyone other than the Haas brothers, John and Otto.

The Board

In its first few years, the Foundation's board consisted of only family members and one or two trusted advisors. Over time, arrangements were made to bring the third generation of Haases into Foundation affairs. F. Otto and his wife Dophie had four children; John and Chara had five. When they were still quite young, Dick Bennett and others gave them briefings and took them to visit organizations which had received grants. Later, the Haas children (and their spouses)—equal numbers from each side of the family—took turns serving as full members of the board. I continued the tradition of educating the third generation of the Haas family, through seminars, speakers, written materials, and bibliographies. At one such meeting, scheduled on a weekend because the office would be closed and the staff absent, I arranged for them to hear from Waldemar Neilson and Paul Ylvisaker, two of the most shrewd and knowledgeable experts on philanthropy in the country, and I made sure they visited other foundations and attended conferences, such as the annual meeting of the Council on Foundations. By the time I approached retirement, John Haas had stepped down as chairman, turning leadership over to his son and his brother's daughter-in-law. One of my final tasks was giving them a thorough review and analysis of previous Foundation activity and as much advice and information as I possibly could about their new responsibilities.

The practice of inviting a few carefully selected outsiders (i.e., non-members of the family) to join the board had begun before my time, and during my tenure, they constituted a majority. They were outstanding individuals, representing the very best that Philadelphia had to offer. Among their number were physicians, judges, professors, and community leaders from all parts of the city. A list of those who served as outside board members during the years I was president appears in Appendix IV.

I believed that the entire board needed to be more involved in setting the goals and priorities of the Foundation's grantmaking program. The chairman agreed, and together we convened the first board retreat in 1982, at the Morris Arboretum in Chestnut Hill. The retreat was planned for a full day, but it lasted only half that time. There was limited interest in this kind of strategy session: it was new to the board members and several of them did not attend. Still, it was a beginning. The retreat in 1983 lasted a full day and attendance was better.

Over the next five years, the retreats evolved into sessions of two-and-a-half days and required overnight accommodations. The discussions grew more spirited and there was greater participation. Some board members even assisted the staff in planning the agendas. One year we focused on philanthropy itself: how to design grantmaking that was more creative, responsible, and responsive. Before each retreat, we sent out a briefing book which contained a detailed summary of the issues to be discussed, biographical information on speakers and panelists, and a schedule of working sessions and social events.

When we were planning major initiatives, we usually invited authorities in the field to address the board. For instance, during the early stages of considering grantmaking in the Caribbean area, a former United Nations official and an internationally known economist gave presentations at the 1987 fall retreat. Further staff study and consultation led to the idea of a global environment initiative with a Caribbean focus, and in 1990 we convened two panels of experts who gave presentations in both June and October. The panelists included representatives of the London-based Centre for International Environmental Law, environmental planning organizations, and the National Park Service. Sessions like these were invaluable: they improved the grantmaking process, helped to clarify board and staff relationships and responsibilities, and enabled the board to make informed decisions about the major initiatives which I will describe later.

I felt it was important for the board to recognize those who did most of the day-to-day work on proposals and programs, so I made sure that all program staff members not only attended but participated in the retreats, making presentations or answering questions. These sessions provided one of the rare opportunities for board members to assess staff quality and for the staff to discover board members' interests, opinions, and areas of expertise. Although the program officers also attended the regular board meetings (usually five were held each year) in order to respond to questions and defend proposals, these meetings were too short and their agendas too crowded to permit much, if any, informal conversation.

Trouble with a Board Member

Throughout my presidency, my relationships with members of the board were cordial and professional. There was one exception to this general rule: the episode has stayed in my mind because I thought this board member's charges were dubious and actions devious. The opening shot was fired on June 11, a little more than two weeks before a regular board meeting. As usual, the "blue book," containing the agenda and summaries of recommended grants had already reached members of the board. The member in question sent in regrets and included a brief note about how Foundation funds could best be utilized. The second paragraph of the letter was the key:

> ...There are many desperate needs nationally and internationally, but the traditional limitations of this foundation to charities in the Philadelphia area should be observed and a real commitment should be made to this policy.

The second shot was fired on July 31, when the same person sent a confidential letter to the vice chairman, Dr. F. Otto Haas, asserting that there had been major changes in the policy of the Foundation, that they went "beyond operating policy and impact[ed] the basic mission of the organization," and that they had occurred without the advice or consent of the board. The letter noted that the Foundation "has, in the past, declined support to organizations involved in political activities...." Finally, the letter got to the real point:

> ...In light of recent Foundation commitments of $1.2 million over the next three years to the National Urban Coalition, the National Urban League, the national NAACP Legal Defense Fund and NAACP Special Contribution Fund, it is clear the scope of the Foundation giving has broadened from that of a regional foundation confining its grant making to the metropolitan Philadelphia area.
>
> In fact, with the commitment of $500,000 per year for the next three years to the African Development Fund of the William Penn Foundation, our scope has broadened to not only a national level, but an international level.
>
> ...Are we becoming a worldwide foundation? Are we attempting to influence or direct national policy?....Such a break with the 40-year tradition, begun by Otto and Phoebe Haas, warrant (sic) careful examination by those who make major policy for the Foundation...

The third shot was fired on August 2, when Dr. Haas sent a memo to his brother John and me, attaching a copy of the board member's letter, which neither John nor I had received. In his memo, Otto noted that he had told the member that he would forward the letter to the chairman and the president; he closed the memo by asking us: "Would you like to discuss this with him?"

I immediately ordered a study of regional and national grants over the entire history of the Foundation. Among the findings were the following:

- Since the first grant year (1946), a total of 4,546 grants had been approved; 165 (3.6%) were to organizations beyond Philadelphia.
- Of the total of $157,296,427 paid out in that period, $15,364,536 (9.8%) had gone to national organizations, including $6.1 million to Johns Hopkins University for medical research relating to the early diagnosis of cancer (a program authorized before I joined the Foundation).
- During the four years in which I had been president, the Foundation approved 14 national grants and of the $47,460,436 paid out, $1,691,850 (3.6%) had been approved for organizations outside Philadelphia.
- Grants to the NAACP Special Contribution and Legal Defense Funds had been approved by the Foundation board as early as 1971.

It was apparent, to me at least, that this board member was concerned less about national and international grants than about Foundation support for organizations engaged in advocacy, particularly on behalf of minorities. After all, national and international grants had been discussed exhaustively at two board meetings and retreats (in fact, the international thrust had been initiated by the board); the board had approved them, but had also decided to place a limit on the percentage of the annual grant budget which could be used for these purposes.

The basic mistake that this board member had made was in writing a letter to the vice chairman without sending a copy to the board chairman and/or the president. As I indicated earlier, John and Otto were very clear and consistent about their relationship to me and the Foundation. After a thorough discussion of the issues involved, John Haas replied to the board member. In his usual gracious way, John acknowledged the individual's concern, shared the results of the grant analysis the staff had prepared, and gave assurances that the board would continue to proceed "cautiously" and to monitor grants "closely."

We were keenly aware, more than most of the board members, of the dangers of using Foundation grant money for political and legislative purposes. In fact, it was prohibited by law. All of our grant letters included the following paragraph:

The grant is designated for the purposes outlined in your proposal and may not be used for any other purposes, including political or legislative activity. A narrative and financial report must be submitted to the Foundation periodically throughout the term of the grant and at the end of the grant period.

After the exchange of letters, the board member could not have been more open and cooperative, having learned, as others had done before and after, that the Haas brothers were as good as their word. In addition to the organizations mentioned in the board member's letter, the board also approved grants that year to Amnesty International of the U.S.A., Fund for Peace, International Peace Academy, Parliamentarians for World Order Conference Fund, and Professional Organizations for Nuclear Arms Control.

I remember only one other incident involving a board member. It concerned the well-established Foundation policy that the board would consider only proposals for grants of more than a certain amount. Smaller grants could be approved by the president at his discretion, and a list of these grants would be given to the board on a quarterly basis. (I should note that, whatever the amount requested, all proposals were subject to the same staff review process, and recommendations were always made with due regard to how much the board had approved in each grant category for that year.)

During one board meeting—suddenly, without warning—a longtime board member charged that the board was losing control and launched into an attack on the right of the president to approve discretionary grants. He implied that I was abusing my authority by not bringing all the grants to the board for approval. It was rather embarrassing, because this board member should have known better. Research proved that, as in the issue raised by the other board member, he had no case whatsoever: in fact, the number and percentage of discretionary grants I had approved were lower than at any time in Foundation history. I can only guess what was behind his outburst, but probably it was triggered by the unusually high number (39) and total ($955,000) of discretionary grants in that particular quarter. Six months earlier, the quarterly report had listed only 10 grants and a total of $165,000 approved, and maybe he thought those were the normal figures. But there was no set pattern: it all depended on how many proposals we received in a given period and how much was available in the grantmaking budget.

Grantmaking

The Foundation's budget for grants has increased steadily, and at times dramatically, since it was founded more than fifty years ago. In 1982, my first year as president, grant payments totaled $10.5 million. When I retired at the end of 1993, the Foundation had paid out $35.8 million in the course of that year alone; during my tenure I had overseen the distribution of nearly $278 million! Some people may think that there could not be an easier or more pleasant task than handing out money, but believe me that is not always the case, at least in my experience. There are so many human needs, so many good causes: how do you decide what to support?

Like other foundations, we had to establish funding priorities—but by doing so, we inevitably excluded many important and worthwhile areas of need from our consideration. And even within our guidelines, there were always far more requests than we could possibly meet. Finally, we knew that, no matter how hard we tried to be fair or well-informed or consistent, some of our decisions would be wrong. So we had to carry on, knowing that our funds were limited and the staff was not omniscient. Gratifying as much of the work could be, we often had to deal with disappointment, anger, and even despair on the part of those whose proposals we rejected. Not always an easy job.....

In 1986, the board approved new grantmaking priorities, which remained in force until 1996. Remarkably similar to the earlier ones, except for the exclusion of hospitals, medical education, and medical research, the four broad categories in which proposals were considered were: Community Fabric, Culture, Environment, and Human Development (with three sub-sections for children, adolescents, and the elderly). There was also a fifth category, for national and international projects, but here all proposals had to be invited by the staff. Unsolicited requests were politely, but firmly, rejected. Moreover, the board had set a limit of five percent of the annual grant budget to fund such proposals.

In keeping with Foundation tradition, by far the largest percentage of our budget was allocated to Human Development, mainly for educational programs and health services for infants, children, and teenagers. Community Fabric was the second largest category, because it included substantial grants for housing for low-income families, a longterm interest of the Foundation. Also to be found in this category were grants for a great variety of purposes, ranging from improving community relations and supporting the cultural institutions of various ethnic groups, to helping the Red Cross improve its blood services operation and assisting the victims of domestic abuse. Although Culture seldom had as much as 20 percent of the budget, I think that there were few cultural organizations in the Philadelphia area which did not profit from Foundation generosity. Some were internationally known, like the Philadelphia Orchestra or the Art Museum; others were new, small, experimental. Finally, Environment was the single category for which the geographic boundaries were extended to an area with a radius of approximately 100 miles from Philadelphia—in recognition of the fact that the effects of wind and weather, as well as human pollution, are not restrained by arbitrary lines, such as county borders.

What were the most rewarding things we did? What were the big mistakes? I could probably write an entire book about the grants made during my presidency. Almost every single one contains a story of human hope and imagination and enterprise (or, infrequently, some less admirable qualities), and it's hard to select only a few. In view of all that we were trying to do, it's not only quite a challenge to select the "best" or the "worst" grants, but also very presumptuous. For instance, how do you distinguish between those Foundation-funded projects that have made a visible contribution to the Philadelphia landscape and others with no "product" except a healthier baby or turned-on student or happier neighborhood? I simply don't know, any more than do members of the board or the staff, the exact dimensions of any grant's impact on an individual or family or community. If we did, I bet we'd be surprised.

At the risk of overlooking some excellent grants simply because they were small, let me tell you about some of the major efforts the Foundation made while I was president. For the most part, these were "initiatives," programs devised to focus on particular problems or areas of interest. They began with intensive staff research and consultation with experts in the field; once the goals and general strategy had been determined, selected agencies or institutions were asked to submit proposals. Although the program officers did much of the groundwork, I always made sure that the board was intimately involved, from concept through the various stages of development to implementation. Sometimes board members participated in the study process, and in at least one case, they themselves proposed the program.

This was the Basic Human Needs Fund, a response to the severe reductions in federal spending for social welfare in the early 1980s. Touched by the widespread impact of these cuts on individuals and families, the board took the unusual step of allocating $1.5 million from reserve funds—thus not depleting the regular grant budget—for distribution over two years to help provide food, clothing, shelter, fuel, and health care. Before making this decision, the board had had to resolve a number of questions: What about the Foundation's longstanding policy against crisis funding? How could we be sure that these funds would be handled efficiently and would go directly to needy people? Why should private philanthropy undertake responsibilities which by rights belonged to the government?

The urgency of the social problems, combined with the seriousness of the board discussions, resulted in some creative staff work: for the first time, we issued an "RFP" (request for proposals) and sent it to area organizations that had established a good record of service, informing them that no grant monies could be used for general operating expenses. Almost as soon as the program was announced in January 1982, 220 agencies sent in proposals; 78 were selected for funding. The Basic Human Needs Fund was so successful that the board decided to add another $500,000 and extend it for a third year, while it inspired numerous similar programs, here and elsewhere. We also discovered that our strategy had had a number of excellent, but unforeseen, results: agency cooperation, more systematic planning to meet human needs, new emphasis on longterm improvements as well as emergency aid. The RFP strategy was one we used many times in the succeeding years; it proved to be extremely effective.

Just about the time the Basic Human Needs program was ending, we were becoming increasingly concerned about the devastating effects of the unrelenting drought in many countries of Africa. Once again, questions arose about whether and how the Foundation should respond, and once again the board decided to take action. Having weighed the risks of making exceptions to its own rules, the board decided in favor of assisting millions of starving Africans, not by the relatively easy route of supplying food (many agencies were already doing that), but by supporting projects which had some likelihood of providing longterm relief and rehabilitation. A total of $1.5 million was approved for the African Development Fund, and during a three-year period, we found ourselves subsidizing forest management in Zambia, beekeeping in Kenya, and farm cooperatives in Zimbabwe, and a number of other projects.

The African program was approved in 1985—a significant year in other respects. For one thing, it was our first year without F. Otto, who had resigned from the board just short of his seventieth birthday (he remained interested in the Foundation until his death on January 2, 1994). For another, 1985 was the year that the board approved the series of national public policy grants to which one of the members had so strongly objected. It was also the year in which the Foundation began to break away from its forty-year reliance on Rohm and Haas stock. Discussions had begun in 1984, but it is the 1985 balance sheet which shows that William Penn had divested itself of 1.3 million shares of company common stock.

This process continued with another major sale in 1990. In both cases, the stock was sold back to Rohm and Haas. A third sale in 1992 was made privately, however. Divestment was an extremely difficult task, both emotionally and financially. Yet it seemed to me essential, an issue of prudent management: no organization should depend completely on a single investment for its income, and in any case we were not obtaining as much income as we could have derived from a broader portfolio. With the advice of trusted attorneys (one a board member), John and Otto Haas agreed that the assets of the Foundation should be more diversified, and a number of excellent companies were retained to manage our investment portfolio. The board's own investment committee met regularly and did a fine job of monitoring the Foundation's finances.

As I have already said, I demanded a great deal of board members. I wanted each of them to know as much as they could absorb about Foundation activities, past and present, and the staff bombarded them with charts and tables, comparing one year with another, or with mini-essays tracing the history of Foundation grants for such projects as revolving loan funds or the Walnut Street Theatre. The statistical information was fairly easy to compile, once our records had been computerized, and I sometimes wondered whether any overworked board members regretted approving the initial acquisition or the later upgrading of our excellent system. But I was equally eager to educate the board about new ideas—emerging major problems and challenges, and what we might do about them in the future.

I began with a sweeping review and reorganization of the grantmaking program, and at the board retreat in 1986, the staff presented recommendations for new categories, which the board approved. In 1987, we initiated the largest, most imaginative—and ultimately least successful (i.e., relative to its cost)—program the board had ever undertaken, the Philadelphia Ranger Corps. The focus was on Fairmount Park, the biggest municipal park in the entire country and one of the region's most remarkable assets: thousands of acres along the Schuylkill River comprising scenic roads and trails, historic houses, concert stages, and recreational areas. Unfortunately, the city was facing a fiscal crisis, and funds for the park were so limited that the park managers could hardly cope with basic maintenance, let alone the steadily increasing number of visitors.

As we considered ways that the Foundation could assist in preserving this beautiful place, we had a veritable brainstorm: maybe we could combine this goal with another abiding concern, educating and preparing young people for careers. And so we worked out plans for the Ranger Corps. It would recruit local high school graduates, offer them two years of college courses and extensive paid experience in the park, and thus create a trained cadre of rangers to supplement the hard-pressed park staff. We negotiated with the Fairmount Park Commission, the School District of Philadelphia, and Temple University, developed an administrative structure for the program, and calculated the costs for a three-year trial— more than $9 million. This budget included funds for tuition, salaries (full-time during summers and part-time during the school year), the renovation of the historic Ohio House for use as Ranger headquarters, uniforms, vehicles, and state-of-the-art communications equipment. The Foundation board was stunned, but agreed to allocate the necessary funds.

The Ranger Corps gave every indication of becoming a great success. The young people in their smart uniforms were seen everywhere in the park, greeting and assisting visitors, conducting tours, and helping to improve the landscape. During the academic year, they also taught environmental classes in schools throughout the city, and when their own formal education was completed, most of them became regular members of the park staff. What went wrong? A number of things, I think. The small Ranger Corps staff was apparently overpowered by its board of directors, comprised of leading citizens, and appeared unable to take advantage of their expertise and contacts. The Foundation's massive investment seemed to impede rather than encourage efforts to develop fund-raising strategies, and the city's continuing financial difficulties prevented the promised assistance from municipal sources. Conflicts arose between park employees and the young Rangers. At the end of the first three years, the Foundation, reluctantly, provided another $9 million grant in 1991 to keep the program going until its staff and board could reorganize it and raise the necessary funds. It was a sobering experience.

In 1987 and 1988, we implemented several other initiatives, all of them deriving from our longterm interest and experience in the welfare of children and young people. We were prompted by our awareness of some critical problems in poor and minority areas, as well as by a desire to tackle them in a comprehensive way. They included programs to provide pre- and postnatal care for mothers and babies in North Philadelphia; to prevent teenage pregnancy; to supplement the budgets of summer day camps for low-income children with funds for cultural trips and health screening; and to find ways to deter child abuse (rather than dealing with the effects, after it had occurred). The day camp enrichment program continues to this day, although management responsibilities were transferred to the Philadelphia Foundation just before I retired. Meantime, the results of the first round of grants to prevent child abuse were deemed so encouraging by the national evaluating organization that they were published in a Foundation monograph; most of the participating local agencies were awarded continuation grants.

In case you are wondering whether we had any energy or funds to devote to culture, let me tell you about just a few of the Foundation's contributions in this category. For instance, the Walnut Street Theatre (the oldest in the country) would have been demolished and forgotten if the Foundation had not rescued it and poured millions of dollars into renovation and program support over a period of twenty years. A particular favorite of F. Otto's, the Walnut is recognized not only for its handsome building and excellent performances, but also for now having the largest subscription base of any regional theater.

Another theater was also saved by the Foundation, this time in collaboration with the Pew Charitable Trusts. The beautiful old Shubert, just a block away from the renowned Academy of Music, had fallen into near total disrepair although, ironically, the lack of appropriate space for performances was causing serious difficulties, especially for the Pennsylvania Ballet. When engineering and other studies revealed that the cost of renovation would exceed $4 million, the two foundations agreed that it was eminently worthwhile. The William Penn contribution was $1.5 million, and Pew (a very much larger charitable organization) gave $2.6 million. Since 1988, the theater, renamed the Merriam, has been a charming venue for a year-round schedule of local and touring group performances. It is now managed by the University of the Arts next door—an institution in which the Foundation has played an important role. Together, the Merriam and the University of the Arts provided an early and important basis for the development of South Broad Street as the Avenue of the Arts, a project which I will discuss later.

The list of cultural activities supported by the Foundation is so long that I cannot possibly describe them all. Suffice it to say (immodest though it may sound) that the arts throughout the Delaware Valley would have been severely impoverished without the help of the William Penn Foundation. Let me mention just a couple of other grants that we initiated and that I especially liked. In 1985, we conceived the idea of producing a series of guidebooks—on museums and historic sites, on gardens and arboreta, and on public art (i.e., outdoor sculpture—for which Philadelphia has a national reputation, in part because the city requires that one percent of the costs of new construction be allocated for art). We made arrangements with the Temple University Press to produce and distribute for sale three first-class volumes, with essays and photographs by outstanding professionals. (The photographs for the book on gardens, for instance, were taken by a well-known expert, Derek Fell, and the text was written by the former director of the Morris Arboretum, Dr. William M. Klein, Jr.) The results were wonderful: the books are handsome to look at and full of information about our rich cultural resources.

Finally, let me mention Art Now, a project which was designed in order to focus attention on contemporary local artists. The grant was administered by the Philadelphia Museum of Art, which mounted the major juried exhibition, but funds were included for two smaller shows at the Institute of Contemporary Art and the Pennsylvania Academy of the Fine Arts. Before recommending this grant to the board, the staff had made unusual efforts to lay a solid groundwork—for instance, by traveling to museums elsewhere to discuss similar projects and by consulting a number of artists themselves about their needs and hopes. The Art Museum show in 1990 was magnificent, but there were a couple of amusing aspects to this project. For one thing, the *Inquirer* art critic took it upon himself to write a scathing piece, questioning or condemning the way the exhibition had been organized: I hope, probably in vain, that he was suitably embarrassed when he was informed that every single point he raised had been decided not by naive Foundation staff members but by artists and other art experts. Out of 2,400 entries submitted, only 129 were chosen; understandably those whose paintings and other works had been rejected by the jury were disappointed or angry. Some of them, however, drawing on an honorable tradition in art history, promptly arranged a rival show, coinciding with the first weekend of the one at the Art Museum, and proudly called it "Art at the Armory 1990: A Salon des Réfusés." Such bravado deserved—and received—financial support from the Foundation.

Although many of the Foundation's renewal efforts focused on Philadelphia and a couple of other depressed areas in southeastern Pennsylvania, we did not ignore Camden, New Jersey. Once a thriving manufacturing, industrial, and shipbuilding center, its economic base gradually crumbled, and it acquired the dubious honor of being known as one of the poorest small cities in the United States. Just across the

Delaware River from Philadelphia, Camden had been included in the Foundation's target area from the outset and had become a major concern as early as 1980. Although then-Mayor Errichetti refused funding because of our stringent requirements for accounting (he later went to jail on corruption charges), we continued to work with Camden officials to encourage sound planning and economic progress. Soon, a plan developed for a major Foundation investment, one that would help to restore civic pride and revitalize its economy.

In 1984, the Cooper's Ferry Development Association was established to serve as a catalyst for the renewal of downtown Camden and the waterfront area. (Cooper's Ferry obtained the necessary 50l(c)(3) designation from the Internal Revenue Service within 24 hours, thanks to program officer Roland Johnson. I never knew how he did it.) With Foundation support amounting to over $1 million from l984 to 1991, this organization was able to raise millions more to support new construction, infrastructure improvement, housing, and—perhaps most important—the creation or preservation of hundreds of jobs in the area. Much remains on the drawing board, but much has already been accomplished, such as persuading the state, RCA, and Campbell Soup to invest in capital projects along the waterfront. Only a few years ago, Philadelphians would have simply laughed at the idea of going to Camden for fun, and yet now they do in large numbers, not only by car but by ferry across the Delaware River. One of the attractions is the large entertainment complex built by the Sony Corporation; another is the New Jersey State Aquarium, the board of which I served as secretary for several years.

The Foundation continues to support many neighborhood groups, such as Heart of Camden and Habitat, that are committed to improving housing and social services for needy residents.

As I have already said, the Foundation made increasing use of initiatives in the 1980s, in large part because they allowed a well-planned and comprehensive way to address important issues. Rather than simply waiting for unsolicited proposals to arrive in all their variety, we were able to give focus to and, we hoped, get significant results from the expenditure of Foundation funds. (Of course, we continued to devote a large proportion of our resources to meeting the requests of individual organizations as long as they fell within our guidelines.) At the end of 1989, after a lengthy period of staff research and discussion, I asked the board to consider four six-year, multimillion dollar initiatives—one in each of our regular grantmaking categories. Once again, by way of background, the members were given a detailed summary of past Foundation activity, as well as a rationale for these major new undertakings. They were: the development of South Broad Street as a cultural corridor; the revitalization of a neighborhood in North Philadelphia; grants to colleges and universities to encourage the recruitment, retention, and graduation of minority young people majoring in science, mathematics, engineering, and teaching; and finally a concerted effort to protect the Delaware River.

Avenue of the Arts. Philadelphia's City Hall, an enormous Victorian structure surmounted by a statue of William Penn, straddles the crossroads of the two major downtown streets—Market, running east and west, and Broad, running north and south. Although various attempts have been made to tear it down, it is currently enjoying a wave of public sentiment and grand restoration plans. The two streets have been developed quite differently: Market East is chiefly home to small shops and department stores, and Market West is a canyon amidst office skyscrapers. Broad Street, particularly the blocks south of City Hall, is home to a number of impressive structures: great old bank buildings, the Union League, and above all the beloved Academy of Music.

For a number of years, civic leaders had tossed around the notion of turning South Broad Street into an "Avenue of the Arts," and several organizations had announced plans for construction (e.g., a new hall for the Philadelphia Orchestra). But little or nothing happened, apart from the installation of the University of the Arts in one of the massive edifices (with our help) and the renovation of the Merriam Theater, which I mentioned earlier, and there was no comprehensive strategy for realizing the vision. Soon after I became president, the William Penn Foundation began to give the project some serious thought, and we quickly came up with any number of reasons why it should go forward: to answer the pressing need for more and better space for performing arts groups, including some just beginning to emerge; to offer both local residents and tourists an attractive and convenient location to enjoy a variety of cultural activities; and, of course, the preservation of several outstanding architectural gems. Eschewing rhetoric, the staff and I went quietly about the business of studying the feasibility of the idea, developing plans, and estimating costs for several major projects.

At the fall 1989 board retreat, we unveiled our proposal for South Broad Street (and the three other initiatives). There were three initial components: the renovation of an historic firehouse for use by the Brandywine Graphic Workshop as a neighborhood art center; the transformation of an old bank building into a modern small theater (it quickly became known as the "Arts Bank"); and—dearest of all to me—the construction of a new home for the Clef Club, an organization of black jazz musicians with a long and important history. (The Clef Club is the direct descendant of the old segregated local of the American Federation of Musicians and has numbered among its members many of the great performers in this uniquely American musical genre.)

To manage these projects without taking on additional and probably temporary staff, we hit upon the device of creating the nonprofit Sassafras Corporation, to be run by a well-known local impresario and to have its own board of directors. We also mentioned a couple of future possibilities: the conversion of the old Ridgway Library into a site for the Philadelphia High School for the Creative and Performing Arts (CAPA), and improvements to the street itself, such as better lighting and distinctive subway station entrances. The six-year budget which we presented along with our plans totaled almost $13 million. The board approved it.

Since that November day in 1989, the Avenue of the Arts has become a major object of city and even regional interest. The Brandywine Graphic Workshop firehouse has been completed, the Arts Bank has hosted many concerts and plays, the Clef Club has opened its doors, and, as I write, the jackhammers are busy on South Broad, implementing the imaginative "streetscape" which won a design competition. Even more important, the person who was elected mayor in 1991, Ed Rendell, made the Avenue of the Arts a priority in his plan to revitalize Philadelphia's physical appearance and economic health—thus ensuring not only municipal but state support. By this time, the project was clearly growing beyond the Foundation's desire or capacity to oversee. Mayor Rendell organized Avenue of the Arts, Inc., a public/private vehicle for coordinating all aspects of further development, and I have the honor of serving as its first chairman.

The Avenue now also includes a portion of North Broad Street, where there are a number of significant African American cultural organizations, such as New Freedom Theatre (which the Foundation has supported). The Broad Street portion of the Temple University campus, with its recently renovated Rock Hall (a performance venue for the Esther Boyer College of Music) and its projected Apollo recreational center, is part of this extended cultural area.

Someone asked me how projects on this scale are possible, and I replied by taking CAPA as an illustration. Soon after my arrival in Philadelphia, I became disturbed by the poor location and amenities provided for the High School for the Creative and Performing Arts—almost unknown and difficult to find, in a former elementary school, inadequate space for rehearsals, exhibits, and performances. Similar schools in New

York and other major cities were recognized and respected institutions: why should Philadelphia's budding artists have to "make do"? I continued to ponder this question for several years, and my opportunity to do something about it came after my appointment to the Foundation.

When W. Wilson Goode became mayor, I spoke to him about the possibility of renovating the magnificent old Ridgway Library on Broad Street and turning it over to the School District for CAPA. The building was owned by the city but it was used for only one small recreation department program; most of it had been allowed to fall into dangerous disrepair. Next, I talked with Joe Coleman, then head of city council, and of course I discussed the idea with Connie Clayton, the school system's first black female superintendent. All three were enthusiastic about the prospect, although somewhat concerned about funding it. The Foundation went ahead with several studies—engineering, curriculum, and architectural—to make sure the project was feasible (it was) and allocated $2 million toward the ever-escalating costs. CAPA-Ridgway was included in the capital budgets of both city and school system, state funds were added, and First Fidelity Bank made a major contribution as well. Thanks to carefully planned negotiations, the project which was once only a wild dream is now well on the way to becoming a significant element of the Avenue of the Arts.

North Philadelphia. This area, which lies directly north of City Hall and stretches almost from the Schuylkill to the Delaware rivers, had, in the words of my Temple colleague, Carolyn Adams, and her co-authors, "the dubious distinction of being chosen as the first site for slum clearance under the 1949 federal redevelopment legislation." The population, once comprised of many different ethnic groups who lived in densely packed row houses and worked in thriving local factories, is now largely black and Hispanic and poor. Most manufacturing enterprises have long since departed, leaving decaying buildings and widespread unemployment in their wake. In spite of the efforts of many gallant residents and community organizations, as well as repeated government plans for rejuvenation, North Philadelphia was and is a community marked by grave and complex problems, including a thriving traffic in drugs.

Over the years, the Foundation had made many discrete grants, amounting to millions of dollars, for housing, education, recreation, and health care in this area. For instance, more than $4 million was awarded to the Temple University Hospital and Medical School for a program intended to reduce infant mortality. When I was still at Temple, William Penn and the Pew Charitable Trusts made a major grant to construct playing fields and a track on the campus—on condition that the new sports facilities be made available to residents of the community. We readily agreed, and as a result the facilities have never been vandalized.

The goal of the 1989 initiative, however, was to focus aid on a particular neighborhood around Cecil B. Moore Avenue and, in cooperation with public and private agencies, make a multi-faceted attempt to address its needs—housing, education, human services, and others. The staff and I wanted to create an independent non-profit organization to manage the work there, but without careful negotiations with the affected parties, our program could sooner or later have been torpedoed. I knew from experience that perhaps the biggest danger was the power struggle that could easily ensue with a large sum of money at stake, and I wanted to head that off.

I talked to the mayor, W. Wilson Goode, because his administration had designated the Cecil B. Moore area as a priority. He agreed to work with us and to see that politics was excluded from decision-making on our projects. I then went to the council president, John Street, who represented that district. I explained the proposed plans in detail, assured him that the Foundation would not permit people in the area to use the projects to undermine him or create another political force, and asked that he keep politics out of the Foundation activities. He readily agreed and promised his full cooperation, a promise which he kept. At the time, Street and Goode were often on different sides on some issues. I told each of them of my conversations with the other, and asked them to discuss the matter. Once I had their guarantees that the program would not encounter political interference, I presented the proposal to the Foundation board. The board responded by allocating $26 million for North Philadelphia over a six-year period. I don't know whether the mayor and the city council president talked to each other about our initiative, but I do know that we cleared the way for years of trouble-free work. Although the Foundation program is now officially over, the Beech Corporation continues as an important coordinating agency in North Philadelphia.

As we did with the Avenue of the Arts, we created a non-profit organization, the Beech Corporation, to initiate, coordinate, and oversee the many individual projects. They ranged from summer programs for elementary school students to a construction skills training program for teenagers, from development of the first community-wide planning group to the creation of mini-parks and the planting of trees on the streets. Housing—both renovation of existing buildings and construction of new ones—was a high priority, and we tried to emphasize, wherever possible, the renewal of entire blocks and not just individual homes.

Minorities in Higher Education. Like the two initiatives just described, this one was built upon years of Foundation concern and experience: preparing minority young people to undertake careers (including teaching) in science, engineering, and mathematics. The "pipeline" problem—which is still with us—has been well documented: far too many black and Hispanic students are poorly educated and motivated from grade school on. If they reach college, they tend to stay away from intimidating course work for which they have not been prepared, and many drop out before graduation. The result is that minorities are grossly underrepresented in graduate schools, in the scientific work force, and in science teaching. Many of the Foundation's early efforts to tackle this problem had focused on high school students, providing them with residential summer programs on nearby college campuses or the Saturday sessions sponsored by PRIME (Philadelphia Regional Introduction for Minorities to Engineering). In 1989, we decided on a different approach.

Once the board had approved, allocating $10.2 million for this initiative, the staff identified a number of institutions of higher education which had already made substantial progress in recruiting and retaining minority students who wished to major in the sciences. Three kinds of institutions were on our list: some because they were attended by significant numbers of local students; historically black colleges and universities (HBCUs have produced most of the African American professionals over the years); and community colleges which are the first, if not the only, link to higher education for many low-income students. A list of the institutions we selected may be found in Appendix IV. The Foundation also made a substantial six-year grant to Teachers College, Columbia University, for evaluation of this initiative.

Among the seventeen institutions participating in this program, there was a marvelous variety of approaches: pre-freshman orientation, peer tutoring and counseling, research opportunities with faculty members, summer internships—anything and everything which might encourage the students to succeed in their courses, to set long-range goals, to obtain their degrees, and perhaps to attend graduate schools. In October 1992, the Foundation sponsored a two-day symposium which brought together almost 100 people to compare their experiences, explore avenues for collaboration, and exchange ideas. The symposium was held at the American Philosophical Society (the nation's oldest intellectual honor society), and it was attended by several world-renowned scholars who spoke to the students. It was a thrilling experience for me to see and talk with so many bright and eager young people and their mentors. The strategies employed by some institutions proved so successful that they were extended to entire departments for the benefit of all students. In one instance, the Department of Defense was so impressed by the Tuskegee engineering program that it awarded $6 million for its continuation.

Delaware River. As I mentioned, the Foundation's geographic area for environmental grantmaking was extended in 1986, in recognition of the impact which distant problems could have on the quality of local air and water. We had already supported many kinds of activities throughout this area: canoe trips on the Susquehanna River as part of the Chesapeake "Save the Bay" program; the purchase of farmland in Lancaster County; and the local public radio station's program, "Earthtalk." But the importance of the Delaware River for life, health, and recreation made it the logical candidate for a comprehensive conservation initiative. The vitality of the Delaware watershed—comprised of streams, marshlands, forested areas, and ultimately the bay—was being severely compromised by rapid construction and uncontrolled waste disposal. The problems were compounded by the many but unrelated political boundaries which criss-crossed the region.

The Delaware River initiative attempted to strengthen existing programs and encourage new cooperative ventures. One of our main goals was the creation of a "greenway" along both sides of the river and its tributaries, using such land preservation mechanisms as outright purchase for public recreational use or permanent protection agreements with landowners. We made substantial grants to organizations in both Pennsylvania and New Jersey to encourage the organization of local environmental commissions, and we sponsored the development of a program for visitors to the New Jersey State Aquarium to help them understand the ecology of the river and its tributaries. A key Foundation concern was citizen education and participation in monitoring water quality, all the way from the Delaware Water Gap to the Atlantic Ocean. Under the supervision of the American Littoral Society's Riverkeeper, many young people became involved in this important project through their science classes or Girl Scout troops. So this initiative, like the other three, reached and benefited the younger generation—an aspect which I found particularly gratifying.

The final initiative during my tenure as president was developed and implemented in response to several board members' concern about the global environment. In 1990 both the board and staff participated in discussions with experts (noted earlier in this chapter) on such issues as global warming (the "greenhouse effect"), overpopulation in the Caribbean, and U.S. policies relating to the United Nations Conference on

Environment and Development, which had been scheduled for June 1992 in Rio de Janeiro. In 1991, the board approved a total of $1,200,000 to fund a three-year program, 35 agencies were asked to submit proposals, and ten were selected to receive grants. Among them were the United Nations Association of the U.S.A., the National Audubon Society, and the Delaware Valley Clean Air Council. The projects varied widely: some were focused on educating the public about the need to conserve energy; others involved the strengthening of—to use the United Nations term— non-governmental organizations both here and abroad. Two of the projects were carried out in the Caribbean area, one to expand a coral reef monitoring program and one to improve family planning clinics.

Supporting Grantees with More than Money

Good organizations are not all alike. A number of them, especially small neighborhood or grassroots groups, need technical assistance of one sort or another in order to develop and carry out their programs. They may do excellent work and make a positive difference, but they often lack financial and managerial expertise (usually because they can't afford a full-time professional administrator). For instance, arts organizations may be run by brilliant artists who simply don't have the necessary skills. I can recall one instance when one of the largest and best-known arts groups needed to install a computerized accounting system: the group literally could not keep track of its operating budget, expenses, income, and so on. The situation was remedied when the Foundation made a small grant for equipment, backed up by training—with the understanding that future grants would depend on how well the organization learned to manage its finances.

Technical assistance to a floundering group has frequently made the difference which kept it from going out of business altogether. Many Foundation grantees have found that they needed help in areas ranging from marketing to fund-raising, from developing a mission statement to educating board members, from renovating a building to planning a new facility. Over the years, the Foundation has not only helped individual organizations, but it has supported the development of agencies which specialize in providing technical assistance. An early grant to the Wharton School of the University of Pennsylvania was made in the hope of establishing a resource to help arts organizations, but it proved unsuccessful. However, in 1984, a small grant was given to LaSalle University to plan a regional center which could offer consultant services to nonprofit agencies and help them to become more efficient. A much larger grant two years later established this center, and the Foundation has continued to support it over the years. Other similar grants have gone to:

- the Nonprofit Energy Management Organization, which proposes solutions for buildings (many of them churches) that eat up resources because of inefficient furnaces or poor insulation;
- Community Accountants, which uses volunteer financial experts to unravel accounting problems or set up new systems;
- Regional Housing Legal Services, which works with community development corporations that want to renovate or construct low-income housing, steering them through the maze of funding, zoning, licensing, and other regulations;
- the Greater Philadelphia Cultural Alliance, which tries to bring an "economy of scale" to a number of arts organization tasks, including improving management and selling tickets;
- the Penjerdel Regional Foundation, which organized a Business Volunteers for the Arts program.

Collaboration with Other Foundations

I have already mentioned the rehabilitation of the Merriam Theater as one outstanding example of collaborative grantmaking. Perhaps the most unusual, and continuing, effort of this sort is the Summer Youth Employment and Career/Vocational Exploration program, which William Penn organized more than ten years ago. Each year, funds are contributed by up to 30 other foundations to assist high school young people throughout the six-county area (the number has ranged from 1,600 to 3,400 each summer). Grants are then made to a number of selected nonprofit agencies which line up the summer positions and assign them to students on the basis of their expressed career interests. These positions are strictly limited to professional and business settings (with the exception of the fast-food industry), where students are likely to get good supervision, pay, and experience. College-age monitors are an important part of the program, keeping track of students' job progress and counseling them about their future educational and vocational goals. Until 1995, when administrative responsibilities were transferred to the Philadelphia Foundation,

William Penn was the program manager, usually hiring a graduate student for the summer to observe every aspect of the activities and prepare a detailed report for the funding organizations. Year after year, the success of this program has been demonstrated through such measures as additional hours of summer employment (i.e., beyond the term negotiated by the collaborative) and part-time work during the following school year.

Another joint venture revolved around the historic houses in Fairmount Park, which were rapidly deteriorating. Together with Pew and Bartol, we sponsored a number of studies of ways to maintain the buildings' charm and unique architecture while finding a new role which might make them self-supporting. Shortly after I took office, we helped to fund, this time with ten other donors, a study of Philadelphia's shelter program by the Philadelphia Health Management Corporation. The study became the basis of the city's policy on the homeless. Two of our collaborative projects were directed toward strengthening local philanthropy: the establishment of the Delaware Valley Grantmakers, a professional association for private and corporate funders which has long since proved its worth, and the expansion of the philanthropy collection at the Free Library of Philadelphia. I am pleased that the Foundation is continuing with joint ventures: since my retirement, $2.5 million has been allocated for the Philadelphia Neighborhood Development Collaborative, which is providing technical and financial assistance to selected community development corporations involved in low-income housing programs.

Inclusive Grantmaking

It should be clear by now how strongly I believe that foundations have a special responsibility to encourage and support the development of minority organizations, whether in the arts or social services. Institutions like art museums and major hospitals are clearly vital to any city, but while they may have difficulty in raising adequate funds, they are not likely to go out of business for lack of support. For small community groups, particularly in minority areas, even small grants may mean the difference between life and death for neighborhood cultural centers or local clinics. To create and maintain this sensitivity, foundations must have a diverse staff. Minority staff members, once having gained access to these particular corridors of power, should be ready to uphold the claims of the hitherto excluded, the needs of the often silent poor. As people who have personal experience of marginality, we can also insist that plans be made with, and not for, minority applicants. I remember reading about the response of philanthropists to the 1992 riots in Los Angeles: many were happy to provide emergency aid but said they had no idea how to go about longterm rehabilitation. In contrast, the Irvine Foundation hired a consultant to visit affected neighborhoods and find out what local groups and individuals thought were the most urgent problems and most promising solutions.

If the William Penn Foundation has often seemed to have a bias in favor of programs benefiting low-income and minority groups, that was a deliberate policy and one that I was delighted to implement and expand. Much of the credit belongs to the late F. Otto and Dophie Haas, and to John and Chara Haas, who had an unusual sensitivity to and compassion for the problems of those so much less favored than they happened to be. And there was never any doubt about the sympathies of my predecessor, Dick Bennett: he was always an outspoken advocate for the oppressed and the disadvantaged. When I was being considered as its president, this tradition was, to me, the Foundation's most compelling, most attractive feature.

Over the years, the Foundation has contributed millions of dollars to assist poor people, members of minority groups, and new immigrants. Some grants were of necessity made to the School District, hospitals, and social agencies run by whites, but wherever possible we tried to identify and to fund minority organizations, like the Negro Trade Union Council or Congreso de Latinos Unidos or the Korean Community Development Service Center, for projects of their own choosing. While many grants were awarded for health and welfare purposes—for instance, to assist mothers before and after the birth of their babies, or to expand adult literacy programs, or to provide smoke detectors in North Philadelphia homes—there were others as well. I was always particularly gratified by Foundation efforts to preserve and expand the cultural heritage of minority groups.

The New Freedom Theatre, one such beneficiary, has earned national acclaim for its 25-year history of offering first-rate training and performance opportunities to young African American actors. Philadanco has a similar reputation in the medium of dance. Another grantee was the Village of Arts and Humanities in North Philadelphia. Initially organized (by an Asian woman) to turn a vacant lot into a community park, it has become a center for art exhibits and dramatic productions by neighborhood young people. Taller Puertorriqueño is a flourishing arts center for thousands of Hispanics in North Philadelphia, in large measure because of Foundation support for both its building and its program. Its year-round schedule of art classes and exhibits culminates in a day celebrating Puerto Rican culture with music, dancing, parades, and food.

The Charles L. Blockson Collection at Temple University is one of my personal favorites among minority projects. Charles is a man with a passion—some might say mania—for African American history, and he has been collecting letters and journals and photographs and anything else he can lay hands on which might contribute to the understanding of the black experience. (His collection is one of the two or three outstanding national resources for scholarly research, and I wish he had a bigger budget and larger staff.) The Foundation became involved with Mr. Blockson because of our historical marker project. As it happens, many important African American individuals and organizations have been associated with Philadelphia, but few people, black or white, knew much about them—except, of course, for Charles Blockson. To make a long story short, the Foundation awarded him two grants, the first to identify and acquire state historical markers for significant sites, and the second to compile and print a detailed directory. There are now 65 markers in place, all but one (the African Episcopal Church of St. Thomas) arranged for by Charles. Fifty thousand copies of the directory were published and distributed for use in classrooms and by tourists.

Did the William Penn Foundation succeed in its mission of helping "to improve the quality of life in the Delaware Valley" during the twelve years I was president? Although I can take only a tiny portion of the credit—most belongs to the dedicated board of directors and the hard-working staff—I think the answer has to be "Yes."

In January 1992, John Haas and I made a joint announcement about our respective retirements: his as chairman of the board in January 1993, and mine as president in December 1993. My association with him and many others involved in the work of the Foundation was a source of great happiness and satisfaction.

CHAPTER X
NATIONAL AND OTHER
EXTRACURRICULAR ACTIVITIES

All my life I have been busy, unable and unwilling to be a mere spectator. During my school years, I was into every extracurricular activity offered—music, sports, student government, clubs—and I often ended up running some of them. It was the same throughout my university years, and the habit of involvement has stuck with me ever since. Although I am now officially "retired," my schedule still keeps my travel agent engrossed and my family bemused. But it's wonderful to have the freedom to engage in some of the things I most enjoy: jazz clubs and concerts, reading a wide range of titles, writing, travel, and reviving friendships of long standing in various parts of the country.

I have already described my participation in the growth of the independent black political movement in Philadelphia but—important as that was and is—politics is only one of my many interests and activities. Some have been satisfying and others frustrating, but I have learned so much from these involvements that I think they deserve a separate chapter. First, a word on why I've been so busy. For one thing, I was blessed with physical health, the vigor and stamina that make constant work and travel possible, as well as with almost insatiable curiosity about people and events and places. Much of my time as a child was spent with books, in the library, in the world of my mind. My dreams, fantasies, and aspirations were shaped by my love of books. When I was growing up, my family encouraged me to pursue a variety of activities, and while they demanded high standards of achievement, they were eager to applaud every success. Being small for my age was never an excuse for sitting on the sidelines; on the contrary, I was determined to prove that I was just as fast or smart or tough as the rest of the kids.

But the single most important factor in shaping my life and the choices I made was the color of my skin. African Americans, especially those of my generation, will understand immediately; for them, no further explication is necessary. People from other backgrounds may have some difficulty comprehending the impact of race on millions of their fellow humans beings. Many blacks have been destroyed by it; some have tried to ignore it by pretending it doesn't exist or by lying low; others have made their private peace with it, hoping for justice in a better world or in heaven. But I was born and raised as a fighter, and I can barely remember a time when I was not outraged by the endless, unavoidable reminders of racism. I still am. My education, my various jobs, and my extracurricular involvements have all been energized by my determination to help eradicate racism and empower its victims.

I was, therefore, particularly gratified by my appointment to the Committee on Research and Program Development of the Martin Luther King Center for Nonviolence. The Center was established by Coretta Scott King in order to continue and expand the work for which her husband had given his life. It was directed by Dr. Robert Green, a psychologist who had earned his Ph.D. at Berkeley before becoming one of Dr. King's youngest assistants. I was privileged to participate in its summer workshops and seminars along with such noted figures as psychologist Erik Erikson and civil rights leader Fannie Lou Hamer. Although I was not a convert to nonviolence, I could not help but be enormously impressed by these two people, and in particular by Fannie Lou Hamer, who had suffered extensively at the hands of Mississippi police while she was assisting in voter registration efforts in Greenwood and Winona.

The credentials which brought me to the attention of the school reformers in Philadelphia—experience in the public schools, an earned doctorate from the University of Chicago, being the first black to win the Shankland Award of the American Association of School Administrators—were also noted by some others around the country. Once I joined the Dilworth/Shedd team, which had become the focus of nationwide hopes for urban education's renewal, it was all but inevitable that I would be asked to participate in the work of such organizations as the National Urban League and the National Urban Coalition. The League dates back to 1910, when it was established by a group of black and white individuals to aid blacks who had moved from the rural south to the urban north. Throughout its eighty-six-year history, it has concentrated on job training and education, while also sponsoring programs in housing, recreation, and other areas. The Coalition is much younger, having been organized in the aftermath of the unrest, riots, and violence of the 1960s, by A. Philip Randolph, founder of the International Brotherhood of Sleeping Car Porters, and Andrew Heiskell, then publisher of *Time*. Its first president was John Gardner (later of Common Cause), and its board was comprised of a veritable "who's who" of corporate, public, and independent sector CEOs, including the mayors of Pittsburgh and New York, labor leaders George Meany and Walter Reuther, David Rockefeller, president of Chase Manhattan Bank, and J. Irwin Miller of Cummins Engine. Its agenda was restoring peace with justice to the troubled cities of America. My involvement with both these organizations began not long after I moved to Philadelphia; I am now completing my twenty-eighth year as a volunteer for the League, and I resigned from the Coalition's board in 1991.

In 1968, Whitney Young, Jr., who had recently become president of the National Urban League, was eager to see it become more outspoken on all the issues affecting minorities. To aid him in this task, he called together a small group of black men. I was one. I became a member of the education advisory committee, as well as a regular contributor to the League's annual publication, *The State of Black America*. In 1981, I joined the board of trustees, becoming its senior vice chairman two years later, and I have served as an advisor to all three of Young's successors— Vernon Jordan, John Jacob, and Hugh Price. Jordan, who became president after Young's tragic drowning death in Africa, had been head of the Atlanta NAACP and helped integrate both schools and colleges. After serving as president of the United Negro College Fund, he came to the League, bringing a different kind of energy and excitement. He retired after surviving an assassination attempt and was followed by John Jacob, whom he had recruited. By the way, I think John deserves particular credit: he became president when the "glamour" of civil rights was fading and corporate contributions were dropping precipitously, but he successfully steered the League through a very difficult time.

Also in 1968, but by a different route, I became involved with the National Urban Coalition. John Gardner had commissioned a monograph on citizen participation in school affairs and had asked my friend, colleague, and mentor Luvern Cunningham to serve as editor. With Bruce McPherson, I co-authored a chapter on "Selected Mechanisms of Citizen Participation in Chicago, Illinois, and Philadelphia, Pennsylvania." The following year, my research assistant and I prepared another monograph for the Coalition, this one entitled *Business, Industry and Education: New Resources for Pressing Needs*. In 1972, I was appointed chairman of the Coalition's education task force, and in 1973, I was elected to the organization's national steering committee and executive committee, positions I held until my resignation in 1991.

Gardner's successor as head of the Coalition was a wonderful, gentle man named M. Carl Holman, a poet and playwright who had earned graduate degrees from both the University of Chicago and from Yale. He began his career as a professor of English, and in a more peaceful era he would probably have been happy to stay in the academic and literary world where he was at home. But he believed that the times demanded his participation in the civil rights movement, and he went forward without flinching, although it undoubtedly contributed to his premature death. He founded the *Atlanta Inquirer*, a black newspaper, and served as mentor and adviser to many of the young civil rights leaders, including Julian Bond, Charlayne Hunter-Gault, and John Lewis. In 1971, after several years as a member of the "black cabinet" in the Kennedy and Johnson administrations, he was appointed president of the Coalition. At its twentieth anniversary celebration in 1987, tributes to Carl Holman's vision and commitment poured in from across the country. A year later, he was dead. He was succeeded by Dr. Ramona H. Edelin, who had joined the staff in 1977. As senior vice president for programs and policy, she assumed many of his responsibilities and virtually directed the organization during Holman's final illness, and she is doing an admirable job as president in times which are difficult for organizations like the Coalition. It was an honor to have known and worked with Carl Holman; Ramona Edelin is a close friend to this day.

I had not been in Philadelphia very long when, in 1969, President Lyndon Baines Johnson appointed me to the National Advisory Council on Education Professions Development. I later became the vice chairman. At that time, Harold ("Doc") Howe was in charge of the Office of Education, and Frank Keppel was Secretary of Health, Education and Welfare; they, along with Charles Smith who worked with Howe, were probably the individuals responsible for my appointment. It was a good commission, with lots of controversy and intense discussion about the future training and roles of school teachers and administrators.

Many people have forgotten that Richard Nixon, who was elected president in 1968, wanted to be known as an "education president." Although education did not then have cabinet status (Jimmy Carter created the department in 1980), there was a great deal of ferment and excitement in Washington, in part because of the ramifications of the massive Elementary and Secondary Education Act of 1965. I was appointed to President Nixon's Urban Education Task Force. I served, but disagreed publicly with the first draft of its report because it did not address sufficiently the needs of urban schools and the responsibility of government to deal with those needs. Meantime, the Office of Education had created the National Center for the Improvement of Educational Systems, and one of the Center's experimental projects was the development of "leadership training institutes." These institutes were panels comprised of school personnel from all over the country, each of which studied and drew attention to a particular aspect of school reform. They were clever devices to extend the Office of Education's influence without hiring additional full-time staff, while also incorporating ideas and opinions from the field into the development of federal policy.

In 1969, I was approached about becoming director of the Leadership Training Institute on Recruitment. At the time I was considering whether and when to leave the School District of Philadelphia, and when I learned that this appointment would carry with it a small budget, I decided to accept. The funds from the Office of Education, along with a grant from the Rockefeller Foundation, made it possible for me to move to Temple University and create the department of urban education there. A few years later, I turned over the LTI to Eunice Clarke, an outstanding member of my department.

Two other presidential appointments have come my way. In 1980 President Carter named me to the National Council on Educational Research. This council served as an advisory group to the National Institute of Education, recommending topics for staff research and ultimately policy positions on public education. One of my treasured memories of that period is the luncheon I attended at the White House with a group of leading African American scholars and intellectuals whom President Carter had invited for a general discussion of issues and priorities. Included were Walter E. Massey, then director of the Argonne National Laboratory; Clifton Wharton, chancellor of the New York State higher education system; and Charles Hamilton of Columbia University and co-author with Stokeley Carmichael of *Black Power*. The luncheon was intense and enjoyable—and showed how really bright Carter was (after all, he was a nuclear engineer and one of Rickover's proteges). Many years later, in 1994, President Clinton appointed me to the National Advisory Council for Historically Black Colleges and Universities.

In the spring of 1972, I was asked to serve as the director of the first National Policy Conference on Education for Blacks, sponsored by the Congressional Black Caucus and nine other organizations. The conference brought together 722 people from all over the country: students, elected officials, leaders of civil rights organizations, parents, and community leaders. In addition to members of the Caucus, speakers included Kenneth Clark, president of the Metropolitan Applied Research Center, Harvard law professor Derrick Bell, Cleveland mayor Carl Stokes, and many other nationally known leaders in politics and education. The conference was a huge success, and a number of the conclusions and recommendations are still relevant today. The proceedings were published and mailed to all participants within thirty days, and there was a surplus large enough to fund research on violence and vandalism three years later. Much of the credit for this efficiency goes to Patsy Fleming, my administrative assistant for this project. It turned out that she was related to Allison Davis, the noted black scholar whom I had met while at the University of Chicago. Dr. Davis's work was well-known and revered; he had done classic studies with Robert Havighurst and W. Lloyd Warner.

There was also drama at the conference. On the first day, Roy Innis of CORE held his own press conference in the lobby of the hotel where the meetings were being held. He was annoyed because he had not been asked to participate (his stance on civil rights had changed markedly in the recent past), but his attempt to interfere with the conference failed when our staff and the participants ignored him and refused to talk to the media representatives about him. Another, more serious effort at disruption was made by a delegate from Detroit, who apparently believed the conference agenda was not sufficiently diverse—i.e., it was dominated by integrationists. Although unwilling to take a public position himself, he encouraged young delegates who claimed to be "nationalists" to protest during the session when Dr. Vivian Henderson, president of Clark College and a noted integrationist, was to speak.

At the appointed time, Henderson entered the hall, accompanied by his close friend, M. Carl Holman, president of the National Urban Coalition, Congressman Augustus Hawkins, vice president of the Congressional Black Caucus, Congressman William Clay of Missouri, and myself as chair of the session. The disruptive faction was seated around the auditorium, but we knew who they were and who the instigator was, although he tried to disguise his role. We were ready for them, determined that the members of the Caucus would not be embarrassed and that the conference would not degenerate into a media circus. We had long since made arrangements with off-duty black policemen from Washington and Virginia to provide regular security, but we thought more was needed. Just before I called the meeting to order, the Philadelphia delegation, led by Dave Richardson and Paul Vance, filed into the room and stood along the walls and in the rear. Shortly afterward, Kwame Holman, Carl's son, and six or eight of his friends came in and took strategic positions. Considering that discretion was the better part of valor, the would-be disrupters remained seated and quiet throughout the session.

A social hour had been scheduled immediately following the meeting. As people filed into the reception, there was tension in the air: frowns, glowering, hard looks everywhere. Suddenly, Haki Madhubuti, a poet who allegedly had once been a member of the Black Panthers, made an exaggerated leap into the middle of the room, screaming the first two lines of a poem which included the word "nigger." Silence, stunned silence, settled over the area. Hakim proceeded to recite his poem, which spoke of respect, honor, love, tolerance, brotherhood, sisterhood, humanity. It was over in five minutes. Cheers, tears, hugs, and sighs of relief replaced the hostility. Hakim had transformed the evening, and the party began. Some of us, including Gus Hawkins, Patsy Fleming, and Bill Clay, met with the dissidents and their leader, and arranged for them to have their say the next morning at the closing plenary. Even Roy Innis was invited to participate, but he declined. We retired after midnight with everything under control and, even more important, with a sense of respect all around. We were together on the agenda, despite disagreements. The final session was a love-in, with calls to continue the dialogue.

For whatever reason, Jesse Jackson was not at that conference, but throughout all the years I have worked with minority educators and civil rights activists, he stands out. He is the only person who has consistently and forcefully upheld the importance of individual responsibility, particularly where education is concerned. He has urged young people to stay in school, to do well, to take advantage of every opportunity. And he has repeatedly told parents that they must do everything in their power to see that their children succeed in school. Turning off the television so that they do their homework, he has said time and again, is a key part of educational accountability.

Since my days at the University of Chicago, I had had ties with Harvard, particularly through Dan Lortie, the chairman of my dissertation committee, and later through Mark Shedd. In the summer of 1968, I went to Cambridge for a postdoctoral seminar in educational administration, and while I studied, Lois and our baby daughter Barbra spent much of their time observing the pigeons and other denizens of Harvard Square. Soon after we were there, Harvard, like most other universities, began discussing the feasibility of an academic program in African American studies. The issue there, as elsewhere, was fraught with controversy, with a few individuals adamantly opposed to "dignifying" the history and (in their view) questionable culture of former slaves. Harvard's program was launched as an academic department and was later chaired by the father of professor Lani Guinier. (Ironically, Guinier was unable to attend Harvard as an undergraduate because the single scholarship reserved for a Negro freshman had already been awarded.) Today, the department is headed by Henry L. (Skip) Gates, Jr.; it includes Cornel West, William Julius Wilson, and Evelyn Higginbotham, wife of the noted judge; and it is now probably the premier department in the country.

I served on the Visiting Committee for the Department of Afro-American Studies at Harvard from 1974 to 1978, during some of the tough times, and I was able to observe closely the problems inherent in the implementation of black studies programs and other similar ventures. On some campuses, when such a program was created, it was all too easy to blunt its effectiveness and diminish its credibility by denying it departmental status or by hiring instructors who did not have authentic academic credentials. And of course, as I noted in discussing my years at Temple, even properly qualified blacks were likely to be given "special" appointments which had little authority and did not lead to tenure. For an even longer period, 1981 - 1987, I was a member of the Visiting Committee for Harvard's Graduate School of Education, advising on a host of issues, ranging from recruitment and diversity to student retention and financial aid to, ultimately, placement of graduates. I also served on the advisory board for the Center for Urban and Minority Affairs, affiliated with Teachers College, Columbia University.

As I have already said, the important contributions made by the historically black colleges and universities (HBCUs) can hardly be overemphasized. Although I did not choose to attend one of the HBCUs, I have always been interested in them and concerned about their welfare. Two are located near Philadelphia—Lincoln and Cheyney—and I served on the board of trustees of each university. Cheyney trained many teachers, not only for the Philadelphia schools but for those in Gary and other cities. In its heyday, Lincoln was outstanding in many fields, attracting large numbers of students from abroad as well as across the country. Unfortunately, the university was caught in one of the paradoxes of integration: as new opportunities opened up for African Americans, it no longer attracted the number of top calibre students it had once boasted. Ivy League and other top institutions began to recruit, entice, and accept the best minority students (some of whom would once have gone to Lincoln, Morehouse, Spelman, and other leading HBCUs), luring them with more financial aid and the opportunity to network with the emerging white elite. Lincoln was unable or unwilling to change to accommodate the new realities. During the years I served (1975 - 1978), the board of trustees was comprised of several corporate CEOs, and included one of the du Ponts from neighboring Delaware, but we found it difficult to persuade the administration to adapt. Without any fanfare, eleven of us resigned together. Under Niara Sudarkasa, the president since 1987, Lincoln has begun to reclaim some of its former prestige. Dr. Sudarkasa, who came to Lincoln from the University of Michigan, earned her Ph.D. in anthropology from Columbia.

One of my most interesting associations was with the Educational Testing Service, the Princeton organization which helps determine the educational and vocational fates of millions upon millions of Americans. Over the years I served on several advisory committees and carried out other assignments for ETS. While I have serious reservations about some aspects of its early history, I believe it has made enormous progress. When I first became involved, it was the target of serious and justifiable criticism for its bias toward white, middle-class standards in its many testing programs; but at least some of that criticism should have been directed toward the admissions and employment offices which unquestioningly accepted test results as infallible indicators of future success. Since that time, ETS has exerted enormous energy toward freeing its testing instruments from cultural bias, encouraging minority student participation, and clarifying what test results can and cannot predict. My experiences with ETS led me to write a major monograph on the history of testing in 1993.

For many years, I maintained contact with school districts and state education agencies around the country. I served on or chaired a number of national search committees for school superintendents in Trenton, New Jersey; Berkeley, California; St. Louis, Missouri; and others. I was the first black to be involved in this process in any meaningful way.

From 1986 to 1988, I had the chance to make a small contribution to one of the nation's persistent and perplexing problems—the declining economic status of non-college young people—through my participation in the William T. Grant Foundation Commission on Work, Family and Citizenship. Our interim report was *The Forgotten Half: Non-College Youth in America,* while *The Forgotten Half: Pathways to Success for America's Youth and Young Families* was the title of the Grant Commission's final report. As the latter title suggests, our emphasis was on programs that worked, rather than on frightening statistics and gloomy predictions. It was a rather high-powered group, too: it was chaired by my old friend Doc Howe, who had returned to Harvard, and among the members were Dr. Mary Jo Bane (then a professor at Harvard's JFK School of Government and now assistant secretary of the Department of Health and Human Services), Hillary Rodham Clinton (then of Arkansas), Father Theodore Hesburgh (retired president of Notre Dame), Dr. William Julius Wilson (former professor of sociology at Chicago and now at Harvard), and Daniel Yankelovich (one of the country's best-known pollsters).

At home in Philadelphia, I was continuously involved in civic activities. For instance, I served on the Philadelphia City Planning Commission at a critical time when the issue of whether the city would tolerate real skyscrapers was being discussed. Until then, there had been an unwritten agreement that no building could be higher than the statue of William Penn, which stood atop the monumental City Hall. After well-known developer, Willard Rouse, succeeded, amidst much controversy, in getting this restriction eliminated, he proceeded to construct Liberty Place which, with several more recent additions, has permanently changed the Philadelphia skyline.

Over a number of years, I played a part in an interesting progression of civic groups, beginning with the Greater Philadelphia Movement, once the leading organization dedicated to reforms in the city and (later) in the school system. Founded in the late 1940s, GPM limited its membership to the chief executives of local banks and businesses, all of whom were white and male, and it would be difficult to overestimate its power and influence. But after the educational home rule charter had been adopted and Richardson Dilworth installed as president of the school board (in 1965), many of the key goals of the GPM had been accomplished and, like some other reform groups, it seemed to lose its sense of mission and urgency. Meantime, the events of the mid-1960s—the Civil Rights Act, urban violence—had stimulated the founding of new kinds of organizations, such as the Urban Coalition, in which I became active at both the national and local levels.

In the early 1970s, a new civic group, comprised of younger leaders (including African Americans) and headed by Graham Finney, was formed: the Philadelphia Partnership. Several years later, prompted by similar agendas and overlapping board membership, it merged with the GPM to become the Greater Philadelphia Partnership. I served as a cochairman of the new organization, along with Stewart Rauch (a leading banker, head of PSFS) and John Haas, and Graham continued as its director. By the early 1980s, however, it was widely observed that there were simply too many civic groups in town, each claiming to speak on behalf of the public interest and each requesting corporate and foundation support. When this was documented by a study, an alliance of CEOs was revived under the name of Greater Philadelphia First, Inc. To resolve the potential for conflict with the Partnership, my colleagues, Messrs. Rauch and Haas, Jim Bodine (the CEO of the First Pennsylvania Bank), and I helped to negotiate an agreement to organize the Urban Affairs Partnership to speak on civic matters. Greater Philadelphia First became the city's leading economic voice.

The final merger occurred in 1991, when the Urban Affairs Partnership joined forces with the Urban Coalition. I chaired a committee of board members from both groups which worked for more than a year to bring this about. The new organization, known as the Greater Philadelphia Urban Affairs Coalition, has a board comprised of a cross-section of business, academic, and community leaders. Today, GPUAC plays an important role in promoting all aspects of civic health, under the capable leadership of Ernest Jones, one of the early black graduates of Temple Law School. He had served for many years as head of the Philadelphia Urban Coalition.

I had chosen to move to Temple University in part because of the greater freedom I would enjoy to pursue outside interests. As president of the William Penn Foundation, I was expected to continue and expand the scope of my activities, and I took advantage of every opportunity to do so. I have already mentioned my role in creating the Avenue of the Arts and my continuing involvement in this $300 million-plus project. It includes a new home for the Philadelphia Orchestra; the renovation of the Ridgway Library for the Philadelphia High School for the Creative and Performing Arts (known locally as CAPA); and several new halls for drama and music performances. The Clef Club of Jazz and the Performing Arts is the only facility ever built from the ground up for the study, perpetuation, and celebration of jazz, America's art form. On North Broad Street, a new venue for the New Freedom Theatre (nationally recognized for training black actors and producing the work of black playwrights) is underway. Headquarters are being created or renovated for the Black Family Reunion, the Black United Fund of Pennsylvania, the Coalition of African-American Cultural Organizations, and Greek Row (several black fraternity houses). Tying the Avenue together, both north and south of City Hall, is a magnificent "streetscape," incorporating new paving, lighting, subway stations, and other improvements. The necessary upheaval has irritated numerous travelers (and business owners) on Broad Street, but when the streetscape is complete, with freshly planted trees and flowers, I think everyone will agree that it was all worthwhile. In any case,

Avenue of the Arts is the Philadelphia venture I have most enjoyed, partly because of the many challenges it presents. All of it has been made possible by a combination of state, local, Foundation, and private funds.

A close second choice for my favorite local project is the Pennsylvania Convention Center, one of those enterprises for which the song might have been written—"They Said It Couldn't Be Done." While there had been general agreement for years that the aging Civic Center needed to be replaced, controversy simmered continuously about where a new facility should be located. One of the more daring suggestions was to put it above the massive railroad yards at 30th Street. A site was finally selected (just north of Market Street and a few blocks east of City Hall) and, amid dire predictions of total disaster, work began in 1986 with the appointment of members of the Convention Center Authority. I was one of the city representatives chosen by Mayor Goode (and later reappointed by Mayor Rendell), and at the first meeting I was elected vice chairman, a position I still hold eleven years later at this writing. Other members were designated by the president of Philadelphia's city council, the four surrounding suburban counties, the state legislature, and the governor (the Commonwealth of Pennsylvania had invested heavily in the project).

The project came under fire from some members of the black community and others who felt that the money would have been better spent on housing or health care, but many minority jobs were created both during and after construction. The Authority was committed to affirmative action and we hired the Philadelphia Urban Coalition, which had some expertise in this area, to see that it was carried out properly. Everyone knew that I was on record as promising to help block construction if we did not find a way to be inclusive in our contracts and hiring. We were really proud when our affirmative action plan withstood a court challenge, although Judge Bechtel had overturned other similar plans from the school district and the city.

One day, John Street and Lucien Blackwell, both members of Philadelphia's city council, telephoned me at the Foundation and asked to see me as soon as possible. I offered to go over to their offices in City Hall, but they said they'd come to the Foundation. When they arrived, they told me they wanted to clarify my position regarding some contract and personnel issues and cooperation with other agencies. They had heard one of the members of the Authority describing my views, and they said to each other that it didn't sound like Bernie Watson, it wasn't consistent. The two council members were upset and decided to check immediately on my real position. After they had explained the reasons for their visit and while they were still in my office, I telephoned the person in question. "I called to be certain that you were clear about my position at the last meeting. So many people were talking and the discussion lasted so long that I wanted to be sure we understood each other." His response was "Yes, I recall your statement exactly..... That is what you said, and that is what I understood." There was no confusion.

The Convention Center opened in 1993, on time and on budget. The credit belongs in large measure to Harry Perks, the project superintendent, and someone I had respected and admired since the days when we were both at the School District. It is also one of the most beautiful convention facilities in the country, combining the best of modern architecture and design with the restoration of the magnificent, but long disused, Reading Railroad station. And, contrary to the many voices of doom, the unique Reading Terminal Market—a real Philadelphia treasure—was not only preserved but improved. In my view, the Center is a monument to how much can be accomplished when people focus on a worthwhile goal and hang together through thick and thin. Maybe we should rename it the Pennsylvania Cooperation Center.

I have always been interested in the arts, an interest which began, I suspect, in those early days when my family sang around the piano. Lois and I have always enjoyed attending concerts, operas, and plays, and we have friends who are successful painters and sculptors, musicians and composers. We exposed our children to music, theater, and dance, including ballet. I also served on the boards of non-profit organizations such as Young Audiences and supported African American arts groups. When F. Otto Haas retired from the Pennsylvania Council on the Arts, he nominated me, and I was honored to be appointed as a member and vice chairman of the Council by a Republican governor (Dick Thornburgh) and reappointed by a Democratic one (Bob Casey).

During my seven or eight years on the Council, I became familiar with artistic endeavors all over the Commonwealth, and I am proud that the Council was able to rescue quite a number from near-fatal obscurity or total collapse. Our resources ebbed and waned in rhythm with the prevailing economic and political winds, both in Harrisburg and in Washington, but I think we were able to accomplish a great deal, particularly through our support of emerging artists and ethnic groups. I resigned in 1993, and I was deeply gratified when Governor Casey presented me with the Crystal Bowl Award for the Arts and the Humanities.

There are many, many committees and boards, other than those mentioned in this chapter, on which I once served or still do. I have often been the only black member. I never forced my way in, but when I accepted an invitation to join a group, I raised questions about the lack of minority members. I raised these questions with force and conviction, but without anger or making it personal. Other people attending meetings never forgot I was there. They were often surprised, initially, that I held the same positions as some of the more outspoken and visible community and civil rights leaders.

In a number of situations, I was able to make things happen by working behind the scenes. Because it was well known that I would not change my views to suit a particular audience, I had access to and credibility with many different people. I gave examples, in the chapter on the William Penn Foundation, of how I used this trust to conduct two sets of high-level negotiations: one was to ensure that our complex, multi-million dollar program in North Philadelphia could proceed without political interference; the other was to preserve a beautiful but deteriorating building by renovating it for use as a high school. I learned early on that you could work with almost anyone if they believed you were sincere, honest, and consistent. Another important factor was discretion. What I was told in confidence, whether in the board room or in political circles, I kept in confidence. People learned that they didn't have to worry about hearing something on the street that came from me. I didn't need or want the public attention that comes from media exposure. It was more important to me to get the job done.

I also knew that it is essential to distinguish between a person's point of view and the individual himself or herself. I remember my days at Chicago, when students debated all the time and eagerly adopted the role of devil's advocate just for the fun of it. The arguments were often heated almost to the point of violence, but when they were over, we clapped or laughed and went on our way as friends. To this day, I can have deep and even furious disagreements with people, yet still have cordial relationships with them. I can have at least civil relationships with those whose ideas I find distasteful or worse. It is not only possible but vitally important to understand fundamental differences and continue to oppose one another, without descending to personal attacks. This ability has been especially helpful in dealing with powerful individuals and corporations, whether one-to-one or in the board room.

I have been truly privileged to participate in such a wide range of activities, at home and across the country. Not many individuals have the good fortune to see both the broader, national perspective and to know the local scene intimately, and yet this dual focus is critically important for the successful development and implementation of social policies and programs. My most treasured memories are of the countless people I have met, from welfare mothers to U.S. Senators, who were committed to working together for the common good, for a better America. We did not always agree—in fact, we sometimes argued vehemently—but we respected one another, we built a relationship of trust, and we developed a network of concern. Time and time again, in connection with Foundation as well as other projects, I was able to pick up the phone and talk directly with individuals who had facts I needed or a different point of view. (Of course, I have also been on the receiving end of such calls.) In fact, more than twenty years ago, when the terms "multiculturalism" or "diversity" were rarely heard, I drew on personal contacts with people of every imaginable background to discuss material for *Cross Reference*, the journal I published at Temple.

In Philadelphia, there are many satisfying, *tangible* markers of activities in which I have participated—the Clef Club and the Convention Center, to mention just two. What can I point to elsewhere? Most of the "extracurricular" work I have engaged in, in Washington and around the country, did not produce national monuments, new buildings, or other visible reminders of our efforts. Nevertheless, I will always treasure such experiences as testifying before a Congressional committee about the Foundation's child abuse prevention program, helping to evaluate and improve Title I, working with national organizations to expand opportunities for minorities. In the end, what matters most is not a medal or a trophy, but the knowledge that you cared and that you did your best to help.

CHAPTER XI
SUMMING UP

If I hadn't made a promise to my children, I might never have finished this memoir. Their interest in the events of my life kept me going, even—or especially—when I was sick and tired of the whole project. But whenever I felt like abandoning it, I was reminded that my generation of African Americans has lived through an era of momentous change, and that I have what amounts to an obligation, not only to my children but to many other people, to record some of its effects on individuals, the black community, and the country at large. Again and again, I have been struck by how little people know about the past or how easily they forget. If you were born after the Brown decision and the Civil Rights Act and the bloody struggles for simple justice, then the conditions under which millions of people used to live is ancient history for you. You may well dismiss affirmative action programs as unnecessary, you may believe that equal opportunity pervades the air we breathe, you may assume that "the racial problem" has been solved. We may have won some battles, but the war against ignorance, racism, hatred, and violence is far from over.

The main reason that it has been difficult to write this memoir is that I am basically a very private person. On public policy issues—education, urban problems, human rights, issues about which I care deeply—I am outspoken and sometimes I have been called abrasive. I am happy to argue and debate, whether the audience is large or small. But getting personal is very different. When I began this book, trying to describe my background, my family, the events of my life, I realized how much I have always kept my own counsel, lived inside my own head. My closest friends now tell me that they have observed this for years, thought of me as a loner, not very social. Even my children, despite our close relationship (which continues although they are now independent adults), have casually remarked that I keep things to myself, things that are personal.

My attitude seems almost ludicrous in this day and age, when the most intimate details are revealed on television and discussed in daytime talk shows, but the fact remains that I do not find it easy to share my particular experiences or my innermost views.

I think there are several reasons for this reticence. My family, in keeping with the social conventions of the day, believed that respectable people did not talk about themselves or express their personal feelings in public—or even, sometimes, in the confines of their own homes. I've already noted that my parents could not share with me their sorrow at the loss of their young son, and my father refused to discuss his military experience. And I'm sure that as African Americans they were even more inclined to keep themselves to themselves. They knew, like everyone else in the black community, that their best protection was invisibility.

Then too, I am a "depression baby," a person forever marked by the suffering, economic and psychic, endured by almost everyone as a result of the 1929 stock market crash. Those of us who were born and raised during the depression remember seeing strong, proud men—men who had worked all their lives and taken care of their families—standing around with nothing to do. We saw men who would rather work, at any job at all, lining up at the relief offices or the surplus food lines to pick up whatever the government would provide for needy families. Fortunately, my father never had to "go on relief," but most people were out of work. It didn't make any difference whether you were black or white. Things were really tough, and they didn't change all that much until the country started gearing up to fight World War II.

People like me, depression babies, spent the rest of our lives trying to avoid a repetition of the hardships of those years. Above all, that meant we had to depend on ourselves. We expected to be responsible for our families and for our own future. Even in the good days, when we had regular raises and promotions, we saved and invested and taught our children to do the same. We tried to prepare for the worst, to limit the risks, to insure a reasonably predictable future: owning a home, educating our children, eliminating debt, building a nest egg. We learned to be conservative in our lifestyles, rarely spending more than we could afford and saving something out of every paycheck. If a windfall came—and they were rare—we always put a portion of it away for a rainy day—the day our income ended or an emergency arose. Economic independence was a top priority.

There is another reason for my lifelong reserve. During my early years, I lived in the worlds created by books. I read all the time; I spent hours in the library. Later, when I was an undergraduate history student at Indiana University, I frequented the stacks to find books about black people, books that never saw the light of day in regular classes. Books took me places I could not go, they told me about things I would never have known. I was fascinated by the ideas, the fantasies, the visions, the stories, the knowledge hidden in those books. I would spend hours daydreaming about my future, about other lands, about possibilities only I could envision. Occasionally, I talked to my mother and more often to my closest friend Clarence Currie, but for the most part, I kept my notions to myself. I am still like that to a great extent, telling very few people about my dreams of what could be and what ought to be in this country, in human affairs. I am a private person, but I am determined to keep that promise to my children.....

❧

As I look back over my life and try to ascertain its major themes, I believe I can identify two: my confidence in the power of education to transform individual lives and even society itself, and my hatred of injustice in all its forms, but especially that of racism. As I have already noted, these themes were established early, in my family and my school, and they have played a part in almost every important decision I have made. As I bring this memoir to an end, I want to reflect on my experiences as an educator and as an African American.

An Educator

I made the correct choice of vocation! When I decided to become a teacher, I embarked on a journey that has made my life a joy. My original intention was to pursue the study of law, primarily because I viewed the law as a way to secure justice for people who were denied it, especially African Americans. Most people expected me to become a lawyer: my teachers, my parents, my friends. That's what I planned on doing until my senior year in college, when I realized that enabling young minds to develop could be the most rewarding, constructive, and challenging career possible. I cannot describe adequately what a thrill it is to see young people—whether a junior or senior in high school, an undergraduate, or a graduate student—solve a difficult problem or arrive at an understanding of some complex issue. They might have thought it was beyond them or, even worse, boring, until the moment when they discover that they can handle the problem and can go on to other, more challenging activities. Watching students acquire not only knowledge, but self-awareness and self-confidence, is always gratifying, and perhaps something that only teachers (and parents) fully appreciate. I cannot imagine a more satisfying career.

I have spent a major part of my life engaged in the seldom lucrative but unbelievably fulfilling pursuit of teaching and learning, not just in classrooms but in a variety of settings and through a variety of media. Some of my students brought to class incredible advantages: they were so intellectually endowed that they could accomplish anything they put their minds to. Others came with more deficits and burdens than any American child or youth should be forced to bear, appearing so battered and discouraged that it took Herculean efforts to get them to recognize how truly gifted they were, despite their difficulties.

How sad it is that talent and ability have so often gone unrecognized by those who should have recognized and encouraged them. I have seen and engaged students who have been failed by almost everyone and yet have been able not only to persevere, but to thrive. Sometimes they just needed a friendly smile or a reassuring touch (or, on occasion, a harsh challenge) to open up possibilities even their greatest admirers and supporters could not envision. But I have also seen too many young people become enormous and tragic failures because of the oppressive nature of the society in which they were forced to live. I am outraged by the waste, the criminal neglect of poor youngsters with talent, ability, high ideals, and wonderful dreams, by a society which still refuses to recognize that the most cost effective and intelligent investment we can make to insure our future is investment in the nation's schools. To state it bluntly, the quality of education received by a significant percentage of black, Hispanic, and poor Americans is unacceptable. In fact, it is nothing short of a national scandal, an absolute disgrace.

Education is important, not just because it will prepare you for a job or for graduate programs leading to a profession. Education is the key to unlocking those qualities and talents, those feelings and emotions, that make a person truly human. I don't mean learning to read and write, to compute and figure out answers to problems. These are necessary but not sufficient. I refer here to a wide-ranging exposure to a civilization's creative genius in all its modes of expression: painting, sculpture, music, composition, literature, dance, drama, the visual arts of all kinds. It never ceases to amaze and to infuriate me when citizens, even educators, call for the elimination of the arts when public school budgets are tight. Parents who have the means to provide such "frills" or "extracurricular" activities for their own families should realize that they are equally important for poor children who may never have an opportunity outside the classroom to encounter the arts. Yet when they are a part of the regular curriculum, as they were in my own public school, they can become the motivating force, the spark, that makes the rest of the course work important and exciting.

One of the most heated arguments in education revolves around performance standards. We seem to have forgotten that excellence is a part of our history and our heritage. Our youth are capable of excellence, and that should be held up to them as the only reasonable standard worthy of pursuit. There was a period when it was somehow thought to be unacceptable to achieve excellence, that somehow being a scholar and/or a super achiever placed those black Americans outside the mainstream of struggle. Such notions were self-defeating, and they sent a very confusing message to our young people. We must recognize that a curriculum based on minimum competencies in a society that requires maximum skills is not the answer for black Americans.

Another controversy has to do with the curriculum. Some conservative educators regard the "canon" (what must be taught to every generation) as rigid and unchanging, while liberals are more likely to rush into the latest (and occasionally wild) experiment. I like to think that I am somewhere in the middle, recognizing the merit in both tradition and innovation. In the light of some current pedagogical theories, I need to say that we do not do our children any favor by providing them with fairy tales in the hope that this will build self-esteem. Similarly, we are cheating them when we suggest that misspelled words, ungrammatical prose, and "street talk" are perfectly adequate substitutes for standard English.

Even when sound basic skills have been learned, the work is just beginning. Decoding is not the same as comprehension; comprehension is not the same as analysis or criticism. Addition and subtraction skills, both important and necessary, are not the same as understanding algebra or trigonometry or calculus. General science is not the equivalent of chemistry or physics or biology. My years in the classroom have persuaded me that students know this, just as they know that they can learn, even if they try to convince you otherwise. They can accept and adjust to stringent standards. Although people learn at different rates and in different ways, they can and will learn almost anything when the teacher expects them to do so. Confidence in their ability; realistic goals; intelligent, consistent instruction; fair, supportive, but honest evaluation and grading: in my experience, when these conditions exist, young people always exceed your expectations.

Students must participate in their own education, in the process of teaching and learning. The effective teacher must, therefore, engage the students and keep them engaged until that engagement becomes automatic, self-starting. The students eventually, some sooner than others, become autodidactic; they teach themselves, become learners on their own, frequently without even noticing the change. The truly excellent teacher then becomes a guide who leads, who challenges, who encourages, who supports the learner. The most fulfilling teaching I have done has been of this kind, helping young people to unlock their talents, their abilities, their creativity, their humor—and their acceptance of the notion that they could do almost anything, given enough effort and time. That is the most fun I have ever had as an educator.

The most difficult problem for many educators, parents, and citizens alike is chaos in the schools. They know that learning cannot take place under chaotic conditions. I'm not thinking solely of classrooms out of control or bullies in the school yard or students with weapons. Turmoil can also be created by filthy buildings, missing supplies and equipment, untrained or unsympathetic teachers. But when a few students make it impossible for the overwhelming majority to learn, the disruptive few must be helped to change their behavior or, if these efforts fail, be removed from the classroom. They must not be abandoned to the streets or to correctional institutions, but placed in alternative educational settings until their behavior warrants their return to the regular school. It is unfair to everyone to believe and to act as if every child, even the most troubled or violent, can be served in the same environment.

Black children and youth will not be educated unless black Americans insist that they be educated, and unless blacks participate in the educational process on a consistent basis. For the individual parent, whether the child is enrolled in a public or private school, sustained interest and involvement are necessary. There are thousands of poor, black parents who are doing a commendable, even Herculean, job of rearing their children, encouraging and motivating them to succeed in school. There are thousands of disadvantaged black children and youth who are willing to pay the price for scholastic achievement, for excellence. These students work hard and somehow make it over the difficult and depressing hurdles placed in their path. Black student achievers are almost totally ignored; they are certainly the most ignored of all inner-city youth.

Optimum learning takes place when students are treated as intelligent, thinking, curious, caring human beings. Optimum learning takes place when children and youth believe their teachers care about them and believe they are capable of mastering intricate, complex, difficult, and exciting areas of knowledge. Optimum learning takes place when parents have access to school officials, when parents believe they have some influence over what happens to their children. Optimum learning takes place when the environment is orderly, safe, and open. Optimum learning takes place when all the participants in the process understand and support the same goals and a consistent approach. In short, optimum learning takes place when there is sanity and humanity, whether in public schools or private schools.

Throughout history, tyrants have feared the power of education to free both the mind and the body. In fact, one of the great ironies of the antebellum south was the simultaneous insistence that black slaves were innately stupid—and that strict laws, with severe penalties attached, were needed to make sure no one tried to teach them. I, too, believe in the power of education to liberate the poor and the downtrodden. And I also believe that it is possible to enlighten the powerful and the prejudiced. People are not born believing in racial superiority and hating other people: they have to be taught, just as they can be taught respect and fairness. Over more than forty years, I have participated in the healthy development of thousands of young Americans, and I have seen the contributions that dedicated teachers have made to the welfare of this nation. It has been an honor to have been a part of this enterprise.

❧

An African American

The most important theme running through my life is the persistence and importance of the concept of race in America. For black Americans, race is always there, every day in one form or another, regardless of age, education, station in life, place of residence, vocation, or gender. Yet for most white Americans, it is extremely difficult or impossible to understand what this means. It isn't as if there have been no changes, no improvements in race relations in the United States. It isn't that race weighs black Americans down every waking moment so that they cannot go on with their lives. Quite the contrary, the history of black Americans in the United States has been a glorious history of perseverance, hope, achievement, and sanity amid the insane persecution of slavery, reconstruction, the depression, two world wars, Korea and Vietnam, the civil rights movement, and the assassinations.

In my early years, when inequalities, injustices, discrimination, and open expressions of prejudice and even contempt were regular facts of daily life, we were taught both at home and in school to fight against them; never to accept anything other than first-class treatment; to demand respect. It wasn't always easy or even possible to carry out these admonitions; the resentment was always there. We were taught that we were the equal of anyone. Any assertion to the contrary was a lie, another assault by those who were determined to make us accept the indignities imposed by a racist society. And so I learned that I could be the master of my own destiny, that I could shape my own future in spite of the system. I determined when I was quite young that I would not be a willing victim or have my humanity demeaned. I would do everything that society required to become successful—that included obligations as well as opportunities—and having done them, I would not take any crap from anybody merely because I was black.

When I went to school, I achieved and contributed to the school community. When I participated in school and community and church activities, I did more than my share if that was necessary. When I had jobs as a teenager or as an adult, I became an excellent worker. I paid my bills. I volunteered to serve my country in the armed forces. I voted and participated in our political system. Because my father and my two older brothers died prematurely, I assumed additional responsibilities in my family, for my widowed mother and my younger sister. I worked and earned my educational opportunities. I expected to be rewarded with equal opportunities. When I was not, as most black people of my generation were not, I raised my voice in protest and in anger. I worked harder, and I never let those who tried, and often succeeded, in holding me back forget that I knew it had little to do with my ability, effort, or preparation: it had to do with race and a system based on preferences, unfairness, and an unequal distribution of privilege and power. The outrage that system generated in me became a roaring engine, providing the impetus for greater and more focused efforts to change things and to expand the phalanx of those committed to making this country, our country, live up to the promises and ideals of its most revered documents. That struggle continues to this day. It will end when I draw my last breath.

Not long ago, I was sitting around a conference table with five or six other African Americans, waiting for a meeting to start. The conversation ranged far and wide, small talk mostly, but we drifted into a discussion about race in our lives. One man smiled and said, "It doesn't matter where you are or who the people are, the conversation will eventually get around to race." He was speaking, of course, about any gathering of African Americans, anywhere in this country, and he was right. Over the next several months, I paid particular attention to this phenomenon. We had all known that he was correct, but I decided to check it out anyway with groups that included both women and men, of various ages and backgrounds. It didn't seem to matter, these differences all became subordinate to the importance of race in our lives.

The people there that day ranged in age from the early fifties to the mid-seventies. By any criterion, they were people of achievement and accomplishment. One had graduated as valedictorian of his college class from a selective eastern college where he was the only African American in his class. He had been the only African American on campus when he enrolled. He made Phi Beta Kappa and graduated *summa cum laude*. His distinguished career included stints as president of the medical staff at two hospitals, president of a white medical school and college, and as health commissioner of the fourth largest city in America. One member of the group was an internationally known artist, composer, and producer, as well as co-owner of a major successful record label; he is now deeply involved in housing and economic development. Another was a lawyer, businessman, author and lecturer who, in retirement, produced films, videos and curriculum materials on African and Afrocentric topics. The lone female ran a conglomerate of community-based housing, cultural and educational organizations. There was a successful physician and healthcare provider who once owned seven HMOs and now presides over a family-owned conglomerate consisting of a number of independent businesses, each headed by one of his children, all of whom are well educated in business, law and related fields. (By the way, this gentleman recently bought the plantation of more than 400 acres in Virginia, where his great-grandparents had lived and worked as slaves!) Yet another person had recently retired as chief financial officer and senior vice president of the regional electric public utility. In his earlier career, he had served as the first African American finance director of Philadelphia, chief financial officer of the Philadelphia public schools, and executive vice president of Girard Bank before it was acquired by Mellon.

We had all lived through the days of rampant and demeaning, in-your-face segregation and brutal discrimination. We had all lived through derogatory name-calling, smirks, snide excuses, and the denial of even the most elementary opportunity. Yet, we had all persevered, over-come open and difficult barriers, and succeeded in a variety of fields. More important, we had all managed to hold on to our sense of balance, to keep our sense of humor despite the stupidity and harshness of racism, and to live without hatred and bitterness. Lest there be any misunder-standing, we were angry for most of our lives; some of us are still angry. Every time you took a step forward, another barrier was placed in your path, sometimes in the dark of night so you wouldn't see it until you had fallen in the light of day.

For those of the generation represented in that board room, being born black meant many things:

- growing up with the knowledge that no matter how well you did academically in any field, the choices you had were limited;
- knowing that most elite colleges and universities, especially the private ones, were not realistic choices, unless we were bona fide geniuses with white sponsors or people with incredible athletic skills;
- having to fight for admission to majority universities even when they were state universities supported by our taxes;
- recognizing that certain fields of endeavor were completely closed to us, that certain neighborhoods and housing were unavailable;
- being forced to agitate, even when we were (reluctantly) admitted to the armed forces, for the opportunity to prove that we were capable of flying an airplane or driving a tank or serving on a submarine or aircraft carrier in any capacity other than a cook or steward;
- having to prove over and over again, despite recorded history dating back to the Revolutionary War, that black Americans will fight and can be trusted in combat.

The rules were always different for us. We knew that the liberties taken by others in similar positions were not for us. Our performance had to be superior and above reproach, like Caesar's wife. We knew that if we crossed the boundaries of honesty, propriety, or arrogance, we would not remain in our position, yet we had to exercise the full power of the office or there would be no respect from peers or subordinates. We had to do a better job than our predecessors, we had to pave the way for those who might follow. If we failed, there would not be an opportunity for another African American. For many white people, these operating principles are difficult to understand. It never occurs to them that they have been endowed with privileges and opportunities merely because they were born with a white skin—or, more accurately, because they were not born with black skin.

I am not naive. I understand the problems facing anyone in this country who is born into poverty and without education, and I do not underestimate the many problems that Americans have in common. I was born and raised in a working-class, multiracial neighborhood of poor people without much education. One could argue that today differences in opportunity or quality of education are a function of socioeconomic status and class, rather than of race. It is still true, nevertheless, that the accident of birth bestows upon those with white skin privileges that few, if any, African Americans enjoy.

Black Americans love this country for what it says it stands for and what it promises. It is incredible to many of us, those of my generation, that white Americans still believe that African Americans are somehow "different"; that we are less loyal to this country; that despite four hundred years of doing the hardest, dirtiest, most demeaning, most underpaid, dangerous work, black Americans are looking for a handout, something for nothing. White people still do not understand why many, perhaps most, black Americans do not view the police as friends and protectors, particularly those police forces that have few if any members who look like us. White Americans would be shocked to learn that most black Americans, as a matter of routine, teach their sons how to deal with the police, lest they be killed or maimed for no reason. My instructions to my son certainly helped when he faced what every black father fears: being stopped by police at night just because he was one of three black males on a city street.

It is not that we go around disoriented, unhinged, or depressed by the burden of race. We have long since learned how to deal with it, both on an individual basis and as a group. But it never stops, this preoccupation with race. In social situations, where you might be the only black individual or couple in a sea of white faces, it is not unusual for someone to march up to you, having never seen you before that moment, and start aiming a barrage of questions: How do you know the (famous or powerful or rich) host and hostess? What do you do? Do you live near here? Do you have children? Where do they go to school? I can assure you that these are not friendly inquiries, intended to break the ice. People who do this usually don't bother to introduce themselves.

Perhaps it is a formal occasion and you have on a tuxedo: latecomers who do not know you may very well ask you to get them a drink or take their coats. You may be standing outside the Four Seasons or the Ritz

Carlton, dressed in a Canali suit and waiting for the attendant to bring your Mercedes S Class: that doesn't prevent arriving guests from asking you to see that their bags are delivered to the room immediately. It can happen anywhere. The distinguished federal judge and legal scholar, A. Leon Higginbotham, was once the honored lecturer at a formal affair held in an elegant private club. Just before the guests moved into the room where the lecture was to be given, a striking woman brusquely ordered Judge Higginbotham to get her a scotch and soda. Leon promptly fetched it and handed her the drink. A few minutes later, he was called up to the podium and introduced, and the woman, recognizing her *faux pas*, was so upset that she dropped her glass, shattering it on the floor.

For the first couple of years after I assumed the presidency of the William Penn Foundation, when I attended social events with one of my vice presidents and a senior program officer—both white males—people would walk up to the three of us and immediately address one of the others as president. It became a standing in-house joke. Even in a city where I had certainly not been invisible in my previous positions, some people apparently could not imagine a foundation president with a black face. Even four years into my tenure, one of my staff members was still receiving mail with his name and the title of president.

Once I was visited by a distinguished university president and two of his aides. Although he ran very successful programs funded by the Foundation, we had never met. After shaking my hand, he strode briskly to the head of the conference table, took a seat, and immediately began asking me questions. "I am the first in my family to attend college," he said. "Are you the first in your family also? I assume you are." He then proceeded to tell me a story about growing up poor, as if this cemented some special relationship with me. How, he wanted to know, did I become a vice president of Temple University and head of the Foundation? His aides, who were aware of my background, began to look a little nervous.

I responded by telling him that Marvin Wachman, the Temple president, had given me my big break. I had been a dope peddler until Marvin, recognizing my street smarts, invited me to take a job with the university and attend classes. I wove a fantastic story about my phenomenal and rapid ascent in the university hierarchy, repeatedly saying how lucky I was that Marvin had given me this chance and saved me from a life of crime and probably prison. My visitor was almost mesmerized by my story, but his aides were obviously squirming in their seats.

I abruptly ended my performance and began to talk about programs and funding priorities. Only toward the end of a thirty- or forty-minute business discussion did he (I think) become suspicious of my earlier and completely imaginary account. I am sure the trip back to his out-of-state campus was interesting, as his vice presidents gave him the real story. As soon as they had left, I went downstairs and told two of the program staff, one a vice president, what had just transpired. Both of them laughed; one of them believed it immediately. It took a little discussion before the other realized I was not putting them on. The black staff member was not surprised at the behavior of the college president or at my response.

Two other vignettes will further illustrate. Juanita Kidd Stout was the first female and the first black female to serve on the Pennsylvania Supreme Court. Prior to her appointment, she served several ten-year terms as a judge of the Philadelphia Court of Common Pleas. A list of her honors, national and local, fill many pages of her resume. Attending a large banquet honoring the first black judge to serve on the Louisiana Supreme Court, Judge Stout was seated next to a state supreme court justice, a distinguished white male. They got along famously. The justice observed that he supported women joining the highest ranks of the judicial system, and he congratulated Judge Stout. He allowed, however, that he had some real concerns about these "niggers" being seated: he was not certain that "they" could carry out their responsibilities in a fair and impartial manner.

On another occasion, Judge Stout returned to Philadelphia's 30th Street Station late in the evening, after an event in Washington, D.C., and hailed a taxi to take her home. The taxi driver, a middle-aged white male, immediately launched into a lecture about how dangerous the streets were and that Judge Stout should be careful because the niggers were likely to rape and rob her, maybe even kill her. He explained that niggers didn't work, lived off welfare, and had ruined the quality of life in Philadelphia. Judge Stout was quiet until the cab reached her house. Then, throwing the fare on the front seat, she told the driver that what he was saying was ridiculous: she had worked all her life and she was black. She jumped out of the taxi and ran into her home. Judge Stout is very fair-skinned and people frequently assume that she is white. The Chief Justice made that mistake. So did the Philadelphia taxi driver.

You are reminded, sometimes in strange ways. In the early 1980s, I visited the bank where I often conducted business—checking, savings, certificates of deposit, and taxes. I entered the elevator to go to the floor where I was to keep an appointment with a bank officer. The elevator started, then stopped between floors and moved no farther. I picked up the telephone; it didn't work. I pushed the emergency alarm; it didn't work. I pulled and pushed the red stop button; nothing happened. Then the lights went out. It was around midday, lunch hour, but this elevator was away from the main bank of elevators, because it was the only one for the floor where I had to go.

I remained calm while I banged on the door and called for help. There was no answer. After continuing this for about five minutes, I began to think about what could happen. It was the Friday before a long weekend; when the bank closed it would not open again until the following Tuesday morning. Nobody knew where I was, as I had not mentioned my appointment to my secretary or my family. It dawned on me that I could easily be locked in this elevator for several days. I continued to bang on the door, yell, and try the telephone without success. Finally, after about thirty minutes. I heard footsteps, so I yelled and banged more loudly. A voice said "Are you all right?" I answered "Yes" and explained what had happened. "I'll get help," the voice replied. "Stay calm." In about ten minutes, a maintenance man arrived with a crowbar, got the door open, and helped me out.

I wrote a detailed letter to the chairman and CEO of the bank stating what had happened and suggesting that the emergency systems on the elevator be checked and repaired. I received a nice reply from the CEO apologizing for what had happened and assuring me that it would be looked into. I knew the man, had served on civic committees with him, and had been a good customer of the bank. I had even served as a judge of elections at annual meetings.

Weeks later, I inquired about what had been done with the emergency systems. This time I received a letter from the legal staff informing me that I had no right to know and that they had no obligation to tell me anything. I was furious. I knew that no white person with similar stature would have been treated in this manner. I persisted, to no avail. So I sued them. It was not about money; I asked for no specific damages. I merely wanted an assurance that an elderly person or someone in poor health would not have to endure what had happened to me. To make a long story short, the bank's distinguished law firm assigned one of their black lawyers to fight my suit. Although he had the reputation of never having lost a case, he lost this one in pre-court arbitration. I collected and went about my business. The amount I settled for was paltry; it did not even cover my lawyer's fees, but he had taken the case as a favor to me, out of our friendship. We split the award. It was another reminder of the reality of race in America.

Over the past three decades, I have had more opportunities than most African Americans to interact with white people in a variety of social, civic, and professional settings. My wife and I have been both their guests and their hosts. I have had a wealth of experience in reporting to white executives as well as in supervising white staff members. I have worked with all sorts of individuals, from wealthy entrepreneurs to ordinary working folk, on interracial committees and task forces, and I am as comfortable in white board rooms as in African American clubs. Nevertheless, I find I must always be alert to mistaken ideas or misguided efforts. In spite of their excellent educations and world travels, I have found that many of my white colleagues have been insulated and isolated from the harsh realities of race and poverty.

Some of my fellow board members enjoy enormous wealth, privilege, and power, usually inherited. Others acquired their positions through hard work, education, vision—and luck. For the most part, they are decent people. Comfortable in their circumstances, they treat black people with civility and courtesy, but few have any understanding that their lives are different, more fortunate, simply because they were born with white skin. Even fewer have any idea that a black American of my generation, with talent and ambition similar to their own, seldom, if ever, had the opportunity to attempt—let alone achieve—what they took for granted as the logical outcome of their efforts. It never occurred to them that Ivy League institutions were off limits to almost all black Americans until the 1950s. They did not know that the most gifted black physicians, architects, engineers—you name it— used to be restricted to segregated systems, to practicing in their own communities. Nor did they realize that black graduates of the best law schools—Harvard, Yale, Chicago, Stanford—once had no chance of being admitted to a white law firm. Of course things have changed since I was young, but race is still an issue.

Perhaps most frustrating, to me at least, is that these decent white men and women do not understand how institutional barriers continue to limit opportunities for non-whites. They don't see that routine procedures and thoughtless attitudes restrict access, even when a policy of non-discrimination is supported from the very top. I once listened to a senior official of a large and successful company explain that he was actively recruiting minority candidates for financial positions. Auditing was a convenient entry point, and the job requirements included several years of experience with a (then) Big Eight accounting firm. It never occurred to this official that those firms had few, if any, black or Hispanic employees in other than clerical positions. He wasn't intentionally discriminating against non-whites; he just didn't understand the big picture and the impossible demands his company was making. I have been and still am a member of a number of corporate boards, as well as non-profit boards that include business leaders. I have always considered it my responsibility to help my fellow board members understand the day-to-day realities, the different experiences, of minorities, so that their companies will be able to take advantage of all the opportunities and talents available. It's a matter of mutual self-interest.

To be sure, I have met and worked with some wealthy and powerful people who were very unusual, who made informed efforts to recruit, hire, and promote non-whites at every level. I think of some special individuals. They would be embarrassed if I named them, but they each represent the spirit of equity I think this country needs very badly. They have a fundamental respect for other people, whatever their status or origin, and I have never, over many years, observed or heard of their succumbing to the arrogance of wealth or power, although they have both in abundance. They inspire hope.

❧

This country is as much an ideal, a process, a becoming, as it is an existent reality. Sadly, there is a chasm between most black and white Americans, created by different experiences and almost impossible to bridge. Each group becomes a part of "them": stereotypes, symbols, representations of an imagined reality. Yet the future holds more diversity in language, race and ethnicity, religion, cultural values and perspective. Unless we change, we risk compromising further or losing altogether the ideals and values proclaimed in our most revered documents. We risk our future as a nation, as Americans, as human beings, if we fail to acknowledge the basic humanity, the inherent importance and value of every individual. We need to learn how to respect one another as human beings, regardless of our differences.

I believe that most people, given a chance, will do the right thing; that they would rather work than be dependent; that parents want the best for their children. As a nation, we do far too little to protect our youngest citizens and to encourage and strengthen families, despite the rhetoric to the contrary. I have been outraged at the injustices in other countries—the Balkans, Africa, Central and South America, the Middle East. I was infuriated to the point of trembling and tears, when I visited Yad Vashem, the Holocaust museum in Jerusalem, and confronted a horror approaching that of the Middle Passage. Yet here in the United States, I see malnourished children and homeless adults. I see schools no child should have to attend. I see parents struggling mightily day after day to create a sense of order for their families, trying to make their lives better. In this, the richest country on earth, more of us should be not only angry but ashamed.

Education, racial justice—the twin themes of my life—have also been critically important to Nelson Mandela, the world leader whom I most admire. His vision, his strength, and his unflagging diplomacy made possible the peaceful transition in South Africa, from rigidly enforced apartheid to democracy and freedom. Whether he was in prison or in the president's office, he has consistently declared that all people are worthy of respect and deserve to share in the good society. I am honored to know this incredible and gentle man, and I am proud to serve on the board of the Friends of Nelson Mandela Children's Fund, a Foundation to which he donates half his salary.

Let me close with Mandela's own words, written before he became president:

> The crisis in education that exists in South Africa demands special attention. The education crisis in black schools is a political crisis. It arises out of the fact that our people have no vote and therefore cannot make the government of the day responsive to their needs.
>
> Our march toward freedom is irreversible. We must not allow fear to stand in our way... In conclusion, I wish to go to my own words during my trial in 1964—they are as true today as they were then.
>
> I have fought against white domination, and I have fought against black domination. I have cherished the ideal of a democratic and free society in which all persons live together in harmony and with equal opportunity. It is an ideal which I hope to live for and to achieve. But, if needs be, it is an ideal for which I am prepared to die.
>
> Amandla! Power!

Mandela said it better than I ever could, and his life is a living testament to his beliefs and values. I hope that mine will be seen in the same light.

FACTS ABOUT ROOSEVELT HIGH SCHOOL
Graduates (1931 - 1990): 22,000

Selected colleges and universities attended by Roosevelt graduates:
Arizona, Atlanta, Bowdoin, Chicago, Clark, Columbia, Dartmouth, Fisk, Florida A & M, Grinnell, Hampton, Harvard, Howard, Kenyon, Illinois, Indiana, Iowa, Michigan, Montana, Morehouse, Morgan State, Morris Brown, North Carolina A & T, Northwestern, Ohio State, Purdue, Spelman, UCLA, U.S. Naval Academy, West Point, Western Michigan, Wisconsin

Some outstanding alumni of Roosevelt:
Fritz Alexander: Dartmouth graduate; jet pilot; New York judge
Maurice Baptiste: University of Chicago graduate; Gary City comptroller;
    private businessman
Thomas Barnes: retired U.S. Army officer; mayor of Gary
Maurice Bean: senior foreign service officer;
    Peace Corps executive in Philippines; attorney
Avery Brooks: stage and television star; professor at Rutgers
Chester Davis: chairman, Department of African American studies,
    University of Massachusetts
Rosemary Anderson Davis: executive director, National Medical Association
Cynthia Elliott: dean of students, Smith College
Portia Elliott: professor, University of Massachusetts
Rebera Elliott: physician; poet; author
Eloise Gentry: entrepreneur; educator; president of Gary Urban League
Booker Griffin: promoter; entrepreneur; radio and television commentator; publisher
David Hall: Howard graduate; retired U.S.A.F. general
J.T. and Imogene Harris: newspaper publishers; business owners
Arthur Hoyle: world-class jazz musician; played with Sarah Vaughn, Tony Bennett,
    Johnny Mathis, Oliver Nelson, Sun Ra, Lionel Hampton, and many others
Donald Hubbard: designer of shoes in Paris and other European venues
Bill Joiner: vice president, National Bank of Detroit, Gary, Indiana
John Joyner, Randall Morgan, Steve Simpson, Odies Williams: physicians. Drs. Joyner
    and Morgan are, respectively, past and current presidents of the
    National Medical Association
Emery King: NBC and CBS TV news correspondent
Leon Lynch: vice president, U.S. Steelworkers Union
Cornell McCollum: West Point graduate; retired U.S. Army colonel
Chester McGuire: jet pilot; Harvard professor
Martha "Bunny" Mitchell: assistant to President Jimmy Carter;
    Senior vice president and partner, Fleishman Hillard
Emanuel Newsome, vice president of student affairs, University of Florida

Some of the Roosevelt Teachers I Remember
Haron Battle was a mathematician who (it was rumored) had somehow, in a moment of madness, once received a "B," thereby marring his hitherto unblemished record of

"A's" from first grade through high school; through Morehouse and graduation as valedictorian of his class; through a master's degree in mathematics at the University of Michigan; and through his Ph.D. at the University of Chicago.

Al Beckman made chemistry and physics fun for his students, who loved him. His wife Katherine was a teacher of foreign languages. They were one of several husband-and-wife teams on the faculty.

Charles Bonner was a "wild man" as well as a scholar who made history and government come alive. He scared students so badly that they didn't realize how much they had learned until they took examinations or went to college. His wife Evelyn taught English.

Hope Dennis was a counselor, English teacher, fine writer, and an absolute magician with students.

Lila Duncan made Shakespeare fascinating and relevant. Her husband taught biology and general science.

Ida B. Guy pioneered the development of a speech and drama department that over time produced Genevieve Gray, Frankie McCullough, and Y. Jean Chambers.

Ida B. King devoted her entire professional life to Roosevelt and was legendary for her clothes, her sponsorship of senior class activities, and her senior civics classes.

Ida Mason was a Latin teacher—and everybody's grandmother.

Alberta Newsome, head of the business education department, placed girls in top positions in business all over the country.

Natalie Ousley was another marvelous English teacher who loved all of her students.

Roberta Rowan and Walter Murray were brilliant mathematics teachers.

San Bonita Slaughter and Eva Brooks were music teachers, both graduates of Northwestern University's music school. (Mrs. Brooks was the mother of Avery Brooks, a graduate of Roosevelt who became a Broadway stage and television star, as well as a professor of drama at Rutgers.)

Other legends included Al Brown (civics, government, and social problems), Elizabeth Williamson, Charlene Taylor, Wallace Wells, Arnold Williams, Isabel Coleman, Martha Morgan, Henry Bennett, and Ernest Bennett. There were too many to mention them all, but you always leave out someone equally important.

Athletes

Charles Adkins became an Olympic gold medalist in boxing and the first American to defeat a Soviet boxer in head-to-head competition. A University of Arizona graduate.

Dick Barnett was a member of the New York Knicks NBA championship team. He holds an earned doctorate and heads his own consulting firm.

Lee Calhoun, a gold medalist in high hurdles in two consecutive Olympic Games, later coached track at Yale.

Willie McCarter, Gerald Irons, and Glenn (Big Dawg) Robinson all became professionals with the Los Angeles Lakers, the Oakland Raiders, and the Milwaukee Bucks, respectively.

George Taliaferro led Indiana University to its first Big Ten football championship and later played pro football with the New York Giants. He recently retired as assistant to the president of Indiana University.

Willie Williams was the first athlete to break Jesse Owens' 100-meter world record. He is now a track coach at University of Illinois, his alma mater.

There were literally scores of other athletes who attended top schools and earned degrees: Jim and Tom Floyd, Earl Smith, Robert Stearnes, and Claude Taliaferro, for example.

APPENDIX II

SOME ROCKEFELLER ALUMNI AND THE POSITIONS THEY HELD ON COMPLETION OF THE PROGRAM

Dr. Howard Amos, Deputy Superintendent, Philadelphia

Dr. Ronald Boyd, Superintendent of Schools, Cleveland

June Hairston Brown, Director, Human Resources, Temple University; Executive Director, Main Line Academy, King of Prussia, Pennsylvania

Salvador Flores, Superintendent, Perth Amboy, New Jersey; Superintendent, Chula Vista, California

Dr. Willie Herenton, Superintendent, Memphis, Tennessee; Mayor of Memphis

E. Kenneth Johnson, Director of Title I Programs, New Orleans

Dr. Joseph Johnson, Superintendent, Red Clay Consolidated School District, Wilmington, Delaware

Dr. Theodore Johnson, Superintendent, Middle Township Schools, Cape May, New Jersey; Superintendent, Camden Public Schools, New Jersey

Willis McCleod, Superintendent, Northampton County Schools, Jackson, North Carolina

Dr. Alfred Merino, Director, Administrative Training Program, San Diego State College

William Murray, Superintendent, San Jose, California

Milford Sanderson, Superintendent, White River, Arizona

Calvert Smith, President, Morris Brown College, Atlanta; Deputy Superintendent, Cincinnati, Ohio

Anthony Trujillo, Superintendent, Tamalpais Public Schools, Marin County, California; Superintendent, Chula Vista, California

Dr. Paul Vance, Superintendent, Montgomery County Public Schools, Silver Spring, Maryland

Dr. Laval Wilson, Superintendent of Hempstead (Long Island), New York; Rochester, New York, and Boston, Massachusetts

David Yamamoto, Assistant Superintendent for Personnel, Multnomah County I.E.D., Portland, Oregon

In addition to the Rockefeller program, there were ancillary ones for specific areas of need. Among those who graduated from these programs were:

Dr. Jeannette Brewer (doctorate in early childhood education, University of Pennsylvania), Deputy Superintendent, Philadelphia

Dr. Constance Clayton (doctorate in early childhood education, University of Pennsylvania), Superintendent, Philadelphia, for eleven years

Dr. Arthur Thomas, President, Central State University

BLACK EDUCATIONAL AND POLITICAL LEADERS IN PHILADELPHIA

Sam Evans pushed for greater access and more opportunities before many of the 1960s elected officials and activists had been born or come of age.

Harold Haskins, a gang worker with the famous 12th and Oxford Street gang in North Philadelphia, is now an administrator at the University of Pennsylvania.

Mattie Humphrey, a longtime activist who was trained as a nurse and health administrator at the University of Michigan, recently completed a law degree at Villanova. She was helpful in all my community activities, but particularly (along with Dr. Ed Robinson) in keeping Benjamin Franklin High School students from storming out of the school, after Dr. King's assassination, into the waiting billy clubs of the Philadelphia police. Mattie Humphrey was a real visionary and brilliant woman whose ideas were almost always ahead of those of her peers.

Roxanne Jones led the welfare rights group. Roxanne became the first black female elected to the state senate. She, along with Dave Richardson, were the two most effective and consistent voices for the poor in Harrisburg. It is sad that they are now both gone.

Bill Meek, an outspoken opponent of the "establishment," was director of the Area Wide Council, the required citizen "voice" in determining how federal Model Cities funds should be spent. He attained local notoriety when he was accused of allowing his office to be used for printing announcements of the November 17 (1967) march on the board of education building. His wife Sylvia was a lawyer and the director of education for the Philadelphia Urban League.

Cecil B. Moore, first with the NAACP and then in city council, kept the pressure on.

Henry Nicholas was head of Local 1199c of the Hospital and Nursing Home Employees Union. When he moved to Philadelphia, another powerful and willing voice was added.

Walter Palmer, a member of BPUM, was active in North and West Philadelphia. He was hired by Bill Meek when the Area Wide Council was fighting for control of Model Cities. He graduated from Howard Law School.

Dave Richardson, a ranking black elected official from Philadelphia (a member of the Pennsylvania General Assembly), was the founder and leader of the Young Afro Americans. A young man absolutely clear about his commitment to justice and fairness, he died unexpectedly and far too young, while I was writing this memoir.

Dr. Edward Robinson, the head of the local office of a North Carolina insurance company, held degrees in both business and law. He was an expert on African American history and was especially knowledgeable about the Songhai Empire in ancient Africa. Long before it became popular, he was a strong believer in teaching young black males about their heritage. He was Dave Richardson's uncle.

The Rev. Leon Sullivan and 400 black ministers mobilized the black community through selective patronage campaigns, picketing Tasty Baking Company (Tasty Kake, Inc.) and opposing the construction of the Municipal Services Building until black people were hired or given contracts.

C. Delores Tucker organized political campaigns and helped raise money. She served as Secretary of the Commonwealth of Pennsylvania from 1971 to 1977 and has been chair of the Black Caucus of the Democratic National Committee since 1984.

Alice Walker ran the Alice Rouse Donaldson Center in South Philadelphia and organized young people.

Father Paul Washington, rector of the Church of the Advocate in North Philadelphia and a man who was trusted by everyone. Father Paul was always there, providing sanctuary, advice, leadership, and wisdom.

Rose Wiley organized public housing tenants.

Novella Williams, an outspoken West Philadelphia militant, founded and led Citizens for Progress. She put her life on the line fighting drugs and later became a strong supporter of Frank Rizzo.

Herman Wrice, a former gang leader, founded and led the Young Great Society. Herman took me around the various neighborhoods, identified the gang turfs, and had me observe the urban orientation program developed by his Young Great Society for teachers new to Philadelphia and University of Pennsylvania student teachers.

Many others come to mind. Within the Black Political Forum, George French, Robert Eaverly, Cornelius Stephens, Pearl Sharpless, Elvadean Wilkerson, and Herbert Hutton were deeply involved in voter education, registration, and other activities. Gussie Clark, Marian Tasco, Lana Felton Ghee, and Paul Vance were enthusiastic supporters.

APPENDIX IV

THE WILLIAM PENN FOUNDATION

Outside Board Members During My Presidency

The Hon. Arlin M. Adams: federal judge (3rd Circuit Court of Appeals), president of the American Philosophical Society

Frederick W. Anton, III: president of the Pennsylvania Manufacturers Association and the Pennsylvania Manufacturers Corporation (PMA Group)

Ernesta D. Ballard: founder and president of the Pennsylvania Horticultural Society

Mary C. Carroll: civic leader, founder of Hospitality Philadelphia Style

The Hon. Ida K. Chen: first Chinese woman to serve as Court of Common Pleas judge

Dr. Gloria Twine Chisum: research psychologist; retired head of the Naval Vision Laboratory; trustee of the University of Pennsylvania

The Hon. Nelson A. Diaz: first Puerto Rican to serve as Court of Common Pleas judge; now general counsel for the U.S. Department of Housing and Urban Development

Graham S. Finney: founder and former president of the Conservation Company

Richard G. Gilmore: former city finance director; retired chief financial officer for Philadelphia Electric Company

Paul M. Ingersoll: former president of Fidelity Bank

Stephanie W. Naidoff, Esq.: attorney with Morgan, Lewis & Bockius; former counsel to Thomas Jefferson University

Dr. James H. Robinson (died in 1986): professor of surgery and assistant dean at Thomas Jefferson University Medical College

Robert Montgomery Scott, Esq.: former president of the Philadelphia Museum of Art

The Hon. Edmund B. Spaeth, Jr.: former president judge of the Pennsylvania Superior Court; chairman of Pennsylvanians for Modern Courts

Grace B. Sullivan: founder of the community-based "Miniversity"; wife of the Rev. Leon Sullivan

Professor Anita A. Summers: economist, University of Pennsylvania
The Rev. Paul M. Washington: rector emeritus, Church of the Advocate

Growth in Assets and Grantmaking During My Presidency

Foundation assets:
  January 1982: $133,000,000   December 1993: $673,000,000
Grant payments:
  1982: $10,548,511   1993: $35,770,176
Cumulative total of grant payments 1945 - 1993: $378,711,819
Cumulative total of grant payments 1982 - 1993: $268,968,863
Percentage of 1945 - 1993 grant payments expended 1982 - 1993: 71 percent

Participants in the "Minorities in Higher Education" Initiative
Camden County College (Camden, NJ)
Carnegie Mellon University (Pittsburgh, PA)
Community College of Philadelphia (Philadelphia, PA)
Drexel University (Philadelphia, PA
Morehouse College (Atlanta, GA)
Morris Brown College (Atlanta, GA)
North Carolina A & T University (Greensboro, NC)
Pennsylvania State University (State College, PA)
Rutgers University (Camden, NJ)
Spelman College (Atlanta, GA)
Teachers College, Columbia University (New York, NY)
Temple University (Philadelphia, PA)
Tuskegee University (Tuskegee, AL)
University of Delaware (Newark, DE)
University of Pennsylvania (Philadelphia, PA)
University of Pittsburgh (Pittsburgh, PA)
Xavier University (New Orleans, LA)

APPENDIX V

SELECTED HONORS AND AWARDS PRESENTED TO THE AUTHOR

Human and Civil Rights
National Leadership Award, Children's Defense Fund, 1992
Brotherhood Award, National Conference of Christians and Jews, 1992
Judge William H. Hastie Award, NAACP Legal Defense Fund, 1991
A. Philip Randolph Award, National Urban Coalition, 1991
Drum Major for the Beloved Community, Martin Luther King, Jr., Center for
    Non-Violence (Philadelphia), 1989
Torch of Liberty Award, Anti-Defamation League of B'Nai B'Rith (Philadelphia), 1987
Whitney M. Young Leadership Award, Philadelphia Urban League, 1986
Legion of Merit Award, Chapel of the Four Chaplains, 1982
Benjamin Hooks Award, NAACP Life Membership Committee, 1978

Arts and Humanities

Crystal Award for the Arts and Humanities, Governor of Pennsylvania, 1993

Business Volunteer for the Arts Award, Greater Philadelphia Chamber of Commerce, 1993

Honorary Doctor of Fine Arts, University of the Arts, Philadelphia, 1992

Crystal Award: Man of the Decade, Afro American Historical and Cultural Museum, 1991

Public Service Award, Radio Station WRTI/Jazz 90, Temple University, 1983

Education

Honorary degrees from 21 U.S. universities and one Chinese university

President's awards from Glassboro State College (now Rowan College), Lincoln University, and Cheyney University

George Washington Carver Award, Academy of Natural Sciences (Philadelphia), 1991

Educational Excellence Leadership Award, National Association of Black School Educators, 1989

Hobart C. Jackson Award, Philadelphia Inter-Alumni Council of the United Negro College Fund, 1985

Educational Leadership Award, University of Pennsylvania Graduate School of Education, 1984

Horace Mann Award, Antioch University, 1981

Graduate seminar room and prize in Dr. Watson's name, Temple University, 1981

Selected Professional Memberships

American Academy of Political and Social Science

American Philosophical Society

Kappa Delta Pi

Phi Delta Kappa